THE XANADU SYSTEM

How to get paid $30,000 a year to travel*

*WITHOUT SELLING ANYTHING

BY CRAIG CHILTON

PRINTING HISTORY

February, 1979 -- 500 copies -- First Edition
August, 1986 -- Update segment added to the remaining First Editions
January, 1987 -- 5,000 copies -- Second Edition

Library of Congress Catalog Card Number: 86-51546
ISBN 0-933638-06-X

Published by   Cartoonist:
XANADU Enterprises   Ronald Henley
Box 424   1382 Q Street
East Greenbush, New York 12061   Springfield, Oregon 97477

This Book is Gratefully and Lovingly
Dedicated to
Mom & Dad
and My Brother, Cal.

Their Patience and Assistance
Made the Whole Dream Come True!

ABOUT the AUTHOR

Craig Chilton is a graduate of Central College, Pella, Iowa, and has pursued studies in Geography, Geology, and Anthropology at universities in Arizona, New York, New Jersey, North Dakota, and Mexico City.

He was awarded an NDEA Federal Grant for a special course in urban geography at Rutgers University, during which he conducted field studies in New York City.

Recently, he has completed all course requirements for two Masters Degrees at the University of Northern Iowa (Geography and Geology). While attending school there, he served a term as Executive Editor of the university newspaper, *The Northern Iowan*. In planning his Masters thesis for geography, the author researched an extensive sociological study that took him to universities in each of the 50 states. A book for general consumption is planned as a spin-off to the academic work.

The author has been travel-oriented throughout his lifetime -- a fact readily apparent to readers of his more recent works, of which this Second Edition is his tenth. In 1976 he explored the Alaska Pipeline firsthand during the latter stages of its construction, from Fairbanks to Prudhoe Bay. The result was his seventh book, *7 Days on the Kamikaze Trail*, which provided a unique inside story of life in that dynamic project.

When first attending the University of Northern Iowa, Craig simultaneously worked as a technical writer for the Research & Development Division of Chamberlain Manufacturing Corporation, in Waterloo. The six books written in that capacity were his earliest, providing him a firm foundation for a writing career. The First Edition of *this* book was his eighth published work, followed quickly by the ninth, which was a small guide for RV delivery persons. It followed Energy Hoax II, in 1979, and was designed to help drivers to cope with soaring gasoline and diesel fuel prices.

Before settling on a lifestyle based on writing and travel, Craig served honorably in the U.S. Air Force as a navigator and meteorologist. He then taught elementary school in Arizona and in Lancaster, California. Later, he taught social studies and science at the middle school level in East Greenbush, New York. While doing his graduate work in Iowa, he was awarded an assistantship, the duties of which included instructing undergraduate and graduate students in computer applications and techniques within the field of geography.

Craig is currently completing his first novel -- he hopes to present the most realistic fictional account of nuclear war yet written, and soon will travel extensively in the Soviet Union to complete the necessary research.

INTRODUCTION

Welcome to *XANADU!*

When the original edition of this book first came off the press in 1979, the hit movie of that name was still over a year in the future. The fact that this work is subtitled, *The Xanadu System,* then, is reflective of Coleridge's original concept, when he created the word as the name for an exotic pleasure dome in his work, *The Kubla Khan.*

Over the ages, we have come to regard *Xanadu* as synonymous with the word, *utopia.*

Now... if *utopia* deals with a perfect and flawless world of peace and ease, in which war, hunger, and poverty no longer exist, and wherein Murphy's Laws all have been repealed, then let us apply *Xanadu* to the effect that rapidly manifests itself after one decides to deliver Recreational and Specialized Vehicles.

As author of this book, I must caution you that this lifestyle works best for those who study the entire system, and put its instructions into practice. Simply being hired into this line of work can be an exercise in frustration and non-productivity for the person who works full-time, but earns only $12,000 per year at it. The majority of such drivers unfortunately fit this category -- usually for two reasons: (1) they have never heard of this book, so have not yet learned the practices they need to employ to earn a comfortable living, and (2) *because* their rate of earning is quite low at the outset, most drop out within days or weeks of starting the job, and seek different fields.

It took me well over a year of very lean times before I had learned much of what is presented in this book. Fortunately, I stuck with it, sensing that the earning potential was far greater than the actual returns I saw at the start.

The formal dedication of this book is two pages back. However, this book is *informally* (but sincerely) dedicated to the millions in the United States and Canada who are: ambitious, but unemployed... facing an uncertain future in middle age due to an imminent factory closure... able-bodied and alert in retirement, but suffering within the confines of a fixed income... tired of the rat race and looking for a change... working a seasonal job and seeking employment on a regular basis for each year's otherwise lean months... teachers and college students seeking lucrative summer employment... and so many more...

YOU are the reason I wrote this book. Since it exists only in limited quantity, if you are reading these words, there is <u>no</u> reason you can't benefit from this wonderful lifestyle!

When the first edition of this book was printed in February, 1979, the Second Great Energy Hoax was only a month away. I was blissfully unaware of this fast-approaching disaster, so I began to promote the lifestyle over the airwaves as a talk show guest.

All five talk shows that year were done within the month of March. By the end of that fateful month, the effects of EH II were being felt strongly from coast to coast... and sales of recreational vehicles (RVs) were plummeting.

If RVs don't sell, then drivers aren't needed to deliver them.

The first edition of this book was written *exclusively* on the subject of delivering *RVs*. It was suddenly about as fashionable as a tyrannasaurus rex in the window of Tiffany's. (I stopped doing talk shows, voluntarily.)

The high gasoline and diesel fuel prices resulting from EH II lasted nearly until 1986. Meanwhile, during the earlier years, the RV manufacturers which were destined ultimately to survive were forced to adopt austerity measures. Hundreds of other manufacturers went belly-up within a year or two.

By 1984, recreation vehicles had staged a strong comeback, despite the higher fuel prices. (The same sequence can be seen in the years immediately following 1973-74's Energy Hoax I.)

1986 saw the phenomenon of a return of gasoline and fuel prices to pre-EH II levels. Before this occurred, the RV industry had become more vigorous than it ever before had been, so this new factor simply improved the situation beyond everyone's reasonable expectations.

In August, 1986, I decided to return the first edition of this book to the marketplace, so this was done, after I had inserted updated information into it. After a series of talk shows throughout Atlantic Canada and Northeastern United States, the remaining copies of the first edition were quickly sold.

Lest anyone wonder how I was able to actively keep my finger on the pulse of this lifestyle during the lean years... I did it in July, 1979, by switching to the delivery of *beverage route trucks!*

Manufacturers of luxury vehicles are constantly haunted by the vagaries of the economy, and the whims of Big Oil. If gasoline prices suddenly skyrocket, or the economy hits the skids, they are among the first to go down the tubes. Recognizing this, I decided in 1979 that if I were to preserve my carefully-cultivated utopian lifestyle of driving and writing (and thereby avoid having to return to full-time teaching *(ugh!)* or some equally distasteful form of the rat race), I would have to modify things.

So it was that I discovered a new adjunct to RV delivery -- the delivery of *other* types of *specialized vehicles*. Society will always require the presence of such vehicles as fire trucks, hearses, delivery vans, and beverage trucks -- to name just a few... and nearly all of these are *driven* to their destinations or dealerships.

In 1979, this book listed 333 places where people could seek work, delivering RVs. In 1987, over *850* manufactures and transporters are listed -- making *this* edition *100% Energy Hoax-proof*. If you enter this line of work, you need never stop, for as long as you enjoy it. All of North America may now become your back yard.

Welcome to *XANADU!*

VITAL INFORMATION
About This New, International Edition
for 1987

When the earlier book was restored some months ago to the marketplace, I was surprised at the interest it aroused in those who heard about it. Before very long, a pattern emerged... it became evident that this lifestyle was capable of bringing about a dramatic improvement in the lives and earnings of many people.

In a short time, the remaining supplies of the book became very low, and it was obvious that a reprinting was necessary -- *soon*.

A choice became clear. I could either rework every mathematical computation in this book to perfectly fit the conditions existing at the end of 1986... or I could allow many of them to remain as *examples* of the points being presented. (Their original purpose had been to serve as examples, but of course in writing the *first* edition, *that* year's data had been used: data which fit 1979.)

It was decided that several of the examples using 1979 data would be allowed to remain, with this caveat being entered at the beginning of the book to enable the reader to be aware of this situation. In this manner, it became possible to bring out a new edition of the book as 1987 begins -- rather than as much as two months later -- which would have been the alternative.

Many, many people have told me during these last several weeks how their lives had been changed for the better by discovering this lifestyle. So in the process of ordering my priorities, I elected to *completely* revamp the Job Market segment: Appendix A. This will enable those who desire to obtain this book and put it to use immediately to do so *months* sooner.

Even though these steps were taken, <u>most</u> of the book was revised dramatically in the process, and entire new segments were added. For example, Part VII is new to this edition.

Also, this is finally a *truly* International Edition, listing virtually every single existing manufacturer and transporter company in Canada (and even one in England!).

Please keep all these points in mind as you use this book, and it will serve you well for a long time to come.

Best wishes to all of you... in all walks of life... in your pursuit of this most unique and enjoyable lifestyle!

TABLE of CONTENTS

Dedication

About the Author

Introduction

Vital Information About This New, International Edition for 1987

Table of Contents

PART I

GETTING THE JOB

- - - - - - - - - - - - - - - -

1

AVAILABILITY OF WORK

This is a complete placement manual and guide for one of the most incredible jobs on earth. It is the type of position that most people dream about, but do not realize exists.

The position is almost unknown to those outside of the field, simply because people almost never give conscious thought to the *way* recreational and specialized vehicles reach their respective dealerships and destinations.

Chances are you have never seen a motorized vehicle of a recreational or a specialized nature being transported on a truck. That is because they almost never are, due to their size or height. Almost invariably, they are *driven* from their hundreds of points of manufacture, to their thousands upon thousands of dealerships and customers, throughout the USA and Canada.

Only in two ways do people generally learn about this lifestyle:

A. Something causes them to realize that they *haven't* seen such vehicles being trucked. Perhaps they've heard the author of this book as a talk show guest. Or maybe they notice a "transporter", "manufacturer", or "dealer" license plate on a fire truck, or an RV. And make the association.

B. By word of mouth. Until late 1986, this is how *most* prospective delivery drivers first heard of the lifestyle. From those who were *already* doing it.

As of early 1987, more and more people are becoming aware, thanks to the author's frequent appearances on talk shows throughout the land, discussing the subject. Some concern has been expressed to him in this regard, often as a question asked on the air. It usually goes something like this:

"Don't you think all this new public awareness will cause saturation of the job market, making it difficult for a new driver to enter the field?"

The answer is, surprisingly... "Probably not."

Many factors need to be considered here. As a prospective driver, you need to understand these, and what they mean to you, both now and in the future.

First off, no one knows how many "road rats" there are[*]. *No one!* The Bureau of the Census would probably be very hard pressed even to *guess* the number that are citizens of the U.S. -- simply because their data would mix them up very thoroughly with *truckers*. There's a *world* of difference between the lifestyles of road rats and truckers, but it's highly doubtful the Census Bureau makes the distinction.

---

[*] "Road Rat" is simply a *fun* term used by delivery drivers of RVs and specialized vehicles to distinguish themselves from truckers -- much as someone who lives in a desert community often calls himself a "desert rat". The term was coined in the first edition of this book, and over the last 7 years has come into increasingly common use. (In *no way* is it a derogatory term.)

The best we can do is make an educated guess, based upon the number of manufacturers in existence, the large number of transporter companies which serve many of them, the rate at which vehicles are produced, and the frequency with which one can spot them out on the highways and byways. (We're all over the place, out there, if you know to look for us, and can recognize us when you see us -- usually through use of a special type of license plate, or the lack of one. Paper stickers sometimes are used instead by some states, usually in the front or back window.)

As you will see in this book, some road rats work directly for manufacturers. Others for transporter companies. Some work for both, continually, since most such drivers are independent contractors -- and that *usually* makes them free agents. (In which case, it is up to the driver whether or not he works for more than one company. This is discussed in detail in Part V.) And... there are untold thousands of road rats who work directly for the dealerships that *receive* the vehicles from the manufacturers. Such deliveries are known throughout the industry as:

> CPUs -- Customer Pick-Ups, and
> DPUs -- Dealer Pick-Ups.

So -- how many road rats are there, altogether? It's only an educated guess, but there are probably close to 50,000.

AT THIS POINT, IF YOU HAVE NOT YET READ THE INTRODUCTION
*TO THIS BOOK, PLEASE DO SO NOW. THE INFORMATION IT CONTAINS
IS VERY IMPORTANT TO YOU, IF YOU WISH TO ENTER THIS LIFESTYLE.*

Strange as it may seem, a great advantage to you in seeking work of this type is the fact that the level of pay received by the vast majority of road rats is down in the root cellar somewhere. *Most* road rats earn less than $15,000 per year working on a full-time basis. Many of them earn less than $10,000.

You must be wondering by now why this book's title indicates you can earn at least $30,000 per year when most who are employed in this lifestyle are at or below the poverty level.

First of all, most of them have never heard of this book. Having a copy of it is no guarantee of success, either. One needs to *use and understand it*. As it says in the Introduction, unless one is very lucky, he can either employ the techniques described herein and earn at the rate of $30,000 to $50,000 a year, right from the start, or he can get into the field without being armed with this information... and work his way up out of the poverty level after a year or more, from learning the techniques the hard way.

Most who are faced with doing things the hard way drop out. That is *one* reason there is so much turnover within the driving corps of manufacturers and transporter companies. There are other reasons, too.

No one knows how many road rats are retirees, but this writer estimates the number to be around 30%.

*IF A RETIRED PERSON IS IN REASONABLY-GOOD HEALTH, HAS A VALID LICENSE, A
DECENT DRIVING RECORD, AND ENJOYS DRIVING -- THERE IS NO NEED FOR HIM OR
HER TO BE LIVING ON A RESTRICTIVE "FIXED INCOME"!*

This point cannot be made strongly enough!

If you are retired, and a loved one has given you this book as a gift, you just may have been given a new lease on life! Many road rats continue in this lifestyle until their late 70s. Many reach their 80s before heading for that rocking chair.

The fact is, the rocking chair is literally a deadly foe if you have retired recently. The retiree who keeps active and enjoys a healthy zest for life has a <u>much</u> better shot at a long and happy life than does the person who becomes sedentary. If you don't believe this writer, ask *any* doctor!

Fortunately, most retirees know this.

Unfortunately, most retirees *also* find that their age makes them unemployable in most fields.

Most fields.

But not *this* one!

There is no upper age limit for road rats.

And... retirees are strongly *desired* as drivers by prospective employers!

Most companies want drivers who are stable and mature. Careful drivers. The retiree is perfect in these regards. So they are *eminently* employable. Many companies make it a policy to have *only* retirees in their driving corps. Some of these are mentioned in Appendix A.

Let's look at the average person who reaches age 65. For many, that age means mandatory retirement, while for most others, age 70 is the limit. Perhaps all through his lifetime, a person dreams of travelling, but hasn't managed to do it due to his rat race job and its all-too-short vacations.

For him, the world of travel has simply been in his future.

He just didn't realize it until now!

As a retiree, he can travel to his heart's content... and get *paid* for it.

No "fixed income" problems!

And now he can get out to explore those national parks, or visit friends and relatives in distant places.

And he can set his own schedule. Drive full-time, part-time, occasionally, or even just take a rare trip, now and then. It's easy to negotiate such things with most employers!

Okay... back to the original question. What does all *this* have to do with the availability of work for those seeking to *become* road rats?

Just this. Retirees may be discovering a new career or lifestyle when they become road rats, but their age makes this career a rather temporary one. Ten or 15 years, *tops,* for most. So the turnover rate is <u>rapid</u>. And *that* makes this a field that is *constantly* easy to get into.

Let's take a moment to examine the effects of all that exposure to the fact this lifestyle exists, via the media.

If 30,000 people hear a talk show in which this subject is discussed, most who are interested will purchase the book. Perhaps 40 people do this.

Out of that 40 people, perhaps 20 will read it *thoroughly.*

And perhaps 4 of *them* will decide to become road rats.

That's a total of four new delivery drivers out of 40 books purchased, or one in ten.

You recall, my estimate for the total number of road rats working at any given time was around 50,000.

In January, 1987, 5,000 copies of this (second) edition of the book were printed. It could easily take all year for these to be sold, but let's say they're gone after ten months. That is an average of 500 books per month, from the sale of which 50 readers decide to become road rats.

Out of 50,000 road rats in the field, nearly one-third of whom are retirees, and the majority of the remainder are poorly-paid because they haven't learned how to make the lifestyle pay well, what do you suppose the monthly turnover rate probably is?

My guess is that it is perhaps 5,000 or more per month -- *far* more than the mere 50 you need it to be, to have simply an *even* chance to get started.

As for the 29,960 people who heard the show, but *didn't* buy the book (in this example we just used)... this lifestyle isn't for everyone. So it's true that that many more people now are *aware* that this lifestyle exists... but almost *none* of them will *ever* compete with you in the job market.

Now -- what if you are a *college student,* or a *teacher?*

It's all good news! You are in demand!

Specialized vehicles and RVs are manufactured and delivered *all year 'round...* but the volume is *greater* during the *summer months*. This gap is largely filled by college students and teachers, who have their long vacations at this time.

Two quick examples.

I know a teacher who has used the original edition of this book since 1980, and has *averaged* between $11,000 and $12,000 *each year* since he started driving, in earnings from this lifestyle -- *over and above his annual teaching salary.*

And... one manufacturer polled for this edition complained that he sometimes found it difficult to find a student on short notice, to drive a vehicle for him. (He's listed in Appendix A. Students take note -- there are probably many more in there just like him!)

There is no *upper* age limit for this work... and the *lower* one is most frequently age 18. So this is a gold mine for most students! An ambitious student attending a college which charges $12,000 per year can actually raise that much annually, simply by becoming a summertime road rat!

The methods described in this book are *not* complex. Once you start driving, you will find nearly all of them second-nature to you within two or three weeks. You will become a very skilled road rat in that period of time, to the point that most functions of your new job will have become automatic.

As a skilled and successful driver, you quickly will gain job security. Keep doing your job right, and your future is assured. In the fresh air of the Great Outdoors, which is all yours, there is no "rat race" climb up the corporate ladder, and no competition for your job.

You can sit back in a comfortable bucket seat, drive, and see all North America on a perpetual vacation-with-pay beyond most people's wildest dreams!

There is a surprising number of differences between trucking and RV delivery, as shown in the table on the next page. RV driving has almost all the advantages of trucking, and practically none of the disadvantages. It is both interesting and important to note that *most* of the advantages enjoyed by the RV road rat are also applicable to the road rat who delivers *other* specialized vehicles.

In the back of this book are several Appendices, designed specifically to provide you with all the data you need to secure a good position and to make good money from the start, and on a continuing basis. The first of these (Appendix A) is the gateway to this bright, new world. It provides you with names, addresses, and phone numbers for nearly every RV and specialized vehicle manufacturer, and transporter company, in the USA and Canada. Most listings additionally include names of people to contact regarding employment as a driver. *And...* many of these listings include toll-free "800" numbers you can use in your inquiries.

There are over 850 potential employment locations from which to choose.

An interesting aspect of becoming a road rat is the versatility you will gain. Here are a few of the unique advantages:

1. Many companies allow drivers to take vacations, or days off, at will, on fairly short notice. Sometimes on even a few *hours'* notice.

2. Most road rats have complete freedom to choose any reasonable route to their assigned destinations.

3. Many drivers have a wide latitude of choice as to their destination from the trips available at any given time.

4. Drivers set their own hours. No more "9-to-5" or other similar syndromes of the rat race. They drive when they feel like it, stop when they feel like it, and sleep when they feel like it

5. With a galaxy of 850 potential employers, the road rat can easily gain access to most of the North American continent, including all of its beaches, national parks, and other points of interest.

Selecting a Company

There are two general types of employers. These are:

A. Manufacturers of RVs and other specialized vehicles

B. Vehicle Transporter Companies.

Significant differences exist between the two which should be considered before you apply for employment. These are as follows:

1. *Pay Scale* --

Manufacturers generally pay their drivers more than transporter companies, for good reason. If a manufacturer wants to ship a unit, he will expect to pay a fair amount of money for the service.

Should the manufacturer choose to pay a driver directly, the driver would retain all of the money left over after the run as his profit.

Typical earnings for such a driver would range between $250 and $350 (after expenses, but before taxes) for delivery to a point 1,000 miles distant.

COMPARISON:

Trucking vs. RV Delivery

TRUCKING	*RV DELIVERY*
Special training or apprentice-ship is required.	No training needed.
Chauffeur's license.	Ordinary operator's license.
Frequently must maintain tight schedules.	Normally set own schedules, within reason.
Experience normally required.	No experience necessary.
Investment frequently required.	No investment necessary.
Often restricted to certain highways and routes.	No route restrictions; usually go wherever cars can go.
Loss of time at warehouses during loading & unloading of freight.	No down time at warehouses; check-in usually takes only a few minutes.
Trucks normally haul freight.	RV itself is the payload.
Major repairs cost days or weeks of lost time.	Worst breakdowns usually cost 1 day or less of lost time.
Repairs can be very costly.	All repairs are under warranty.
Much paperwork is required.	Paperwork is minimal.
Many must seek lodging.	Lodging is *never* an expense.
Insurance costs are burdensome to owner-operators.	Insurance is always provided by the company.
Seeking new loads at destinations is source of much time loss & aggravation to owner-operators.	Return or continuing runs, or return transportation is normally established before destination is reached.
Few luxury items included.	Many luxuries are standard.
Cruise control is unknown.	Cruise control is common feature.
Automatic Transmission rare.	Nearly all RV's are automatic.
Older models provide a rough, bumpy, tiring ride.	Ride is always smooth and comfortable.
Trucks are harder to handle & require more physical effort to drive.	Most RV's have power steering & handle as easily as cars.
Truck payments are a monthly burden to owner-operators.	No payments to make, or job-connected financial obligations.
Only the most luxurious trucks have spacious beds.	Most RV's have large, comfortable beds to sleep in.
Trucks must stop to weigh at all open weigh stations.	Only occasional weigh station stops are required upon entry to certain states.

Many manufacturers, however, choose to subcontract one or more transporter companies to handle their deliveries.

A transporter company is therefore a *broker*. After it picks up a unit from the factory, it assigns a driver to the run, and gives the driver a *portion* of the money paid by the factory to make the shipment. The transporter company is the middleman, and must of course make a profit to stay in business.

Driver pay averages about half of what he earns when working directly for a manufacturer. For delivery to a point 1,000 miles distant, then, he can expect to earn between $125 and $175, on average.

Either way, the *factory* still spends close to the same amount of money to make a shipment. (In paying a transporter company, it may spend slightly more, in some cases. This is a trade-off of more money spent, in return for less responsibility to the drivers.)

Once a transporter company assigns a driver to a run, that driver is *its* employee or subcontractor. The driver works directly with the transporter company in the event any difficulties arise. The transporter company provides the factory with a buffer between factory and drivers, and sometimes between factory and dealers.

This book will not attempt to discuss which method is optimal for the *manufacturer*. Every factory has its own unique characteristics, policies, and structure. Only a manufacturer can decide which method of shipment best suits its own system.

The bottom line is this: Many factories have their own drivers, and many employ the services of one or more vehicle transporters. A few even combine the two methods.

In most cases, a driver can expect to receive more money for each mile he drives for a factory, than for the same distance covered for a transporter company. If this were the only factor, there would be little point in seeking employment with a vehicle transporter. But there are other, equally important factors.

2. *Availability of Runs* --

Normally, factories are not wildly enthusiastic about having their drivers working for competitors *in the same immediate vicinity,* when runs are not available. Neither, for that matter, are transporter companies. Both like to have drivers that they can count on when they are needed. (*Interlock* is an advanced means by which drivers *can* work for more than one company -- but from *different* regions. *Distance* makes the difference. See Part V.)

Upon occasion, if a driver works directly for a factory, and that factory has no units to ship for a period of time, the driver could be hung out to dry. (Factories call it "laid off".) This is a difficult situation, and holds the potential of fiscal disaster for the driver, if it should persist.

No matter how high the degree of regard a factory may have for a driver, it is an economic fact of life that it can't pay him if he can't do any work. One could hardly expect that.

However... transporter companies generally serve *more than one factory*. If one of these factories has a slump, vacation, or production problem, the transporter company still receives enough business from the other factories to keep all its regular drivers busy. (During periodic times of surplus, on the other hand, most transporter companies can call upon a list of local residents who are willing to take runs on an occasional or part-time basis. These frequently are retired persons.)

Working for a transporter company affords a driver an additional measure of job security not available from many factories.

3. *Benefits* --

Fringe benefits are almost exclusively within the domain of manufact- urers. Some factories offer none, and others offer such benefits as health and life insurance, vacations with pay, and even the use of an RV while on vacation. It seems as though no two factories are alike with regard to benefits provided. Also, some factories extend benefits immediately, while others give them as seniority is earned,

Although few transporter companies offer even minimal fringe benefits, the positive aspects of being in their employ should be kept in mind.

4. *Employment Status* --

Nearly all transporter companies have a staff of *contract* drivers (*i.e.,* independent contractors). A *payroll* driver is a rare bird indeed. Technic- ally, one who works on a contract basis is hired each time he makes a run. His application is kept on file, but in reality, he is unemployed every time he completes a run, until he contracts for his next one.

The reality of this situation is not nearly so worrisome. While the driver continues his normal, good job of making deliveries, he is a valued employee. As with any regular work, he would never be fired (*i.e.,* not given a new run) without just cause.

Many manufacturers use independent contractors, and some hire drivers as regular (payroll) employees. Payment still is almost universally based on miles driven and types of runs made. Either way, a driver is subject to lean periods with no income, if production declines or stops.

5. *Unions* --

At this writing, I know of no RV or specialized vehicle delivery drivers who belong to a union, either as factory employees, or as transporter company employees. Nor have I ever met a driver who has been approached by a union for this purpose, or who has shown the least interest in belonging to one. Most delivery drivers consider their working conditions excellent, and their pay reasonable for work done. There is virtually no discontent to my knowledge, based on a decade of observation.

Only *you* know the answer to that question... and it is an answer you might not fully decide upon until you have digested all the material in this book.

However, there are some important points to ponder, besides those discussed in the Introduction, and elsewhere.

It's a sad commentary on our society, but evidently America still has a lot of growing up to do. According to a U.S. Government report issued in the mid-1980's, at the rate women currently are approaching a status of receiving equal pay for equal work in the workplace, they can expect to finally be treated fairly by the year 2035. Fortunately, 2035 seems to have arrived long ago with respect to the delivery of vehicles. I have neither seen nor heard of any instance where a woman working as a delivery driver for a company has earned any less than her male counterparts.

What's in it for the foreign tourist? Oddly enough, perhaps a great deal. Most tourists coming to the USA expect to spend a bundle in the process of touring this large nation, and certainly don't consider the possibility of *earning* money while they are here. But it *can* be done -- and in the road rat business, that is *particularly* serendipitous. Travelling around the country is the name of the game for the tourist... and getting *paid* to do it would have to be the best of all possible worlds.

However... there is *one* (not-always-so-minor) obstacle to be overcome, called the *Green Card*. This is the document, issued by the U.S. Dept. of Immigration, that a foreign visitor must secure before he or she can legally work for compensation in the USA. (Canada likely has a similar law.)

This is far from being a hopeless situation, because companies frequently are in the position of needing competent drivers at a time when none seems to be available. Should the tourist come along at such a time, it is altogether possible that a Green Card can be secured for him or her on the basis of the company's need.

It certainly can't hurt to ask -- based on the experience a girl from Australia had a few years ago. I had met her on a bus in Alabama one day, and the following day she was hired by the company in Indiana for which I was then working. She worked for them for five months before she took her earnings and went on a tour of the world. (Her original plan, having just graduated from college, was to take a one-month vacation here.) Since that time, she has returned periodically to deliver more RVs.

If you are in the rat race, there's hardly a better way out of it! This stress-free, laid-back lifestyle can enable you to step back away from the rut you've been in, and look over your options in life. Few people aspire to be road rats all their lives, as fabulous as the experience is. But you may wish to combine it, as I have, with other activities. I love to write, but the pay sometimes leaves much to be desired, or else it comes in a "feast-or-famine" manner. As a road rat, I've gotten many of my best ideas for future writing while driving down the road, and I can stop to write whenever I want.

Great for professionals and executives, too. I know a lawyer who doubles as a road rat... and a banker who met the girl of his dreams this way, and got married!

2

GENERAL REQUIREMENTS

The minimum requirements for becoming a Road Rat seem almost too good to be true. (Which is logical, because the position *itself* seems too good to be true. That's okay. The feeling of awe at having such an idyllic job can last for *years!*)

It is likely that perhaps as much as 95% of the population age 18 and over can qualify.

There are practically *no* educational requirements. I have known some moderately successful people in this field who are totally illiterate.

Sex discrimination is all but non-existant. Most companies have female drivers, and their pay and working conditions are equal to those of the men.

There are only five basic requirements which you must meet in order to be hired:

1. *Minimum Age: 18 --*

   Some companies require a driver to be 21, and a few may still require age 25 (although I know of none of the latter). There is no maximum age, which makes this an ideal field for retirees who enjoy travelling.

2. *A Degree of Maturity --*

   As with any position involving responsibility for valuable property and the well-being of others, a normal amount of good judgment and common sense is expected of the employee.

3. *A Valid Driver's License --*

   A valid operator's license from any U.S. state or Canadian province, or from another nation when accompanied by an International Driver's License. Any class license is sufficient; this job does not require the driver to have a chauffeur's license, although some companies may require this in line with their own policies.[*]

4. *A Relatively Good Driving Record --*

   Even a history of accidents or moving violations may not stand in your way with many employers, if it can be shown that your record in recent years or months is good, or if accidents were not charged to you.

---

[*] Ordinary operators license normally is fine for delivery of most RVs, and smaller specialized vehicles. However, if one plans to deliver the larger vehicles, such as fire trucks and beverage route trucks, a chauffeur's license is needed.

5.   *Reasonably Good Health --*

Many companies ask that their drivers who travel interstate have a Department of Transportation (D.O.T.) physical examination, and carry a health card to this effect (furnished by the employer). The exam can be performed in minutes at nominal cost, by any medical doctor.

Getting hired can be an amazingly easy task. Frequently, simply walking into the prospective employer's office and stating your purpose is sufficient, and more than once I have been hired in less than two minutes this way. Even more surprising is the fact that many companies will hire you sight-unseen on the strength of a phone call... another experience that I have personally enjoyed.

During the course of the interview, make it known that you plan to use *The Xanadu System* and are prepared to buy a bus pass. Even if the dispatcher is not yet familiar with this book, he should be quite familiar with the benefits accruing from his drivers' utilization of this method. Your willingness to pursue the position in so professional a manner should be quite advantageous.

A few other pointers:

1.   Don't take "No" for an answer. If the company isn't hiring, inquire *again* every other day or so. If there is more than one company in your area (or in the region in which you wish to work), make the rounds regularly. (Whether or not your first application is in person, follow-up calls by phone work very well.)

Many of those who secured lucrative jobs on the Alaska Pipeline back in the '70s first lived in Fairbanks for up to five weeks, applying daily. Perseverence pays off.

2.   Don't be a prima donna. If a manufacturer that pays 60¢/mile has no openings, while a transporter company nearby which pays 30¢/mile is willing to hire you, sign on with the transporter company. Later, the factory may hire you on the basis of your experience, or you may be able to set up an *Interlock* (see Part V) with another factory in a distant region. *GET STARTED*... and *then* improve your situation as time progresses. Your employers will admire your initiative.

Remember, though, to do the best job you can, for whomever you are working. Work as hard for 30¢/mile as you would for 60¢!

3.   Tell your prospective employer right up front what you can do for him. Where vehicles are being moved, there is room for all types of drivers... full-time, part-time, vacation-time, those who are on call if needed... even the one who might drive only once in the proverbial blue moon.

If the company knows what you can do, and can count on you to do it on the basis you specify, you have given him what he needs most: stability.

For example, if you know that you want to take two or three days off between runs as a general rule, at your destinations, tell him that this will be your pattern. It will help him immensely in his scheduling.

PART II

PERFORMING THE JOB
- - - - - - - - - - - - - - - - - -

1

GETTING STARTED

Most companies make no provision for intensive orientation, student runs, or a period of apprenticeship. The basic requirements of the job are quite simple, and your new employer generally (and correctly) assumes that you have sufficient intelligence and driving ability to perform adequately.

While most employers would *like* to see their drivers stable and successful, they simply do not have time to teach a ground school. It is up to *you* to get paid $30,000/year and up, as a Road Rat.

This book is the "ground school". Your own initiative will enable you to earn the good money.

Shortly after you are hired (perhaps even *immediately*), you will be assigned a coach to drive. As an RV driver, you'll probably drive one of these four vehicles:

1. *Class "A" Motor Home --*

   This is the most deluxe type of coach on the market. All have in common the general appearance of a solid, rectangular, box-shaped unit, with no cab visible. Most of the Class "A's" currently built range from 25-35 feet in length, and are more streamlined in front than most of the earlier models. These are the heaviest types of coaches made, ranging up to about 9 tons in weight. The majority of these are built on the Dodge chassis.

2. *Mini Motor Home --*

   These somewhat lighter coaches are built on RV truck chassis, generally of four makes: Chevrolet, Dodge, Ford, and GM. Universally, they have a truck cab, with a cabover bed section over the driving compartment. This type of coach currently is enjoying tremendous popularity. (The minis is known in the industry as Class "B".)

3. *Micro-mini Motor Homes --*

   These are miniature versions of the minis, but are <u>considerably</u> smaller. Most are built on a Datsun or Toyota chassis, and their popularity is on the rise.

4. *Van Conversions* --

Many companies take basic van bodies and convert them
into miniaturized motor homes. Some even build their own van
bodies. There is a wide variety in floor plans.

Your dispatcher will explain the handling of the paperwork, most of
which deals with getting the dealer's signature and sometimes a check.

Not too much structure and routine is necessary in the Road Rat
business, which is one of the main beauties of the job. However, you will
want to establish a pattern as early as possible of being able to find
yourself *en route* somewhere on *Sundays*. *Arriving* on a Sunday will leave
you with down time until the dealer opens on Monday morning, in most cases.
(Some dealers *are* open on Sundays, however, and most of these will check
you in on that day. Once you have learned who these are, you can plan
accordingly.)

It normally is bad luck to arrive at your dispatch office on a Saturday,
because many companies will not be able to dispatch you again until Monday
morning, and you'll lose the weekend.

If you are fortunate, you will find employment with a company that *can*
dispatch you again, automatically, whenever you arrive -- night or day,
weekend, or holiday. (Some companies have night watchmen on duty that perform
this function.) Lucky indeed are the drivers who are able to establish this
arrangement, for it enables them to earn thousands of dollars more over the
course of a year.

Some drivers work out of their home towns, and prefer to be home on
weekends. This is your choice, of course, but it is a lifestyle pattern that
probably will cause you to earn substantially *less* than $30,000/year. Most
drivers in this category are married and have families. The single drivers
and male-female driver teams (see Chapter 6 in this Part) tend to favor the
more profitable course of working all the time, and taking occasional days
off as they select them.

The Legalities

Your company will issue you a *license plate* or two to use continually.
(California uses one plate. Indiana uses two, front and rear. Other states
vary.)

Most states are very tolerant of the way you display them, as long as
they're in sight. (In California, I usually prop it up against the inside
of the front windshield.) Some places are more strict. Decatur, Indiana,
for example, shows no mercy. Transporter companies handle deliveries there,
and vehicles are always being shuttled around town, to and from the factories.

In 1977, it was common for units to be moved within town without plates -- but by 1978, if a driver was caught driving without both plates displayed properly, he could kiss $41.00 good-bye. (In the case of having two plates, putting one in the rear window will suffice.)

Transporter companies, and some factories, will furnish you with a *cab card* as well, which documents your company's authority to make interstate deliveries. You should always carry this where you can reach it easily.

Your license plate normally will have *reciprocity* with most states. This means you can travel through such states as though you were driving your own car.

Some states, however, share reciprocity with few other states. Arizona, Montana, and Nevada are good examples. Be sure to check with your dispatcher and learn the states that have special requirements. Generally, upon entering these states, it is necessary to stop at a permit office, weigh station, or court house and purchase a "caravan permit".

Don't take chances and try to evade the requirement. Failure to get a required permit can have grim results. For example, in Montana, fines vary according to the county in which you are driving. The permit for a driver having Indiana transporter plates, crossing more than 400 miles of Montana, costs $10. In certain counties, should he be stopped and not have a permit, the *fine* can be as high as $500.

You always will be reimbursed, either by your company or by the dealer (according to your company's policy).

Route Selection

*Road Rats roam America's
Wonderlands at will !*

Most companies give drivers total freedom of choice in selecting their routes. In return, wise drivers are careful not to abuse the privilege. (For example, travelling 700 miles on a run from L.A. to San Francisco, which is about 400 miles by the direct route, would be considered abuse.)

There are three very important reasons why one would not want to vary his route by any <u>excessive</u> distance:

1. At almost 10¢ per mile for gasoline, side trips can eat into your profits very rapidly.

2. While travelling a *reasonable* number of miles is therapeutic and keeps one feeling like he is always on vacation, an *excessive* number of miles costs him so much in *time*, he might miss a run, or leave later than he otherwise could have. Sooner or later, that lost time can result in loss of earnings.

3. Extra miles piled up on the odometer will aggravate the *dealer*, who then is likely to aggravate the driver's *boss*. Drivers have to please the folks on both ends, and extra-long trips can catch him right in the middle!

However --- even an idyllic job such as this could become old if one always were forced to go the shortest and/or fastest way.

Three good examples of *acceptable* variety would be:

1. A visit to Crater Lake National Park en route from southern California to Portland, Oregon.

2. A ride up the California coast on California Route 1 from L.A. to San Jose.*

3. A trip down the Natchez Trace Parkway from Tupelo to Jackson, Miss. en route from Indiana to New Orleans.

A good rule of thumb on taking the scenic route is this:

Never add more than 15%, and keep it below 10% if possible.

Odometers can be inaccurate by as much as 15%, and occasionally, even more. Chances are good that nothing would be said if your odometer indicated 863 miles on a 750-mile run (15% extra), but 825 miles (10% extra) would be better.

The longer your assigned distance, the more opportunity you have to sightsee without adding more miles.

Once, on a trip from northern Indiana to Vancouver, B.C., I observed that the Dakotas were due for an ice storm, and planned a new route. My normal routing for

---

* One of my more anxious moments occurred during a run like this. A vulture swooped down directly in front of a mini I was driving, and frantically flapped northward in an effort to escape impending doom. For a moment, I had visions of completing my tour of California Route 1 with a mangled buzzard sticking out of the cabover's windshield like a figurehead on the prow of an old sailing ship! (He was bruised by the light impact that followed, but everything except his pride survived intact.)

the B.C. run was from Chicago to Seattle via I-90 and I-94 (across Wisconsin, Minnesota, North Dakota, Montana and Idaho), but this time, I elected to go straight west on I-80, all the way to Utah, and then cut northwest on I-84. I figured it just *had* to be hundreds of miles longer, so I sought and gained my dispatcher's permission to use the route (to miss the storm) and to be reimbursed by the company for the extra miles upon my return.

It was 100 miles *shorter* that way.

I felt lucky my dispatcher didn't request that I reimburse *him!*

Incidentally, a commonly-asked question is, "Why are the RV's *driven* to the dealerships? Isn't it difficult for the dealer to sell new units with all that mileage on them?"

You also will hear that question frequently, so here's the answer.

Those miles are actually a *selling* point. When a potential customer asks about them, the dealer points out three things:

(1) Most factory defects show up within the first several hundred miles. When the unit was driven to the dealership, it was evaluated by the driver. If any significant problems developed, this gave the dealer (or one en route) the opportunity to have them corrected, saving the customer the headache.

(2) The unit has had a good, steady run, and now is well broken-in.

(3) That method of delivery saved the customer money. Most other methods, such as by truck or train, would have cost substantially more, and those costs would have been passed on to the customer.

However, *few* or *no* miles on the odometer is even *better!* (In poker, that would be like having a royal flush, compared to having a full house.) Most dealers stop just short of doing handsprings when a unit arrives that way!

Units that arrive mileage-free, however, are rare. The odometer would have had to fail (usually a broken cable) after the unit left the factory. Then it was an "act of God", and legal. (*It is strictly* <u>illegal</u> *to* <u>disconnect</u> *the speedometer cable!*)

An example of this was a unit from southern California that was once delivered to a Reno dealer with no miles on it, due to the usual cause; the speedometer cable was broken.

Unlike *most* dealers, this one became very upset and *insisted* that the miles *must* show before he could sell the vehicle. After calling the driver's boss on the phone, a solution was reached.

After the broken cable was repaired, the driver was assigned to drive out into the Nevada desert on I-80 for 150 miles, and then return, putting a total of 300 miles on the unit. The driver made additional profit on his run as a result, but what a waste of gasoline!

I wonder, if that ever happens again, if the dealer will think to hook the cable to an electric drill, and run up miles the cheap and easy way?

Back to the selection of a route...

There are other factors worthy of consideration. One of these is cost of gasoline.

If one drives from Decatur, Indiana to Denver, Colorado, there are two equally-good Interstate highways he can use: I-80 across Iowa and Nebraska, or I-70 across Missouri and Kansas.

Since the mileage by either route is approximately the same, one must look for other aspects.

Cost of gasoline becomes the primary factor in making this decision. Gas prices in Iowa are high, and they are exorbitant in Nebraska. Gas prices in Missouri and Kansas are among the nation's most reasonable. One can easily save $15.00 in gasoline expenditures by using I-70. Once one gets used to prices along various routes, he can calculate a *rough estimate* of cost, based on known distances and average performance of units.

For Example:

Point of Origin	Destination	Primary Route	Average Gas Price en Route	Anticipated Gas Mileage	Approximate Distance
Decatur, Ind.	Denver, Colo.	I-70	60¢/gal.	5.5 m.p.g.	1,250 miles
Decatur, Ind.	Denver, Colo.	I-80	67¢/gal.	5.5 m.p.g.	1,250 miles

To estimate your gasoline cost for each route, use this formula:

$$\frac{\text{Approximate Distance}}{\text{Anticipated Gas Mileage}} \times \text{Average Gas Price en Route} = \text{Cost}$$

Using the formula provides this information for the two routes:

Via I-70: (1,250 ÷ 5.5) x .60 = $136.36 ⎫
Via I-80: (1,250 ÷ 5.5) x .67 = $152.27 ⎬ Difference in Cost: $15.91

The difference in the cost estimates is your estimated potential saving. By using I-70, you can reasonably expect to save close to $16.00.

The above specific example may save you much money that otherwise would be wasted through trial and error. A substantial price differential for gasoline has continued for several years along these two Interstates. You can *count* on I-70 being the less expensive route.

Availability of Services is another factor to consider when planning your route. If you have a breakdown along a major highway, such as one of the Interstates, you are never far from assistance. An alternate route may be shorter, but less-travelled.

An excellent example would be a run assigned to Boise, Idaho, from Los Angeles.

By using I-15 and I-84, the entire trip could be made on the Interstate System -- but this routing would be about 200 miles longer than the more direct route across the center of Nevada. The trans-Nevada routing is nearly all desert, however, and in several places, the distance between services is in excess of 75 miles.

The desert can be unbearably hot in the summer, and bitterly cold in the winter. But during spring and fall, temperatures are moderate. In this case, *climate* becomes the major factor in one's decision as to whether or not to use a well-travelled route.

Comparatively few units have breakdowns that would force one to stop out on the road and seek emergency service, so during the mild months, he should go with the odds, cross Nevada, and save the 200 miles. During the rest of the year, he should play it safe, spend the extra $15 to $20 on gasoline, and hope he can avoid having to take more runs to Boise during *that* particular season.

Circumventing the Tollgate (Legally)

Whenever you can, it is good practice to avoid toll highways. *Someone* will save the money, and depending upon the company you work for, that someone could be *you*.

Appendix D provides several good alternatives to some of the toll roads and turnpikes.

Look for Shortcuts

Carefully studying the road map before making a run can reveal shortcuts that might normally be overlooked, because we are used to assuming that Interstate highways always provide the shortest distance between two points.

For example, drivers going southwest on I-69 from the area of Fort Wayne, Indiana, can save 8 miles on each such run by taking the Indiana Route 67 South exit (Pendleton) and proceeding on *that* route to I-465 at the east side of Indianapolis. Upon joining I-465, going southbound, one is located only one mile north of that highway's junction with I-70, westbound.

A Final Tip Before You Start

Visibility to the rear can be a real problem to Road Rats in wet weather, because RV outside mirrors and the back window all blur and get dirty quite easily.

Problems of misting, icing, frost, etc. can be minimized and nearly eliminated by coating the mirrors properly with an application of "Rain-X Glass Treatment" before you leave. It's a good idea any time you think you'll encounter wet weather along your route. The application takes only one minute.

Many "Bingo" or "King Oil" stations, or truck stops sell "Rain-X". Or write to:

Rain-X   Tel. (312) 468-1700
Unelko Corporation
727 E. 110th Street   (Average retail price: $5.00)
Chicago, IL 60628

2

GETTING THE MOST FROM A UNIT

The greatest commonly-occurring problem encountered with coaches is their notoriously poor gasoline mileage.

There are various methods by which a driver can usually improve the mileage he will get during a run, and thereby increase his earnings. Some methods are better than others, but some of the basic ones used by many drivers are as follows:

1. Lean out the mixture in the carburetor.
2. Advance the timing by 8 . (NOTE: This may cause dieseling; i.e., the engine may continue to run after the ignition is turned off.)
3. Set the idle at 700 rpm.
4. While en route, shift *manually*, especially when climbing long and/or steep grades.
5. Drive 40 mph for the 1st 100 miles; 45-50 mph for the 2nd 100 miles. Then kick it hard through the gears to get the carbon out.
6. Overinflate the tires.

It is a good idea to reverse some of the above procedures immediately before delivering the unit. Such as retarding the spark again, if dieseling has been occurring.

If nothing else, be *sure* to restore normal pressure to the tires before delivery, or the unit might get *sold* that way, and the customer could incur abnormal tire wear.

A controversial method not listed above, but practiced by many drivers, is flipping over the lid of the air cleaner. This allows air to go *around* the filter, thus having the effect of leaning out the mixture. However, the author advises *against* it, based on the advice of a chief mechanic at an RV manufacturing plant:

"It's a good way to burn the coach down around your ears. With an extra-lean mixture the carburetor tends to backfire easily, and with the cover inverted, the flames can escape through the air cleaner and ignite the fiberglass of the doghouse cover.

"Furthermore", he asserted, "the procedure makes a negligible improvement in mileage, at best."

If a coach *does* catch fire, it can be consumed very rapidly. On one occasion, a driver in Indiana had parked a Class A motor home in front of his house while he went inside to get his luggage. When he stepped outside again about two minutes later, the coach was blazing away merrily like a log in a fireplace. (Fortunately, the investigation showed that the fire had been caused by faulty wiring.) Because a coach can rather easily become a fire hazard, it is a good idea to place one's luggage near the side door of the coach, so that it can be removed in a hurry.

If you feel inclined to use any of the above methods, or others you may hear about or devise, do so with utmost discretion. If is strictly against the policy of many companies to employ some of these procedures. Those that have no specific policy at this time might feel compelled to establish such guidelines if gas-saving procedures were employed too blatantly by their drivers. Learn your company's policies on these matters, and proceed accordingly.

Facilities and Luxuries

It would be a shame to make a living driving America's most luxurious vehicles and not be able to enjoy the luxury features.

Many of the features are at your disposal, and others are not. For example, use of the toilet is almost universally taboo. There are few things that irritate a dealer more.

Similarly, use of the shower is strongly frowned upon.

Most of the other facilities are usually available for the drivers use, depending largely upon individual company policies, and subject to logical limitations, as follows:

1. _Radio_ --

    Units range from those having _no_ radio to those with AM/FM stereo sets having 8-track or cassette tape players. There are probably _no_ companies that restrict the use of these. (Enjoy!)

2. _Air Conditioning_ --

    A majority of coaches have dash air. Normally one feels free to use it. The only restrictions one is likely to encounter apply to roof air conditioners.

    In order to run the roof air unit(s), one must run the auxiliary generator. (Most of the time, units that have roof air also have the generator ready to use.) The generator runs from a gasoline engine, which draws its fuel supply directly from your gas tank. While it is running, one can expect to sacrifice up to one mile/gallon of fuel economy.

    A few companies restrict or prohibit running the generator due to the presence of a meter which counts the number of hours the generator has been run. This meter cannot be turned back, and many dealers dislike having a number of hours showing on it.

If there is no company policy, use good judgment. To save money *and* keep the dealer happy, use the roof air unit only on really hot days, when you need it for comfort. (Most dealers accept this.)

Occasionally, you will get a unit without dash air, or in which dash air does not work. Nearly all mini-motor homes have wing windows which help to cool the driver's compartment, as well as having vents. (If you use the wing windows, *don't* direct the air flow directly at yourself. *Bees* tend to be hurled at the driver at high speed, this way.)

Also, avoid opening the windows while moving, if the windows have screens. The wind blast tears the screens loose from their mountings, ruining them.

3. *Furnace* --

It may be worthwhile to use the unit's furnace to keep warm during wintertime runs -- mainly for periods of sleep. Check with your dispatcher first; some factories do not check the gas lines before shipment, leaving this chore to the dealer. Occasionally, a propane line that hasn't been checked can *leak*. If it leaks while a driver runs the furnace, he can blow himself up.

If the lines *have* been checked, and it is safe to use the furnace, one then must decide whether or not it is cost-effective to use it during sleep periods. This depends mainly on the number of hours one expects to sleep during the run. Usually it is necessary to introduce at least three gallons of propane into the tank in order to have sufficient pressure to run the system. (This will cost a minimum of approximately $3.00.)

For one's money, he will get several hours of toasty heat throughout the unit, at whatever temperature he selects on the thermostat.

There are two alternatives:
   (A) Let the engine idle, and allow the cab's heater to provide the warmth. This method costs approximately $1.00/hour in gasoline. (Keep a window cracked to avoid carbon monoxide.)
   (B) Bundle up in a thermal sleeping bag. If a driver owns one that is rated for low enough temperatures, he can save substantially throughout the winter.

In conclusion, the methods available, from least to most expensive, are (1) sleeping bag (2) furnace (on a long run, from some factories), and (3) idling the engine and using the heater.

4. *Refrigerator* --

   May be gas, electric, or a combination capable of both. The electric
   one will require running the generator, reducing overall gasoline
   mileage. The gas one will require the purchase of propane. One
   should check on company policy, and then decide how much he plans to
   use it.

5. *Range; Oven; Microwave* --

   Most companies prefer these not be used, to prevent the possibility
   of spilled or burned food, etc. (Check with dispatcher.)

6. *Ash Tray* --

   Smokers should carry a portable ash tray along, and keep the one in
   the unit clean and new-looking. (Some companies don't mind if the
   driver uses the unit's ash tray. Check with dispatcher.)

3

THE CARE & FEEDING OF BREAKDOWNS

A new motor home, like a car, sometimes has manufacturing defects which usually manifest themselves during the first several hundred miles it is driven. When these occur, breakdowns present the Road Rat with the only real problems he usually has, while *driving*.

Breakdowns can be classed in four categories:

Class I   --   Major Delay. (Unit incapacitated for several days or weeks.)
Class II --   Long Delay. (1-2 days)
Class III --   Short Delay.(Minutes to hours)
Class IV --   No Delay. (But special vigilance or actions are required.)

As a rule breakdowns can be traced to either of two sources: (1) The *chassis* manufacturer, or (2) The *coach* manufacturer. Breakdowns that occur out on the road, which require professional service, usually are corrected by a dealership representing the chassis manufacturer. If the chassis warranty does not cover the work (due to a fault caused by the coach manufacturer), arrangements for payment usually can be made between the service manager and the driver's dispatcher. In this manner, nearly all breakdowns can be corrected at that service center.

On rare occasions a breakdown may occur wherein if a driver can pay for the service, he can get underway much faster. A good example of this would be loss of transmission fluid due to a ruptured hose to the transmission cooler. This might be fixed on the road, rather than require a tow. In such instances, the driver should check with his dispatcher. If the dispatcher agrees to the suggested course of action, and to reimburse the driver, then the driver can pay the bill and get a receipt.

It is a good idea to carry an extra $75-$100 on all runs, or a major bank credit card, for this purpose. This occasionally can save the driver from having to wait while money is wired to him by his company.

All breakdowns requiring professional repair (except minor items like headlights and fan belts) should be reported to the dispatcher *before* the work is started. (Company policy on this may vary. Check with your dispatcher upon being hired.)

The majority of chassis used in the motor home industry today are built by Dodge. Therefore two publications by Chrysler Corporation are very helpful. Road Rats should secure these and keep them in their luggage:

Dodge Recreational Vehicle Service Nationwide Directory
    (Form #81-305-5001 - Free)
Dodge Truck North American Service Directory
    (Publication #81-370-6421 - 50¢)

These may be ordered by Publication number from:
                Chrysler Corp.
                Box 40
                Detroit, Mich. 48231

It may be possible to secure similar directories from Chevrolet and Ford.

There is no way to predict the frequency of disabling breakdowns (those that require repair in a garage), but the author's experience has been about one run in 20. Frequency of breakdowns requiring an overnight stay were about one every 8 months.

As we know, there are too many types of mechanical difficulties to detail here. Some of the more likely ones are as follows:

CLASS I

These, the worst of all possible breakdowns, normally involve the total loss of one or more of the three major units on the drive train -- engine, transmission, or differential.

1. *Engine* --
    Severe damage or destruction is associated with either an internal defect (failure of a piston, connecting rod, bearing, etc.), or to loss of lubrication.

    Obviously, the oil level should be checked regularly, when buying gasoline. (*Some* units use substantial oil, such as one that required 17 quarts between Indiana and Saskatchewan -- 1,400 miles!)

However, a unit may lose its oil pressure suddenly and dramatically. Be able to recognize abnormal engine sounds when they begin. Loss of oil pressure causes a clattering noise. If shut down *immediately,* damage can probably be avoided. Sudden loss in pressure normally is due to one of three causes, all of which should result only in a Class III Breakdown:

    (1)   Loss of oil pan plug
    (2)   Blown gasket on oil filter
    (3)   Oil pump failure

2. *Transmission* --

As with the engine, transmission failure due to defective internal parts is rare. Loss of lubrication again is the major villain.

If the transmission has a supplemental cooler, fluid loss could result from a loose or broken line. Loss of fluid results in transmission slippage. Stopping immediately generally results in no serious damage (only Class III Breakdown).
Sometimes, a unit leaves clouds of smoke behind upon climbing a steep hill, resulting from transmission fluid leaking onto the hot exhaust system. (Transmission fluid smokes like crazy when heated.)

A serious leak could result in overhaul of the transmission -- a Class I breakdown. But a slow leak can be closely monitored, and fluid added as necessary (This is a class IV breakdown.) Frequently, slow leaks will stop en route.

3. *Differential* --

Failure here is rare, and almost invariably a result of poor or nonexistant lubrication. A driver with sharp ears *may* detect, as he travels, an unusual whine in the background. The only possible remedy is to *stop immediately*, and check all fluid levels, *starting* with the differential.
If the rear end *does* go out, it is likely to be very sudden and dramatic -- a very loud, metallic, rending sound, accompanied by loss of drive train power. Result -- a tow to the nearest qualified dealer, and, as in all Class I Breakdowns, the unit must be left there. The driver continues to his planned *Interlock* point, or back to home base.

CLASS II

These delays are unusual, occurring either as a hasty repair of a Class I Breakdown, or as a long, drawn-out repair of what normally would be a Class III Breakdown.

Most breakdowns (fortunately) fall into either this category, or Class IV.

1. *Electrical Discharge --*

   Check for a loose fanbelt. If belts are tight, a more serious
   problem (such as a faulty alternator) could be present. In that
   case, stop at the first authorized dealership en route, if during
   the daytime.

   If the discharge happens at night, headlights will drain the
   battery quickly. Get to the first town. If no dealer is open,
   locate the appropriate dealership, park in the service drive,
   if possible, and get a good night's sleep. (Pray that this
   doesn't happen on a Saturday night, or the eve of a holiday
   weekend!)

2. *Electrical Fluctuation --*

   If the ammeter flicks wildly and frequently back and forth from
   "charge" to "discharge", go to a dealer and ask him to check first
   for the possibility that the wire leading to an auxiliary battery
   in the back of the unit may have become fused against the exhaust
   manifold.

3. *Faulty Alternator Bolt --*

   Thanks to a manufacturing defect which manifested itself in 1978,
   a Road Rat may be driving serenely down the freeway one moment,
   and find himself confronted an instant later by a sound somewhat
   akin to a hundred banshees, slugging away at steel drums with pipe
   wrenches. He pulls over and stops, expecting the worst. Instead,
   he finds that his problem is probably only irksome -- *if* he is
   prepared.

   Throughout 1978, there were many cases of alternators mounted in
   Dodges in such a manner that too much stress was imposed on the
   upper bolt. It became common for this bolt to shear off, right
   at the engine block, en route. (The author experienced this on
   many runs: two of them were in succession.)

   Fortunately, most of the time this can be *temporarily* corrected.
   The wild racket occurs when the bolt slides forward through the
   alternator housing and contacts the *fan*. (The speed of the fan's
   rotation is the saving factor; the blades contact the bolt constantly,

preventing it from being thrust forward, doing real damage. Drivers should carry at least one 5/8" nut, which they can screw onto the threads remaining at the end of the bolt. This keeps the bolt from sliding through the housing and contacting the fan.

In this configuration, the alternator rides at about a 10-degree angle from the horizontal, placing strain on the *belt*. (It is likely that you can reach your destination with good alternator function, and an unbroken belt -- but be sure to make the dealer aware of it.)

4. *Engine Overheating* --

The most common causes are (1) loss of coolant, and (2) dilution of coolant, during hot weather.

Loss of coolant usually is traceable to a ruptured hose; this can be repaired at any garage. It can also be caused by overheating due to a broken fan belt. That also is easily remedied. Both situations could easily require a tow, however, should the malfunction occur any distance from a service station or garage. *(It pays to belong to AAA!)*

If the level of coolant is stable, one should test the potency of the mixture. Coolant is most effective when it is mixed approximately 50-50 with water. If overheating is a problem with a filled system, but the mixture is weak, the driver should drain some off, and add pure coolant to restore the mixture to full potency.

(Dilution of coolant can be the result of (a) plain water having been introduced into the system, initially, instead of a coolant mixture, or (b) repeated additions of water, due to slow loss of coolant.)

If overheating *still* persists, in hot weather, it sometimes can be controlled by keeping engine r.p.m.'s up. If caught in slow or stop-and-go city traffic, this can be done by driving in a lower gear, or shifting to neutral and revving the engine while waiting for traffic to move. (Often, the fan will provide enough air flow through the radiator in this situation, to prevent boiling over.)

5. *Undesired Paint Job* --

This can result from crossing a freshly-painted highway center stripe. A driver can lose several hours, working with turpentine and rags, to undo the damage. (Sometimes, highway departments give little or no advance warning, so steer clear of any lines which *look* too bright and fresh!)

6. *Carburetion Problems* --

Sometimes, an engine may begin running sluggishly, providing greatly reduced power. It may even die, and not re-start. Here are three of the possible reasons:

> (1) Carburetor float is stuck.
> (2) Engine is flooded.
> (3) Beaded chain to the cruise control may be hung up in the wide-open position.

Unless the driver is a mechanic, he undoubtedly will have to seek assistance to correct a carburetor float problem.

Engine flooding is correctable by the driver, in most cases. The standard procedure is to turn off the ignition and wait a few minutes before again trying to start the engine.

If that doesn't work, this method is almost foolproof:

A. Remove the doghouse cover (*i.e.*, the engine cover).

B. Remove the air cleaner.

C. Be sure no gasoline is lying on top of the engine. If the engine *has* flooded this badly, mop up the gasoline with a rag or paper towels, and discard these well away from the coach.

D. Open the windows of the coach for ventilation. Wait until all fumes have been dispelled.

E. Using a *Vise-Grip* or a pair of locking pliers, clamp off the end of the fuel line tightly, after disengaging it from the carburetor.

F. Try to start the engine, while watching the end of the gas line to be sure fuel isn't being forced past the clamping device. With no new fuel reaching the carburetor, the engine should fire up quickly. Then, it may run for as long as a full minute before it exhausts the supply of gasoline already in the system.

G. After the engine dies, turn off the ignition, re-attach the fuel line, and replace the air filter and doghouse cover. The unit now should start readily, and perform normally.

If one has a unit with cruise control, the chain may get hung up on an engine bolt or similar hindrance, and thus become stuck in the wide-open position. This is most likely to occur if one attempts to increase power while the cruise control is engaged, such as while climbing a hill. The effect is the same as having a jammed accelerator. If this has occurred, it is easy to remedy:

A. Turn off the ignition key and pull off the roadway.

B. Remove the doghouse cover and free the cruise control chain from its snag.

C. Replace doghouse cover and resume trip normally.

7. *Failure of Taillights and/or Clearance Lights* --

If taillights fail, so, usually, do the clearance lights. They frequently are on the same circuit.

Sometimes, replacing a fuse will correct the problem. However, if the defect is in the wiring, a driver could lose much valuable time getting it fixed. Usually, in the case of faulty wiring, the most cost-effective solution is as follows:

A. Determine that brake lights, directional signals, and **4-way** emergency flashers are still functional.

B. Drive as much of the run as possible in daylight.

C. If it is necessary to drive at night, turn on the **4-way** flashers. If the police see you, they generally will assume the true nature of your problem, and not stop you. If they *do* stop you, chances are they'll only require that you get the problem corrected -- and most of the time, they allow a period of time (such as 48 to 72 hours) in which to do it.

Your odds of getting to your destination unhindered are excellent.

CLASS IV

1. *Air Conditioner* --

Air Conditioners only Fail when One is Crossing the Mojave Desert in August!!

Most coaches have air conditioners. When you are assigned a unit that is so equipped, you stand about a 75% chance of reaching your destination with it still functioning properly, if you use it. Occasionally, an air conditioner is inoperative when one receives the unit, but more often, it either will lose its freon or its motor will fail en route, if you receive a defective one. There is no reasonable solution for the problem -- and as a result, some runs seem very warm indeed.

2. *Cruise Control Malfunctions --*

If one is assigned a unit that has a cruise control that works precisely, he can consider himself lucky. *Most* cruise control-equipped coaches have one of these problems:

(1) Cruise control is not precise. After braking, the act of re-engaging the cruise control (by depressing the "Resume" button) causes the coach to cruise at a speed either slightly faster or slower than before. (Most of the time, it is slower.)

(2) Cruise control lags. After initially punching in the desired speed, the unit stabilizes at a speed several miles per hour slower.

(3) Cruise control disengages intermittently of its own accord.

(4) Cruise control sometimes will not maintain speed uphill, and on steep grades, may disengage after unit reaches a low rate of speed (usually around 35 mph).

(5) Cruise control inexplicably fails en route, and will not re-engage.

(6) Cruise control sometimes will disengage when one or the other directional signal is used.

(7) Cruise control disengages when 4-way flashers are turned on. (This defect is present in the *majority* of cases, but not 100%.)

(8) Cruise control is inoperative throughout the entire run.

The most common problem is (8). The frequency of occurrence seems to vary according to the make of the coach. Some manufacturers check this function thoroughly before shipment, and others overlook it consistently.

NOTE: If the speedometer cable breaks, the cruise control will disengage instantly, causing unexpected deceleration. For this reason, it is good practice for one to rest his foot on the accelerator (without pressing down) while passing another vehicle on a freeway. Then, if the speedometer cable were to break just as he pulled back in front of the slower vehicle, he could instantly maintain speed, manually, and avoid being rear-ended.

3. *Blown Fuse --*

One must decide whether he wants or needs the disabled function. Replacement fuses are found at most service stations, or the driver may elect to carry his own supply.

4. *Disabled Radio --*

If the *FM* radio works, but the *AM* band is dead, the AM antenna may be loose. The antenna lead, in that case, often is found dangling down around one's feet. Plugging it back in restores the function.

Winter Storm Procedures

If one is caught in a blizzard, there are few vehicles better equipped to weather the storm than a motor home. Certain procedures are recommended if one becomes stalled in a snowstorm on the open road:

1. If there is propane in the tank, use the furnace as the primary source of heat. If the supply of propane is low, run the furnace intermittently, or set the thermostat quite low, in order to conserve the fuel.

2. If visibility is low, stay with the vehicle unless you have warm clothing and can see shelter nearby.

3. Keep an inside light on, and flash your headlights occasionally, in the universally-understood distress signal (3 long flashes - 3 short ones - 3 long ones; "S.O.S.", in Morse Code).

4. If it is necessary to run the engine for heat, have a window open slightly, and keep the exhaust pipe free of snow. This reduces the carbon monoxide hazard.

5. Do exercises to keep from falling asleep.

CONCLUSION

Simple replacement of common parts (such as headlights, fuses, fan belts, etc.) normally does not require one to seek out a dealer representing the chassis manufacturer. When one replaces such a part, he should *get a receipt,* and *retain the defective part.* (Most dispatchers have had experience with unscrupulous drivers at one time or another, and presenting him with both of these items upon your return will keep you above suspicion, and assure you of reimbursement.)

4

LIVING OUT OF A SUITCASE

*Truck Stops Frequently are
One's "Home Away from Home"!*

Short-term drivers (two to ten weeks or so) will find it easy to work anywhere on the continent, no matter where they live, just by carrying a suitcase or two.

Those who plan to work for several months or years will find that they need a place to use as home base. Those who have their own homes can continue in this fashion, returning home periodically to "re-group" (leave unnecessary items, replace clothing, etc.)

If a long-term driver has many belongings, he may do well to put everything he doesn't need into storage, and then rent a sleeping room close to his dispatch office. The combined cost of renting a room and paying monthly storage fees generally is less than the expense of renting a house or a large apartment.

When a driver spends 90% or more of his time on the go, he needs to find quick and economical ways and places to eat and to meet personal needs, such as showers and laundry.

The least-expensive way to eat is the same as the one he probably practices if living at home: he shops at supermarkets. Careful shopping yields a wide variety of good and healthful food that can be eaten on the road, such as fruits, many vegetables, luncheon meats, cheese, nuts, milk, soft drinks, etc., etc. The biggest limitation is food that needs to be heated or cooked.

Having a small, styrofoam ice chest is very beneficial. Without it, one is limited to buying food that requires no heating *or* refrigeration. The ice lasts about 24 hours, and costs about 50¢/bag in most places.

It is a good idea to purchase two or three flexible plastic sandwich containers having tightly-fitting lids. With these, one can store everything needing refrigeration from salads to luncheon meat without danger of seepage inside the ice chest.

(You are embarking on a perpetual vacation. Why not make it a *picnic,* too?)

Showers and laundry facilities can be found at nearly all of the large truck stops. The showers range in cost from free to $1.00 or so. Soap and towels are provided. A *few* truck stops are even thoughtful enough to furnish washcloths, as well. Their washers and dryers are frequently less expensive than those in laundromats. (Toss your clothes in and watch a favorite TV show in the trucker's lounge, or take a shower while you wait.)

The Union (76) Oil Company has a large chain of *TruckStops* blanketing the nation. These usually are clean, and most offer the services stated. (You can pick up a free 192-page *Union 76 National TruckStop Directory* at any of their *TruckStops*.)

A good hot meal is welcome now and then, so enjoy yourself seeking out new worlds of cuisine while you travel. You'll probably come up with your own list of favorite eating places.

Security on the Road

Once, at a gas station in San Bernardino, California, at 1:30 a.m., I was surprised when five Chicano youths barged into the rest room and made off with my wallet. (An hour earlier, it had contained $700.00, but when it was stolen, it luckily contained only $4.00. The biggest loss was my driver's license!)

Something like that happens only *once.* Since that time, I have carried *two* wallets. One is an empty dummy, while the other one contains I.D., cash, etc. The *real* wallet is never where anyone would ever find it, while the dummy is always in my pocket.

The next time, if ever, I am held up, all the thief will get is a worn-out, worthless wallet containing nothing but a note making pointed references to his immediate ancestry.

You may never get robbed (it has happened to me only once in my life) -- and let's hope that you are not. But, should it happen, your seeing the thief get a *dummy* wallet would be considerably more satisfying than seeing him get away with your *good* one!

Many companies lack a clear-cut policy regarding picking up hitch-hikers, but most frown on or prohibit this. Check with your dispatcher.

Even though I've never had any trouble with hitch-hikers, I generally avoid picking them up as I often carry several hundred dollars worth of highly-negotiable *cash* on a run. Probably 999,999 out of every million hitch-hikers are okay, but with all that cash in the coach, I figure, "better safe than sorry."

* * * * * * * * * *

5

DELIVERING THE UNIT

Immediately upon reaching a destination city, it is wise to pull off the road and reorganize. Invariably, you will have things to put back into suitcases (such as sleeping bag, CB radio, radar detector, etc.), and you will possibly need to shave and clean up as well. Service station rest rooms are handy for this, if you're in a hurry.

When you arrive at the dealership, locate the person in charge of checking in new units, so that he knows you are there. Dealerships can be busy places.

Check-in of the unit can take a minute or two, or up to an hour of meticulous inspection, depending upon the dealer and his mood.

Remove your luggage from the coach before he inspects the interior. When removing your luggage, *be sure to remove your license plate(s) and put it/them into your suitcase!* (Most companies have arrangements for assessing a fine of from $5 to $25, to cover costs, and to act as a deterrent to forgetting the plate(s).) It is the easiest mistake for a Road Rat to make!

Leaving One's License Plate is a Cardinal Sin!!

Most dealers are *very* cooperative and helpful. Most will even provide drivers with transportation to the nearest depot. (I have many happy memories of dealers throughout the land who have really made me feel welcome!)

Unfortunately, there are a few dealers (perhaps 5%) who seemingly have a sadistic streak that manifests itself when drivers are present. Perhaps one dealer out of 20 will purposely cause drivers to miss busses or planes, and/or force drivers to resort to taking a taxi to the depot or airport.

The other 19 out of 20 make up for it in graciousness and hospitality.

Typically, a dealer will ask you if you have noticed anything wrong with the coach. This puts you right on the hot seat between your company and the dealer. It is a reasonable question, but a very thorough answer could lead to a whole list of warranty claims to your factory.

As a general policy, I unhesitatingly provide the dealer with full details of any *chassis* discrepencies, but wait until *specific* questions are asked about the *coach* -- and then give honest answers to those questions. This procedure usually satisfies all concerned.

Depending upon the instructions provided by your dispatcher, you either will receive a check for the coach and/or the freight, or have the dealer sign flooring forms for the bank. A third procedure is for the dealer simply to sign a delivery receipt.

Dealers in some of the larger cities, such as Portland, Oregon or Tacoma, Washington are frequently situated directly on city bus routes. In these cases, it is common for drivers to use this service to reach a depot or airport. Riding city busses (especially crowded ones) is awkward when carrying suitcases, so you will want to plan ahead if possible, and check your luggage in a coin locker at the depot before you deliver the unit.

6

TEAM DRIVING: PROS & CONS

The availability of work competes with the social life of the Road Rat, whether the driver is male or female. Sufficient work is available to keep a competent driver working almost daily, 365 days a year! When one can earn an average of more than $100 a day as a full-time driver, the temptation to work constantly and ignore the formation or maintenance of relationships with members of the opposite sex is very strong. Yielding to this temptation results in a reluctant acceptance of loneliness.

With a little luck, the enterprising Road Rat can have his cake and eat it, too. If one were able to team up with a companion, both drivers could earn good money, and loneliness would fade to a dim memory.

Road Rat Love... The Greatest Way to Enjoy America!

The team need not just be boyfriend-girlfriend. There are many husband & wife teams already working that way. Sometimes, a couple will apply simultaneously, and be hired together.

There is a drawback. Anyone working *singly* who follows the principles in these pages can easily expect to earn $30,000 a year. With harder work, and/or higher-paying companies for which to work, the potential for up to $60,000 exists! However, for reasons given below, a *couple* working together **can expect to earn substantially less**, *per person*.

Assuming the couple is compatible with respect to maintaining a steady mutual pace and lifestyle, certain factors still present either member of a couple from earning as much as he or she could, if working singly:

1. *Differences in Destinations* --

Much of the time, a couple working for a large factory or transporter company can receive assignments in pairs, either to the same destination, or to dealers in closely-neighboring communities. There will be times, though, when this is impossible. In order to stay together, one driver will have to pass up a run and ride along in the same unit with his/her partner, and suffer a loss of perhaps two or three days of work. Or, they can accept two runs in the same direction; the one with the shorter run can deliver first, and then ride along with the partner to his/her destination. If the two destinations are hundreds of miles apart, the member having the *longer* run may have to lose a day by waiting for the other driver to check in the unit.

EXAMPLE:

Brad and Annette arrive at their dispatch office in Los Angeles at noon on Tuesday. Brad is assigned a run to Sacramento, while Annette gets a run to Tacoma, Washington. They depart at 1:00 p.m.

Following a leisurely drive up I-5, they reach Sacramento at 11:00 p.m., and shut down for the night. Tacoma is 15 hours of driving farther north.

If the dealer in Sacramento checks Brad in at 9:00 a.m., it will require until midnight to reach Tacoma, even though they share the driving.

Delivery in Tacoma takes place on Thursday morning, and they arrive back in Los Angeles Friday noon.

If the drivers had been working *singly,* Brad would still have delivered in Sacramento Wednesday morning, *but,* he would have arrived back in L.A. for a new run that same evening. Even if he didn't get a new run until Thursday morning, he would have saved at least 24 hours.

Annette, meanwhile, could arrive in Tacoma in time to deliver *her* coach late in the afternoon on Wednesday. (At an *average* driving speed of 50 mph, it would require 23 hours to cover the 1,150 miles from L.A. to Tacoma. That would allow five hours for sleeping. Experienced Road Rats generally can *average* closer to 55 mph while driving. If Annette did *this,* she could drive to Tacoma in 21 hours, which would provide her seven hours for sleep along the way. More than enough.)

A third alternative, of course, when offered widely-separated destinations is to split up and run them singly. This becomes complicated, however, in regard to getting together again. They could stay out of phase in their arrivals in L.A. for several days.

For this reason, if partners *do* choose to split up for a run, a better alternative might be to accept two runs of approximately *equal distances,* even though in *different directions,* so that they could join up at home base simultaneously. Annette, for example, could take the Tacoma run as before, but Brad might be able to take a unit to Albuquerque, N.M. Both units could be delivered Wednesday afternoon, and the partners could meet in L.A. Thursday evening.

Acceptance of the plan to occasionally run separately is a key to making good money.

2. *Breakdowns --*

If a couple works together constantly, the amount of down time due to breakdowns will nearly double for each member, because twice as many units are being driven as by *one* driver, working *singly*. A breakdown under this arrangement stops *both units.*

It is obvious that even *if* a couple could *always* get runs to the *same* dealers, *all the time* -- which is improbable, they *still* would be making less money, *per person,* by working together, than if they worked singly, because of Factor #2 -- they would be sharing their down time from breakdowns!

If a couple wished to stay together continually, and were willing to settle for a comfortable joint income, they could run together driving two units whenever practical, and share the driving of *one* unit whenever two units going to the same location were *not* available.

It would be reasonable to expect that such a working arrangement could bring in a joint income of $40,000 - $50,000 per year. That's a *minimum* of $20,000/year, per driver, if total earnings were divided evenly between the two members. That's a very comfortable income, and the arrangement provides constant companionship.

That's the best of all possible worlds!

PART III

ENERGY HOAXES -- THE GREATEST THREAT TO YOUR LIFESTYLE

The original edition of this book rolled off the press in February, 1979 -- just one scant month before the advent of Energy Hoax II.

Therefore, mention was made on that edition only of the "Great Energy Hoax of 1973-74". Now that we have experienced a second one, we tend to number them, as we do World Wars. The 1973-74 hoax thereby is known as Energy Hoax I (or, EH I), and the one of 1979 is EH II.

As I write these words in late November of 1986, I sincerely hope that history doesn't repeat itself and present us with EH III in February, 1987 (a month after <u>this</u> book is released)!

Just in case it does, though, either now or later on, this book is designed to enable you to withstand the storm and retain your lifestyle. You might have to work at it, however, if you happen to be engaged in the delivery of recreational vehicles at the time. EH II dealt a disastrous blow to the RV industry, leaving it reeling for years before recovery was complete. If we see an EH III, the same thing is likely to happen again.

Forewarned is forearmed, so if you see a new energy hoax looming, <u>that</u> is the time to start looking for a job with a manufacturer of a more indispensible specialized vehicle. Don't wait until the Energy Hoax has chucked you out into the street, or you'll likely find yourself competing for the job you want along with thousands of other hungry RV drivers.

In preparing this 1987 Edition, I nearly deleted all of Part III because the material seemed to have become very dated over the eight years since it first was presented. However, it was interesting to look back and see how differently we perceived this problem then, and so it is presented once again to you, completely unchanged, for two reasons. It is an item of some historical interest, and... it provides an interesting backdrop against which to examine the situation as it is today.

At this writing, the 55-mph speed limit is still a reality... but so is the Tenth Amendment of the U.S. Constitution. And in 1987, I still firmly believe that if even <u>one</u> state were to rebel against what I call "federal blackmail" by raising its speed limit, and then fight for its rightful federal highway funds in the U.S. Supreme Court, citing the 10th Amendment, that would restore normal sovereignty of the individual states virtually overnight. Wyoming came close to doing this, and in 1986, for a few hours, Nevada actually <u>did</u> raise the limit for a few hours along I-80. Unfortunately, they backed down when the federal government moved to carry out its threat. Perhaps Nevada was unaware of the tremendous clout it had waiting in the wings... in the form of a document far stronger than the U.S. Congress.

One last word... federal blackmail has begun to crop up in other areas, such as pressuring states to adopt seat belt laws. It would seem vital to our well-being as a free people to see an immediate halt to this unscrupulous means of circumventing our Constitutional rights... before matters get completely out of control.

1

THE "ENERGY CRISIS": HISTORY'S GREATEST HOAX

They called it a "crisis", but in reality it was a hoax. Not an ordinary hoax, but a massive one of unprecedented proportions.

Looking back on the supposed "Energy Crisis" of 1973-74 through enlightened eyes, one only can feel stunned and marvel that this, the greatest hoax ever to be perpetrated upon the Free World could have been pulled off successfully. It would seem that in order for this to have happened, a strongly-united coalition of political and industrial forces would have to have worked hand-in-hand with the leadership of all the major news media. Otherwise, there would have been a significant leak, and the entire cruel, criminal trick upon hundreds of millions of people would have blown sky-high right in their faces.

Unfortunately for all of us, the 3-way coalition presented a powerful united front, and Lincoln was very nearly proven wrong in his historic statement, "You can't fool *all* of the people, *all* of the time."

Only a relative handful of people realized that the "Energy Crisis" was in fact a hoax, right from the start. Apparently, none of them were in a position to do anything about it.

Half of our victory in World War II can be attributed to shot, shell and bravery. The other half can be credited to an extremely well-orchestrated media blitz right here at home. All the Powers-that-be -- political, indust-rial, and media -- combined forces to the extent that they totally convinced the American people for *years* that we were up against a very formidable, horrendously cruel and vicious enemy against whom we could very well lose unless we poured virtually every ounce of our physical and economic strength into the war effort. It was an emotionally-charged appeal to meet a very *real* crisis head-on, and it worked.

If the same tactics had been used at the start of the Vietnam War, we probably would have won the conflict within two weeks. However, for some reason, the Powers-that-be decided that victory in this instance would be undesirable, so the media fostered and nurtured an ambivalence on the part of the people. Instead of the united front against a common enemy that was sought during World War II, polarization resulted instead. Never was Vietnam considered a true "crisis". "Crisis" is a trigger word. In the case of Vietnam, as far as the Powers were concerned, the reaction to a "crisis" was clearly the last thing they wanted from the people.

In 1973, though, it was "crisis" time again. This time, the enemy was supposed to be the nasty old Arabs, who purportedly were boycotting our importation of Middle East oil.

Instantly, we were in the throes of an "Energy Crisis."

Isn't it amazing how all our channels of petroleum distribution broke down so quickly that within a few scant *days*, gas stations either were out of gasoline completely, or else had to ration it? No matter, of course, that *weeks* must pass in actuality from the time the oil leaves the wellhead in the Middle East, until it comes out of the pump at your local gas station. In a crisis, amazing things can happen.

While all of this was going on, heads were shaking in many places over some rather incongruous events. Such as the filling of underground tanks in abandoned or former gas stations by oil companies because all *their* gasoline storage facilities were *full,* for example. Or the fact that petroleum-import-ing tankers were forced to drop anchor and stand by for days or weeks off the American coastlines -- for the same reason.

Ask the "little guy" in the petroleum industry in New Jersey, Texas, Bakersfield, California, and even Montana -- and he'll tell you the same thing.

We never had an "Energy Crisis". At the very most, we had a very elaborately-controlled *distribution* crisis -- thoroughly contrived by Big Oil.

Just about that time, enough Americans *should* have been putting two and two together to conclude that there was something rotten in Houston -- except that the same investigative reporters who were carefully ignoring the mounting evidence of the Great Energy Hoax were having a field day with *Watergate!*

Throughout his political career, President Nixon had been called lots of things, but seldom was he ever regarded as a stupid man.

Yet, Nixon allowed himself to be slowly crucified for more than a year for a petty, bungled incident that easily could have been forgotten by everyone a week after it happened.

Those who remember Harry Truman can well imagine he might have handled Watergate simply by getting on nationwide TV and saying something like, "Well, folks, we screwed up. I'll fire those responsible and publicly apologize for their actions, and we can get back to the things that are important."

The fact that Nixon didn't handle things this way left many wondering about his intelligence.

The extent of Big Oil's political clout in the world may well stagger the imagination.

Throughout the Great Energy Hoax, Nixon staunchly regarded it as a crisis in his public statements, and played his role well. Yet, one wonders how he possibly could have helped but know the truth.

The entire Watergate saga may have been a red herring of monstrous proportions -- a diversion that lasted just about as long as the supposed "Energy Crisis" did -- keeping the people's minds off the possibility they were being conned.

And Nixon? He may well have known all along that he was being politically sacrificed. No one really knows *how* powerful Big Oil is, but its power is *immense* at the very least.

Ultimately, the "Energy Crisis" was declared over. (After all, why wear out a good trigger word? It might have to be used again someday!)

When the dust had settled, a good many small, independent oil companies were bankrupt and dead, with the giants of Big Oil raking the soil over their graves. (Most "cut-rate" chains today are fronts for the major oil companies, and owned by them. For example: *Big-Bi* is *Mobil; Go-Lo* is *Gulf,* and *Bingo* is *Exxon,* just to name a very few.)

In addition, prices of gasoline and diesel fuel had found new levels -- double the previous ones.

At the height of the Hoax, *Federal Blackmail* of the states became more than ever an established way of life following an almost gleeful race by bandwagon-riding members of Congress to romp, stomp, and trample all over our constitutional rights in forcing upon us a mandatory (and nonsensical) 55-mph speed limit.

And so, in the ruins of our constitutional rights, amidst the trauma of double-digit inflation in the wake of doubled prices for petroleum derivatives, the Powers-that-be calmly and quietly declared the "Energy Crisis" ended. Now, they said, we have an "energy *problem*" instead.

They were wrong.

Now we have a *crisis*. But not in *energy*.

2

AMERICA'S *TRUE* STATUS: AVAILABLE ENERGY TO SPARE

What about the *current* status of energy in the USA?

Even if we consider only our *petroleum* reserves, we're not in half-bad shape. Early estimates by Big Oil had the reserves under Alaska's North Slope alone pegged at being sufficient to meet this nation's petroleum demands for as long as the next 500 years.

One must remember, though, that these were pre-Energy Hoax estimates. Presumably, at that time, the Hoax hadn't been hatched yet in the minds of the Big Oil Powers-that-be.

Today, of course, Big Oil claims that our North Slope oil reserves will meet only 11% of our petroleum needs, for only the next 30 years, and then be depleted.

While doing a story on the Alaska Pipeline during the summer of 1976, I spent some time at Prudhoe Bay.

There, amidst all the activity and structures associated with the center of Alaska's oil boom, something was conspicuously missing.

Where are the wells?" I asked. "I don't see any *pumps!*"

There are no pumps up here, my hosts replied. "Much of the North Slope is underlain with oil. All you have to do is tap into it. It's an artesian type of flow. There is sufficient pressure that you just drill a well and cap it. The oil flows by itself."

Many sites on the North Slope are underlain with oil. And it's 200 miles from the Brooks Range to the Arctic Ocean. A vast, gradually-sloping shelf of land 200 miles wide and several hundred miles long.

Big Oil claims all this oil will be gone in 30 years.

Anyone out there believe in fairy tales?

The pipeline itself, incidentally, appears quite capable of serving us well for hundreds of years, with proper maintenance.

Sources in Texas have assured me that the still-untapped wells in the vast Permian Basin promise perhaps even more oil than Alaska's reserves.

The Federal Government surely knows how much oil we have. And the Arabs are no dummies; *they* know. Only one group of people is being kept in in the dark. America's population. After all, *we're* the ones who *use* this resource -- and pay the price Big Oil demands.

Science can make giant strides in this country when the chips are down. The Space Race is an excellent example. We have electronic wonders that wouldn't have evolved until the 21st century, if not for the Space Program.

Similarly, if we ever *were* faced with a *real* energy crisis, science could move quickly in the pinch to provide us with alternate sources of energy. No *true* energy crisis could ever develop overnight. We would have whole decades of warning. Plenty of time.

Our Bright Energy Future

Today, science is rapidly expanding the field of catalyst technology. Catalysts are chemicals which change the time of a chemical reaction. They either speed it up or slow it down -- without being affected themselves by the reaction.

Scientists realistically expect that through the discovery and implementation of new catalysts, they soon will be able to produce *twice* as much gasoline from a given quantity of petroleum than previously has been possible with conventional refining processes.

Ultimately, they believe that we will be able to produce gasoline from sources *other* than petroleum.

Every source of energy on this planet can be traced back to the sun. Radiant energy from that continuous fusion reaction in space warms the earth's surface, keeping molecules moving rapidly in all substances.

In the case of the oceans, this means that the water remains a liquid, subject to motion in the form of tides, waves, and currents. All three of these can be drawn upon as important sources of energy. It's the same with the atmosphere -- energy can be tapped from the wind.

All of these are sources ultimately derived from the sun. They are second-generation sources of solar energy.

Development of means to harness primary solar energy to suit our needs also is in the works.

Nuclear energy is a reality right now, but the way we are going about it is exceedingly wasteful.

The nuclear reactors currently in use consume enriched Uranium as fuel. Through various extraction techniques (such as the gas diffusion process which produces the majority of our nuclear fuel, at Oak Ridge, Tenn.), the isotope U_{235} is extracted from quantities of refined Uranium.

U_{235} -- the *fissionable* isotope of Uranium -- makes up only a *trace of* the Uranium provided by nature. Most of the element Uranium is composed of the isotope U_{238}, which is *not* fissionable.

Through the enrichment process, a metallic Uranium is produced which has a high enough U_{235} content to be fissionable.

Today's nuclear power plants simply use up this fuel. When it has been depleted, it is gone forever. In short decades, planet earth could be totally devoid of all fissionable material.

But -- the controversial breeder reactor (to which President Carter was opposed) would *convert* much of the U_{238} in the fuel supply into Plutonium, which is a fissionable element that does not exist in nature. Such a reactor would produce *more* Plutonium than the U_{235} content that goes in. This Plutonium then could be used to fuel present and future nuclear power plants of the conventional type. This would *extend* our supply of fissionable materials sufficiently to assure us of abundant nuclear energy for 1,000 years or more.

I wonder who is financing the opponents of the breeder reactor, and nuclear power in general?

The energy source that particularly intrigues me is *Hydrogen*.

Try as we might, we could thrive on energy from Hydrogen for a billion years, and not make a dent in the reserves.

Where, then, you may ask, are the reserves? Look toward any lake, stream, or ocean, and think of the formula for water: H_2O. Each water molecule is composed of two atoms of Hydrogen and one atom of Oxygen. With our technology, these elements are easily separated.

As a fuel, Hydrogen is absolutely pollution-free, and contains nearly as much latent energy by weight as gasoline.

Very logically, you probably wonder where we might get the power to operate the plants that would produce the Hydrogen. Remember that *thousand-year supply* of nuclear energy?

When one burns something in earth's atmosphere, Oxygen supports the combustion. That which is burned, becomes *oxidized*. The product that results from the burning is an *oxide*.

If you were to burn Hydrogen, as in an internal combustion engine, for example, you would get hydrogen oxide. No other by-products or wastes. Just that one compound out of the tailpipe and nothing more. Hydrogen oxide. There is a more common name for it, however.

Water.

* * * * *

HOW TO *NEUTRALIZE* FEDERAL BLACKMAIL

America's founding fathers realized that a central (federal) government was necessary, but feared the consequences if their creation were to gain too much power. For this reason, the U.S. Constitution was written to provide explicitly that any powers not actually specified as being within the domain of the federal government are automatically delegated exclusively to the individual states.

During the Great Energy Hoax, Congress knew very well that it could not legally enact a federal 55-mph speed limit. Such an act would have been beyond its constitutional authority.

Federal blackmail of all 50 states resulted.

Congress deliberately circumvented your federally-guaranteed constitutional rights by *threatening* the states with loss of their federal highway funds.

Those highway funds come from *our* tax dollars, which we entrust to the federal government, which is supposed to act merely as a broker. There is no way that Congress should be able to hold potential loss of *our own money* over our heads like a Damocles Sword.

But it happens just that way. And the majority of members of state legislatures in every single state are such gutless wonders, that *not one state* has yet challenged this Congressional decree!

All it would take is just *one* state. One state out of 50, to stand up to Congress and say, "We are reinstating our normal speed limits. Try to withhold our highway funds if you wish, but we will challenge the constitutionality of your action in the U.S. Supreme Court under the 10th Amendment of the U.S. Constitution."

Such an action by that one courageous state would accomplish two very important things:

1. The federally-mandated 55-mph speed limit would fall apart overnight like a house of cards. Federal blackmail wouldn't stand a chance against a highly-publicized, state-backed challenge in the Supreme Court.

2. It would put Congress soundly in its place, causing the swift demise of other, less-obvious forms of federal blackmail, and discouraging attempts to fabricate new ones.

We constantly are bombarded with propaganda, such as: "55. It's a Law
We Can Live With." And: "55. It's Not Just a Good Idea. It's the Law", etc.
(Most originate with the Ad Council, which works hand-in-glove with the Federal
Government.)

However, the fact remains that 50% of all highway deaths are caused by
drunken drivers. Ironically, there is virtually no federal pressure to
reduce or eliminate *that* very substantial problem.

That kind of thinking ranks right up there with such federal concepts as
subsidizing tobacco growers while banning cyclamates -- because the latter
caused cancer in *a few* rats that first were *engorged* with it.

PART IV

GETTING HOME

- - - - - - - - - - -

1

FINDING THE BEST METHOD

Unless you were independently wealthy before becoming a Road Rat, you will find some methods of returning from a run far superior to others.

Some methods are so abysmal, you probably wouldn't last two weeks.

One method is so *good,* it will enable you to earn at least $30,000 a year, *after* paying the cost of return transportation.

Unless you are able to establish *Interlock* (Part V) before you start, you will find that more than half the miles you travel will be on return trips to your home base -- the town and office out of which you work.

Several options for accomplishing this are open to you:

Option 1 -- Drive Out - Fly Back --

This is a super way to do it *if* you like the idea of working all the time and having *little* to show for it.

On nearly all runs of 300 miles or more, you will find that flying home will save you scads of time, and enable you to make many more runs within a given period of time.

But there's a hitch! The plane tickets will cost you scads of money. In many cases, the air fare will cancel your profits completely!

Example: You are given a run from Fort Wayne, Indiana to Denver, Colorado -- a distance of roughly 1,250 miles. You receive a total of $225.00 to cover all expenses. The amount of cash remaining when you return is your profit.

Let's consider that you're in top form, and have had plenty of sleep. If you are able to get two or three hours of sleep en route, you can leave early on Monday morning and deliver the following morning. (The time change(s) are in your favor, going west.)

If your unit costs 9¢/mile to drive, your gasoline cost will be $112.50. Exactly half your money will be gone.

So you hop a jet plane back to Fort Wayne, and arrive the same afternoon (Tuesday) -- in time to take out a new run on the same day.

So far, so good. *But* -- Your plane ticket cost you $116.00.

The run *cost* you $3.50.

(If the trip took 60 hours, you spent 5.8¢/hour of your *own* money from *before* the run, and therefore *earned* nothing.) This does not include meals eaten while you were away.

Ever see that poster of the exhausted cat with his paw draped over a cheerful, alert-looking mouse? It says, "The rat race is over. The rats won!"

In this case, they are not talking about Road Rats. No self-respecting Road Rat would inflict such punishment on himself.

Masochists, maybe.

But not true Road Rats.

Some people fly home from all their runs. They usually don't last long.

There is a *very important exception* to the example given.

There is no upper age limit for Road Rats, and many people in the field are retired. This job affords retirees the opportunity to continue doing productive, enjoyable work. They can set their own pace, tour the entire country in luxurious motor homes, and then jet back in comfort. Their *actual* source of income might be from Social Security, pension funds, savings, etc., or any combination of these.

In short, they don't need the money. They are Road Rats for the sheer joy of working at something they enjoy.

Retirees need not be concerned with earning $30,000 a year. Regardless of their flight home, they will have made enough money on an average run to eat in a nice restaurant, or see a good show. It's the ultimate way to retire; One remains productive, combined with a perpetual travelling vacation.

Of course, a retiree who establishes *Interlock* will earn thousands of dollars annually, in spite of himself! (See Part V.)

Option 2 -- Drive Out - Return by Rail --

Railroad buffs are crazy about this one, and I can understand this. I *love* to travel by train. The cars are spacious, and when one is tired, the click-clack of the wheels will lull him to sleep.

It's too bad that rail travel is fraught with many disadvantages.

I'm sure you know railroads in the U.S.A. aren't what they used to be. During the last 20 years, passenger rail travel has declined so sharply, it probably wouldn't exist today, had it not been bailed out by the federal government.

The image of railroads today is bleak:

- -- Less than 500 communities are served, by Amtrak's own admission.
- -- Certain entire *States* have no Amtrak service (Maine, South Dakota, and New Hampshire).
- -- Trains frequently run late, or are cancelled.
- -- Trains must travel slowly through many areas, because railbeds have deteriorated badly.
- -- Food served is even more overpriced than in bus depots.

  -- Trains run infrequently (Many cities are served
    by only one or two trains per day.)

  -- Cars often have poor climate control, and are too
    warm or cold for *normal* habitation.

  -- Rail fares usually are higher than bus fares.

  -- Unlimited travel passes cost substantially more per
    day than similar bus travel passes.

All of these elements, combined with the fact that *many runs
are assigned to cities not served by passenger trains,* makes the
train an unfeasible and undesirable means of return transportation.

  In the Denver to Fort Wayne return trip example, one-way rail
fare would cost $97.00. (Round trip is only $112.00 if return is
made within 40 days, but the likelihood of a Road Rat taking a train
away from his office is extremely remote.) If the gas cost $112.50
(as in the example given in Option I), this would leave a final profit
of $15.50 left over from the original $225.00. (The return trip takes
25 hrs., 25 mins.; trains leave Denver daily at 6:20 P.M. and arrive
in Ft. Wayne at 7:45 P.M., following a 2 hr. 35 min. layover and
change in Chicago.)

Option 3 -- Drive Out - Return by Trail Car --

  A trail car is driven by a non-RV driver who follows two
or more RV drivers to their common destination, and then provides
transportation back home.

  The system has the advantage of furnishing RV drivers with
immediate non-stop transportation home, since all concerned can
share driving the return leg.

  The disadvantage is the *cost* of the service.

  Typically, all RV drivers on the run pool their money, from
which all gas (including that for the trail car) is purchased. All
drivers (including trail car owner) share equally in the profits.

  Again, let's use the same Denver run for an example.

  Three RV drivers are paid $225.00 each to run from Indiana
to Denver (1250 miles).

  In this example, we are assuming that each RV costs 9¢/mile
to drive, while the car costs 4¢/mile *each way:*

Total Money Available:	$ 675.00
Gasoline Cost (RV's):	$ 337.50
Gasoline Cost (car-out):	$ 50.00
Gasoline Cost (car-return):	$ 50.00
Total Gas Cost:	$ 437.50
Total Profit:	$ 237.50
Total Profit per person($237.50 ÷ 4):	$ 59.38

Option 4 -- Drive Out - Drive Back (Tow Car) --

Many drivers own a small car which they tow behind the unit to their destination.

The advantage is ready transportation for the return trip.

The disadvantages are numerous, and add up to overwhelming costs.

Using any other option for return transportation, a Road Rat *never* needs to own a car, unless he spends much of his time (such as weekends) at home. So *every* cost associated with the car, including insurance, is extraneous, and therefore can be included when comparing return costs via other methods.

In the Denver example, using the same figures outbound as in the previous examples, suppose the car costs 3¢/mile to drive, in terms of gasoline only. (Most such drivers use compact cars that get good mileage. A cost of 3¢/mile at gasoline prices of 65¢ per gallon figures out to 21.5 miles per gallon.) In addition, he must figure costs of depreciation, repairs, parts, tires, and insurance.

Hypothetically (but realistically), a driver with a tow car that works 330 days and drives 100,000 miles *each way* per year could expect to spend the following for his return trip:

Tire Wear: (@ $50/tire, 8 tires/year, minimum).

$$(\$400.00 \div 165^{*}) = \qquad \$ \quad 2.42$$

* (number of days spent driving home)

Parts Repairs:	$600.00 (minimum) ÷ 165 =	$ 3.60
Insurance:	$200.00 ÷ 165 =	$ 1.21
Gasoline:	3¢/mile x 1,250 =	$ 37.50
	TOTAL	$ 44.73

TOTAL COST OF RUN: $112.50 x $44.73 = $ 157.23

TOTAL PROFIT: $ 67.77

On the *surface,* this may appear more economical than the previous three options. However, the driver here puts himself in the difficult position of having to *drive constantly.* He never gets a break, unless he chooses to make more down time for himself between drives in order to get needed rest -- which he obviously *must* do. (In order to drive 330 days out of the year, therefore, he realistically would *have* to absorb 35 other days as down time -- unless his secret identity is Clark Kent.)

Finally, a tow car requires an *investment,* while most other methods of operating as a Road Rat require *no* investment.

This is a *rat race* -- the very thing most new RV drivers would like to *get away* from!

> *NOTE:* Some companies furnish a company-owned car as a tow car. This system certainly reduces the disadvantages, but the bottom line question is -- Does the driver get paid enough to merit his driving twice as many miles? The answer generally is ... No!

Option 5 -- Drive Out - Return via Bus (One-way ticket) --

Busses serve nearly 30,000 communities in the USA alone, while Amtrak serves only about one in 60 of those. Airports, too, are found mainly in larger communities, and the smaller the community having an airport, the less frequent are the schedules that serve it.

The only problem with Option 5 is the *type* of ticket the Road Rat purchases.

Both Greyhound and Trailways offer special "bargain" one-way fares, from point to point within each system (i.e., one cannot buy a *Greyhound* ticket of this type to a city served only by *Trailways,* and vice-versa).

These tickets really *are* bargains for the casual traveller who seeks only to travel to a point far away -- but they present no bargain to the Road Rat.

They are bargains only when you consider that *regular* one-way fares are *more* expensive. There is a much *less* expensive way for Road Rats to ride, as described in Option 6.

As this book goes to press in February, 1979, Trailways offers its one-way ticket for $65.00, and the Greyhound one sells for $69.00. With such a ticket, one could even travel from Key West to Seattle (over 3,600 miles.) It is reasonable to expect, based on past performance, that these fares will be higher during the summer months when it is again a seller's market.

Looking again at the Denver-Ft. Wayne example (given the same outbound data as before):

Cost of return:	$ 65.00	(minimum, via Trailways)
Total Cost of Run:	$177.50	($112.50 for gas, plus bus tickets)
Total Profit:	$ 47.50	($225.00 - $177.50)

> *NOTE:* Drivers buying such one way tickets should purchase the ticket(s) through to the coast (or border) to the closest city in an approximate straight line with their actual destination. The destination should be designated as a *stop-over point* when ticket is purchased.

When a ticket from Denver to Fort Wayne costs $65.00, but the same ticket from Denver to New York, or better yet, Portland Maine would *still* cost $65.00, why not go all the way. In Fort Wayne, the driver might be able to locate someone within the 30-day life of the ticket who wants to go to New York or New England, and sell it to him.

Option 6 -- Drive Out - Return by Bus (Unlimited-travel Bus Pass) --

Both Greyhound and Trailways offer a ticket granting the holder unlimited travel until its expiration date, on almost every scheduled bus in the USA and Canada. Most of the smaller, independent bus lines honor the *Ameripass* and the *Eaglepass*.

Both major bus lines *usually* charge the same price for their passes, and offer the same types with respect to the amount of time it is valid.

On January 25, 1979, the two bus lines offered the following tickets (compared here with the prices of Amtrak's *USA Railpass*):

Duration		Amtrak *USA Railpass*	Greyhound *Ameripass*	Trailways *Eaglepass*
7 Days	--	(None)	$ 99.50	$ 99.50
14 Days	--	$169.00	(None)	(None)
15 Days	--	(None)	$149.50	$149.50
21 Days	--	$219.00	(None)	(None)
30 Days	--	$259.00	$199.50	$199.50

All passes are for unlimited travel. Bus passes can be used on *nearly all* bus lines in the USA and Canada, but not Amtrak. The *USA Railpass* is good throughout the Amtrak System (in Canada: to Montreal, only), but *not* on any busses.

The best deal for Road Rats is the *30-day* bus pass. Figuring the average month as 30 days, it costs $6.65/day to maintain the pass.

The next chapter will show that the *actual* price per day for long-term Road Rats is $6.55/day, so we'll use *that* figure in the Denver-Fort Wayne exemple.

Using the same outbound figures, the round trip costs on the Denver run, for a driver using a bus pass is as follows:

Return Transportation: $ 16.38 (2.5 days @ $6.55/day)*
Total Cost of the Run: $128.88 ($16.38 + $112.50 for gasoline)
Total Profit: $ 96.13 ($225.00 - $128.88)
Daily Profit: $ 38.45/day

* Even though the pass is used for *transportation* for 1.5 days, it still had to be *maintained* during the trip out (assuming it wasn't first *purchased* in Denver, on *this* run).

1987 Update: *These prices change constantly. The 1979 prices here were kept for example only. Please check prices with carriers.*

CONCLUSION

The Fort Wayne-Denver run used as an example in all the above Options assumed payment was from a *transporter* company. Payment to the driver was at the rate of 18¢/mile. (Part I, Chapter 1 discusses aspects of working for factories vs. transporter companies.) *

If a driver worked steadily for this hypothetical company for a year, took 30 days for vacation and/or down time, and left immediately upon returning each time, he could expect to average $12,880.75 per year.

The rate per mile and round-trip time expended are typical for runs of that length for a transporter company.

Using the figure of 30¢/mile, as paid by the average *RV manufacturer,* * the figures for all the Options have been calculated for our sample run to Denver, and the Total Profit and Daily Profit are recorded in the table below. This enables you to compare factory earnings to transporter company earnings. But more importantly, it allows you to see the dramatic savings of using Option 6 as a method of return, over Options 1 through 5.

	Transporter Co. -- $225.00 (@ 18¢/mile)		*RV Manufacturer --* $375.00 * (@ 30¢/mile	
	Total Profit	Daily Profit	Total Profit	Daily Profit
Option 1	- $ 3.50	- $ 1.40	$146.50	$58.60
Option 2	$15.50	$ 6.20	$165.50	$66.20
Option 3	$59.38	$23.75	$171.88	$68.75
Option 4	$67.77	$27.11	$217.77	$87.11
Option 5	$47.50	$19.00	$197.50	$79.00
Option 6	$96.13	$38.45	$246.12	$98.45

Using Option 6, at the above rates of pay, a Road Rat can reasonably expect annual earnings as follows (based on 330 days/year of work):

Transporter Company : $12,688.50
RV Manufacturer : $32,488.50

The title of this book states that one can earn $30,000 a year. This, as you have discovered, was a *conservative* estimate. The potential for *over* $30,000 has already been demonstrated.

The *best* is yet to come, in Part V: *Interlock!*

---

* *1987 Update: The older pay scale tables are presented here as examples, but pay varies with companies, and in general is far far higher today than you see here. Check with potential employers. (Many examples like this are used in this new edition, and can be used very efficiently by simply substituting current figures that companies can furnish you.)*

2

THE VERSATILE BUS PASS ---
PUTTING IT TO WORK FOR YOU

The *XANADU System* <u>depends</u> upon continual use of an *unlimited-travel bus pass,* as described in Option 6, in the previous chapter. Since the purpose of this book is to inform its readers as to how to make *good* money while travelling, there is no point in further discussion of any second-rate methods.

Until mid-December, 1978, both Greyhound and Trailways offered a two-month ticket for $325.00. The recent change to maximum pass duration of only *one* month was an expensive one for the bus lines' most regular customers:

COST DIFFERENCES: 1 and 2 Month Bus Passes

Type of Ticket	Number Needed Per Year		Ticket Price		Annual Cost	Daily Cost
1-Month Pass	12	x	$199.50	=	$2,394.00	$6.55
2-Month Pass	6	x	$325.00	=	$1,950.00	$5.34
		Difference in Cost:			$ 444.00	$1.21

Hopefully, this may only be a temporary period of unavailability for the 2-month tickets. (Tariffs change frequently, and these $325.00 passes may be on the market again within a few months.)

Bus pass users should be aware of certain regulations and procedures pertaining to their tickets. Being informed can easily save a driver between $150 and $200 a year.

1. A one-month ticket is figured on a *calendar* month basis -- not a 30-day period.

2.   Travel days do not include the date of sale, even though one *can travel* legitimately on the date of sale. For example, if a one-month ticket is purchased on May 3, it should be marked to expire on June 4. (This provides 32 days of actual travel across a 31-day month, or 31 valid days across a 30-day month.)

If a ticket agent insists on selling you a pass that does not comply with these time frames, you have several choices open:

(1)   See the Terminal Manager and explain that the agent is not following the tariff requirements. He can usually set it right, but you'll need an extra 15 minutes or so to go this route.

(2)   Go to another pass-issuing depot, if convenient, and buy the ticket there.

(3)   Purchase the pass as the agent wants to issue it, but be sure that the date of sale is both correct and legible. When the book runs low on coupons, seek an agent who will reissue it with the *correct* expiration date punched or marked.

3.   Be sure that the issuing agent marks the ticket with his validation stamp. This validation goes on the back of the *first* page (the identification page) of the Greyhound *Ameripass,* and on the cover of the Trailways *Eaglepass.* The presence of this stamp is meaningless to some agents, and important to others, so don't take a chance.

4.   Try to plan your runs so that your bus pass expires very shortly after an arrival at your home base. If you can time your arrival home to coincide with the demise of the ticket, you will save $6.55 per day for as long as it takes you to drive to your next destination. Savings of $13.10 to $19.65 are realistic between passes.

(*NOTE:* A bus pass expires at *midnight* of its expiration date. If you are on a bus at that time, the bus driver has the right to put you off at the first depot he reaches after midnight. Many drivers will require this.)

If you could manage an average of $13.10 between passes, each time one expires, you would save a total of $157.20 annually on transportation.

A bus pass has incredible versatility, but all too many passengers are not fully aware of this. Much of this versatility comes in the form of one's being able to ride the busses of competing lines. Certain rules govern this:

1.   To ride a bus line offering *parallel service*, the Road Rat needs to obtain a *diversion sticker* from the issuing bus line. (Parallel service exists when two or more bus lines serve the same destination point from your point of origin. In some large cities, such as Las Vegas, and Portland, Oregon, Trailways and Greyhound have a supply of *each other's* stickers on hand, but most places don't make them quite that convenient.)

Greyhound *Ameripasses* require the *gray* sticker; Trailways
Eaglepasses require the *pink* sticker.

To obtain a sticker, one usually needs only to request it from
the ticket agent.

2.   Diversion stickers are *not necessary* if one plans to travel on
a competing line over a route *not served by the line that issued
the ticket*. *BUT* -- some agents don't know this. If in doubt, get
a sticker. With one, you *can't* go wrong -- but without it, you can
find yourself stranded. Some drivers and agents don't know the rules.

3. Some depots *never* seem to have diversion stickers, which
causes many problems for travellers needing to ride competing
lines. (This is true of the Trailways depots in Fresno and
Los Angeles, California, and Daytona Beach, Florida, among
other places.)
When this happens, bus pass users are at the mercy of the bus
lines. There is no substitute for the diversion sticker.
Only the bus lines, themselves, can correct this deficiency.

Bus Line Liability

Bus lines assume no liability for lost or stolen tickets. Safeguard
your bus pass as though it were cash. If the ticket were to be stolen,
chances are excellent that the thief could use it, himself, for the rest
of its natural life.

In theory, names and addresses are recorded on bus passes to make them
non-transferable... but in reality, I have had a ticket verified against my
I.D. only twice in three years. Both times were at the Los Angeles Greyhound
Depot.

Bus Riding for Fun & Profit

Believe it or not, bus riding *can* be both enjoyable and profitable!
The book you are reading was planned and outlined by the author while
riding home from runs. Over *half* of this book was even *written* that way.
Bus riding need not be down time at all. It can be a time for you to
pursue *other* objectives.

Most people riding busses don't do so as a way of life, so you'll find
that *your* lifestyle amazes them. To *them*, a long bus ride is a necessary
evil -- they can hardly wait to reach their destination.

For the Road Rat with substantial bus-riding experience, time telescopes
dramatically. A two-day ride from Seattle to Chicago (2,100 miles) *seems*
to take only a few hours and cover maybe 200-300 miles, if you are busy with
a pet project.

While not working on a project of some sort, there are other options, such as:

1. Visiting with passengers
2. Playing cards
3. Reading
4. Writing letters

...just to name a few good choices.

Best of all, you may find a traveller of the opposite sex with whom to share your seat. And maybe, just *maybe* -- you'll be lucky enough to meet someone so unattached, that you can recruit and team up with him/her.

An excellent example of this is a girl I met in the Birmingham, Alabama Greyhound Depot in February, 1978.

She was a registered nurse from Sydney, Australia and was touring the USA on an *Ameripass*. The opportunity to become a Road Rat expanded her horizons to include places busses don't normally go. After working with me for five months, she took her accumulated earnings and went on to tour the *world*.

The chance to meet someone under similar circumstances happens infrequently -- but it *does* happen.

Riding in Comfort

The occasional bus passenger doesn't ride long enough to learn the many ways in which bus riding can be enjoyable and comfortable. Here is a list of bus-riding tips to help you learn *both* the advantages and the disadvantages of various ways to ride:

1. *Aspects of Riding in the* Back *of the Bus* --

   A. Large seat to sleep in (3 seats wide) if bus is uncrowded.

   B. The last three rows of seats is the smoking section (except in New Jersey, Oregon, Utah, and certain parts of California where smoking on busses is prohibited by state law or local ordinances.) In these cases, people generally turn the rest room into a smoking lounge. (It seems that only about one bus driver in 100 has a sensitive enough sniffer to detect it -- and most of them don't care about what they can't see. In many cases, I have observed *them* smoking -- even in Oregon and Utah!)

   C. The fun-loving crowd usually gravitates to the rear. (For those who are interested, the largest pot parties I've ever seen have been on commercial busses. Once, nearly everyone on the bus was smoking it openly, in pipes, joints -- you name it!) By 1987, people in the rear still seem more fun-loving and active, but marijuana-smoking has pretty much become a thing of the past. A few occasionally try it, but most bus drivers have little or no tolerance for it.

   D. Seats at the very rear of the bus do not recline. In addition, sleeping is hindered by the flow of traffic to and from the rest room,

- 61 -

noise from the engine nearby, and greater bumpiness due to
being situated over the rear wheels.

2. *Aspects of Riding in the Front of the Bus --*

   A. Best seat for scenery is the right front. (Also called the
   "Suicide Seat" by bus drivers, because in the event of a
   collision, passengers sitting here tend to go for a ride
   through the windshield.) The front seat behind the driver
   is second-best for scenery, but has less leg room. (It's
   ideal, if you happen to be a dwarf.)

   B. The front seats provide for the greatest variety in sleeping
   positions, because passengers won't be walking up and down
   the aisle in that location while the bus is moving. (You won't
   have to worry about tripping someone.)

   C. Front seats are no good for work or reading at night on most
   busses, because they have no reading lights. (This is to
   prevent glare on the windshield that might distract the driver.)
   The lights in the second seats back usually are dim. Full-
   strength reading lights are available throughout the rest of
   the bus. (However, you may wish to consider the fact that the
   younger, more animated crowd generally gravitates toward the
   rear. Not so great sometimes for reading or working, but from
   other aspects, it can be more fun.)

3. *Comfort while Sleeping --*

   A. Carry a lightweight thermal blanket. (Busses frequently are
   cold at night, winter or summer.)

   B. Purchase a plastic inflatable pillow (available from larger
   bus depots for $1.00). When not in use, these pillows fold
   compactly and require minimal space in luggage. (For greatest
   comfort, inflate 2/3 full.) The average lifespan of one of
   these pillows is around 20 days (or nights) of use. After this,
   such pillows usually develop a slow leak and are best discarded.

   C. Acquire a double seat, if possible; thus you can change sleeping
   positions, and even lie down. *Or...*

   D. Find a soft, warm seatmate.

3

CATCHING THE ELUSIVE DOG
(...Jackrabbit, Antelope, and Assorted
Other Critters Bus Lines are Named After)

Assuming you already know how to drive, the single, most vital skill
you will need to develop as a Road Rat is bus riding.

Even in a field where the actual work is like a perpetual vacation,
time is money. No company is going to pay you to cushion home on the bus.
The more you are able to minimize this down time, the more miles you will
be able to drive per month.

The best way to get back efficiently is to plan your return trip as
soon as you get a run. Using the techniques outlined in this chapter, you
then should compile an itinerary for your return bus ride, so that it will
begin a relatively short time after your estimated time of arrival.

For planning purposes, until you get to know your regular dealers, it
is usually a safe bet to allow two hours for check-in, from the time you
arrive at the dealership until you board the bus. Many dealers routinely
will check you in considerably faster, and as time goes on, you will learn
who these dealers are, and be able to plan accordingly.

You will very rarely ever miss a bus if you arrive at the dealership
two hours ahead of its scheduled departure time.

Most new drivers generally start out working for just one company,
and then start to arrange for return runs somewhat later on. Until you
have accomplished this, it will be normal for you to think in terms of
always returning by bus to your headquarters.

The effect of this will be for you to gain familiarity with all or
most of the bus schedules which directly influence your return, throughout
the region that surrounds your home base.

Each town or city served by busses has its own unique pattern of bus
lines that feed into it. If the community is a small one, often this will
ultimately funnel down to just one or two schedules per day which directly
serve the community itself.

Clearly, you will have far greater versatility in selecting return
schedules if you work out of a town or city which is served by multiple
schedules daily. It is even better if the community is served by two or
more bus lines.

It would be both impractical and impossible to present here all the bus patterns and attendant bus riding techniques for every community having an RV manufacturer or a vehicle transporter company. Therefore, this book will deal only with the situation as it applies to just *one* community, in great detail: Decatur, Indiana.

Decatur was selected because of the author's substantial familiarity with its regional bus pattern.

This treatment should be helpful in four ways:

1. It will enable you to learn how to use the <u>Russell's Bus Guide</u> efficiently.

2. It will show you how to develop a familiarity with the regional bus pattern of a community. The type of research that is done to determine the pattern for one community applies equally well for ascertaining the patterns of other communities throughout all of North America.

3. It demonstrates a difficult situation: a community served by only two busses daily. Many other places have far easier access, and very few would be more complicated.

4. It will provide you with a nearly complete blueprint for access to Decatur, Indiana -- a town having a fluctuating number of transporter companies which serve the plants run by Fleetwood Industries. Those who start there as I did will find the specific schedules and techniques themselves to be especially valuable.

* * * * * * *

DECATUR, INDIANA
RETURN TRANSPORTATION ACCESS PROFILE
AND SPECIALIZED ACCESS TECHNIQUES

Location:	22 miles SSE of Fort Wayne, Indiana, on U.S. Routes 27, 33, and 224.
Nearest Airport:	Baer Field, Fort Wayne (south side of city); 18 miles distant.
Access by Rail:	Nearest depot -- downtown Ft. Wayne (*Amtrak*).
Access by Bus:	Two schedules only. Both are on A.B.C. Coach Lines. One midday schedule from Ft. Wayne and one late afternoon schedule from Richmond, Indiana. Both run Monday through Friday only.
Other Access:	Taxi -- Fare is approximately $18.00 from Ft. Wayne. By car, via a friend or fellow employee -- Usually done by pre-arrangement. Usually involves minimum cost of paying for the gas (logically).

Hitch-hiking -- Difficult from downtown Ft. Wayne.
Best procedure for hitch-hiking is to take a city
bus (35¢) to Southtown Mall and thumb down U.S.
27 & 33 from the shopping center's northeast
corner. City busses run approximately 30 minutes
apart on weekdays and less frequently on weekends.
It is relatively easy to get rides during daylight
hours from this location if one uses a prominent
sign that says, "DECATUR". (Those working out of
Decatur do well to carry such a sign inside of
their luggage.)

As you can readily see, the best bet is to ride the A.B.C. Lines bus.
(Like most smaller scheduled bus lines, A.B.C. *does* honor the Greyhound
Ameripass and the Trailways *Eaglepass*.) The morning one is best because it
always arrives during office hours. Depending on the transporter company,
runs frequently can be difficult or impossible to obtain after hours.

Because of the difficulty of access to Decatur at night, most return
techniques are attuned to the successful interception of the A.B.C. Lines
schedule from Fort Wayne.

The Road Rat "Bible" is a publication called <u>Russell's Official National
Motor Coach Guide</u>, otherwise simply called <u>Russell's Guide</u> for short. Not
having a fairly up-to-date edition in one's possession can seriously impair
his advance planning.

There are two good ways to obtain them:

1. Check with ticket agents as you stop in various towns and
   cities on your return bus rides. Often, they will have
   copies that they can give you free of charge which are only a
   month or two old. (Tell them about your job, and let them
   know you use a bus pass. Right after the first of the month
   is the best time to ask.)

2. Subscribe directly from:

   Russell's Guides, Inc., Proprietors and Publishers
   817 Second Avenue, S.E.
   P.O. Box 278
   Cedar Rapids, Iowa 52406

The <u>Russell's Guide</u> contains all existing bus schedules within the
United States and Canada. It even includes Mexico and Central America.

Bus schedules do change, so it is best to have a copy that either is
current or very recent. If you choose to use anything but the latest issue,

be sure to phone or see a ticket agent en route and get your tentative return itinerary verified, to be certain that nothing has changed.

The most radical overall schedule changes occur in late June and early September. Bus lines add special schedules during the summer months to accomodate the extra load of travellers. (Certain express schedules, which can be very advantageous, often exist only during that 10-week period. For example, Greyhound runs a bus across from Denver to Chicago in roughly 24 hours, from noontime to noontime, only during the summer months. Be sure to keep yourself up to date on these changes.)

Selected materials from some issues of the Russell's Guide are reproduced within this chapter to help illustrate its use.

USING THE <u>RUSSELL'S GUIDE</u> TO CONSTRUCT
THE BUS ACCESS PROFILE OF DECATUR, INDIANA

1. Direct Access to Decatur

   To find the busses that directly serve Decatur, one must turn to the "Index to Bus Stations" at the back of the book. All cities and towns that have bus service are listed there in alphabetical order, with the bus lines and Table numbers that serve them.

   Refer to the excerpt at the top of the next page, and you will see that all of the service for Decatur, Indiana is covered by Table 1391. (The table itself has been reprinted below the excerpt from the index.)

   (An interesting contrast can be seen in Richmond, *Virginia* -- also contained within the excerpt from the index, but not circled. That city has a fantastic direct-access profile, being served by scores of schedules from a dozen different bus lines.)

   There is one bus to Decatur daily from Fort Wayne, departing from the Trailways Depot at 11:00 a.m., and arriving at 11:40 a.m.

   From the south, the same bus returns from Richmond, Indiana, leaving at 3:30 p.m., and arriving in Decatur at 5:28 p.m.

   IMPORTANT NOTE: During the months that Daylight Savings Time is in effect throughout most of America, nearly all Indiana times are one hour earlier, since Indiana remains on Eastern Standard Time year 'round. This has had the effect in the past of changing the arrival times of those busses serving Decatur to 10:40 a.m. and 4:28 p.m., respectively. While this is true, these earlier arrival times are quite beneficial to the Decatur-based Road Rat. At this time of year, the afternoon bus arrives in Decatur during business hours.

   At the top of each column in Table 1391 is the reference mark,

Davidsonville, Md..136
▲Davis, Cal...600-625-655
Davis, Okla...▲776-778-▲8423
▲Davisboro, Ga...8184
Davis Bros. Rest., Ga. 172
▲Davis City, Ia...751
Davis Corners, Ia. ▲923-1005
Davis Jct., Cal...8553
Davis Jct. X Rds., Ill...1021
Davison, Mich..▲1454-1485
Davis Store, Va...2808
Davisville, R.I...2023
Dawn, Tex...833
▲Dawn, Va...7950
▲Dawson, Ga...8105
Dawson, Ill...1154-1155
▲Dawson, Minn...958
Dawson, Mont...6312
◊Dawson, Tex...4420
Dawson Cor., N.D.509
Dawson Creek, B.C.
　■Coachways System. 6453-6470-6472-6473-6474
　Greyhound...702
Dawson Springs, Ky..3555
Days Inn. Ky...7750
Daysland, Alta..6462
◆Dayton, Mont..6311
Dayton, Nev...4131
Dayton, N.J...7906
▲Dayton, N.Y...2476-2477
Dayton, O.
　▲■Greyhound...1-23-24-25-216-290-344-345-350-355-365
　A.B.C...1391-1392
　Ill.-Swallow...1221
　Short Way...1424
　Tennessee Trail-

Dearing, Ga. 2792-8184
▲Dearson, Ark...3712
Death Valley Jct., Nev...4128a
Deaver, Wyo...4700-▲8505
De Bary, Fla.
　■Greyhound..165-184
　▲■Trailways, Inc..8080
Debden, Sask...6363
De Beque, Colo..8520-8556
De Berry, Tex...8184-8196
Debolt Jct., Alta..6470
Decatur, Ala.
　▲■Cont'l Trlwys...7998
　▲■Greyhound...23-365
　Trlwys. Thru Rte... 7040
▲Decatur, Ark...759
Decatur, Ga.
　■American Coach3035
　▲Cont'l Trlwys...7960
　▲■Greyhound..161-200-202
　■S.E. Stages...2792-2793
Decatur, Ill.
　▲■Cont'l Trlwys...7073
　▲■Crown Transit.1152-1154-1155-1157-1158
　▲■DeLuxe Trlwys...7073
　Gulf Transp...3689
　Ill. Swallow...1223
　Jacksonville Bus1148
　S.E. Trlwys...7754
　Trlwys. Thru Rte... 7065-7073-7075
　◊Decatur, Ind...1391
　Decatur, Mich...1482
　Decatur, Miss...8598
▲Decatur, Neb...8371
▲Decatur, Tex...8250
Decker Lake, B.C.6472
Decorah, Ia.
　▲■Scenic Hawkeye Stages...920-923

Deerwood, Minn..▲514-▲940b
Deerwood Jct., Man... 6373
Defiance, O...401
Deford, Mich...1486
▲De Forest, Wis...521
▲De Funiak Springs, Fla...420
DeGonia Springs, Ind. 1395
De Graff, Minn...537
De Kalb, Ill...▲558-▲559-1021
▲DeKalb, Tex...8186-8190
De Kalb Jct., N.Y.250
DeLand, Fla.
　▲■Cont'l Trlwys...8080-8092-8105
　▲■Greyhound..164-165-184
　Trlwys. Thru Rte... 7000-7001-7028-7050-7055
Delaney, Ark...758
Delano, Cal...▲600-▲630-▲7095
▲Delano, Minn...537
Delanson, N.Y...260
Delavan, Wis...▲530-▼1103
Delavan Jct., Ill...1157
▲Delaware, O..280-315-345
Delaware, Okla...4016
Delaware, Ont...389-2630-2630a
Delaware Rd., Ia...1004
Delaware State College, Del...122
▲Delaware Water Gap, Pa...258-264
Delburne, Alta...6467
▲Delcambre, La...3432
Delco, N.C..8020-8035
▲De Leon Springs, Fla. 164-165

▲7750
Reynolds, N.D...517
▲Reynoldsville, Pa... 7866
Reynosa, Mex.
　■Autobuses Blancos 4097-4097a
　■Linea Azul...4117-4117a-4118
　■Transportes del Norte...4102
　Cont'l Trlwys...8308
　Valley Transit..4200
Rhinebeck, N.Y... 2515-2538
Rhinelander, Wis.
　▲■Greyhound...521
　▲■Wis.-Mich. Coaches. 1055-1057-1060
　Scenic Trails...955
Rhoadsville Jct., Va... 7968
Rhododendron, Ore... 501-7784
Rhome, Tex...8250
Rhyse, Mo...3708
Ribolt, Ky...7976
Ribstone Jct., Alta... 6464
Rice, Minn...512-514
Rice, Tex...8252-8258
Riceboro, Ga..160-310
Rice Hill, Ore...600
Rice Lake, Wis...◆954-955-▲959-1055
Riceville Jct., Pa..2081
Richardson, Sask..706
Richardson, Tex.▲575-▲8197-▲8428
Richardson Grove, Cal...607
Richard Spur, Okla... 781
▲Richardton, N.D.509
Richardville, N.B.2568
Rich Bar, Cal...1360
▲Rich Creek, Va..7976
▲Richfield, Minn..751-753
Richfield, O...340
▲Richfield, Utah.7012-8556-8560
▲Richfield, Wis...526

Richmond, Ill...530
Richmond, Ind.
　◊■A.B.C...1388-1392
　▲■Greyhound...1-290
　▲■Trailways, Inc..7010
　Trlwys. Thru Rte.. 7010
Richmond, Kan..572-8450
Richmond, Ky..25-360
◊Richmond, Mo..3774
Richmond, O...338
Richmond, Que..2722
Richmond, Tex..585-8211-8258-8262
Richmond, Utah...552
▲Richmond, Vt...1987-1995
Richmond, Va.
　▲Car. Trlwys..7309-7310-7311-7312-7313-7315-7316-7322
　▲■Greyhound...1-2-4-18-130-140-145-151-160-161-170-200-215-220-257-265-285-295-296-320-355-587-595
　▲James River...2806-2807-2808
　▲■Trailways, Inc..7810-7869-7901-7908-7950-7953-7960-7966-7967-7970-7990-8000-8038-8080-8092-8108-8184-8370-8380-8553
　Bristol-Jenkins..3031
　Capitol Trlwys. of Penna...7140
　Gray Coach...2667
　Hudson Bus...2048
　Seashore..3424a-3428
　Short Way...1424
　S.E. Stages...2794
　Trlwys. Thru Rte... 7000-7003-7005-7006-7008-7010-7012-7026-7028
　Twin State...3429
Richmond Hill, Ga... 160-310

REFERENCE MARKS

Dly or *—Daily.
ESuH or °—Daily except Sundays and Holidays.
EssH or)—Daily except Saturdays, Sundays and Holidays.
ESa or ‡—Daily except Saturday.
Mon or a—Monday only
Fri or e—Fridays only.
Sat or ⊢—Saturdays only.
Sun or ⊣—Sunday only.
fhs or ■—Highway stop—does not go into town.
SS or °—Saturdays and Sundays.

All trips operate daily unless otherwise noted.

Holidays

Decoration Day	Thanksgiving
Fourth of July	Christmas
Labor Day	New Year's Day

Warning!

It is dangerous to ignore footnotes & reference marks.

A. B. C. COACH LINES

FORT WAYNE—RICHMOND—CINCINNATI

READ DOWN			READ UP
A05	← Run Numbers →		**A12**
EssH	**1391**		**EssH**
-----	Lv *Chicago, Ill.*...(CT) **GL-IT** Ar		11 35
-----	Ar *South Bend, Ind.*..(ET) **GL-IT** Lv		10 15
-----	Lv *Benton Harbor, Mich.* (ET) **IMB** Ar		-----
-----	Ar *South Bend, Ind.*...(ET) **IMB** Lv		-----
-----	Lv◊*South Bend, Ind.*...(ET) **IMB** Ar		9 00
-----	◊*Elkhart*...(1316)		8 20
-----	Ar◊*Fort Wayne, Ind.*...(ET) **IMB** Lv		6 30
11 00	Lv◊**Fort Wayne**...Ar		6 00
11 40	◊Decatur		5 28
11 54	Monroe		5 14
12 02	◊Berne		5 05
12 10	Geneva		4 57
12 15	◊Bryant		4 50
12 30	◊**Portland**		4 29
1 00	◊**Winchester**		4 09
1 14	Lynn		3 56
1 24	Fountain City		3 47
	◊**Richmond, Ind.** (EST)		
1 40 Ar	Trailways Depot...Lv		3 30
1 42 Ar	Greyhound Depot...Lv		3 30

"EssH", which stands for "Except Saturdays, Sundays, and Holidays".
(See the typical list of reference marks which has been reprinted
to the left of the table.)

Ignoring reference marks can be quite costly in terms of time
and aggravation. Be sure to check these carefully when planning
your itinerary.

Throughout the Russell's Guide, all times shown in light type
are a.m.; **bold face** figures are all p.m.

2. Normal Connections to Decatur via Ft. Wayne or Richmond

Both Fort Wayne and Richmond can be seen on the Greyhound Lines
map on page 87. While Richmond is not shown on the Trailways map
on page 88, all of Richmond's service can be located in the "Index
to Bus Stations", as illustrated on the previous page.

The key to reaching Decatur is to first reach Ft. Wayne or
Richmond. This can be done in a normal, straightforward manner,
or in some cases, special techniques can be employed.

First, the usual ways.

A.   Refer to Table 280, on page 117. (This is reprinted from a
summer schedule, so Ft. Wayne times shown are one hour earlier
than during the winter.) You can see that three Greyhound
busses run from Chicago to Ft. Wayne daily.

None are favorable to connect with the southbound A.B.C.
bus, which departs at 10:00 a.m. during the summer.

Trailways does not serve Ft. Wayne directly from Chicago.

B.   If you are returning from the east, Greyhound has a highly-
desirable schedule from Toledo, Ohio (see Table 401) which
arrives in Ft. Wayne at 9:15 a.m. That gives you one and
three-quarters hours to reach the Trailways Depot, six blocks
away, to catch the A.B.C. bus.

C.   Coming from the south, if you board the Greyhound bus that
leaves Indianapolis at 7:15 a.m., you will arrive in Ft. Wayne
with 25 minutes to spare for the A.B.C. bus (see Table 401).

3. Special Access Techniques

Because it is normally undesirable to attempt to reach
Decatur during the nighttime hours, your method of approach can
either be expensive or totally free.

Your *Ameripass* or *Eaglepass* provides you with a freedom granted

Greyhound Lines, Inc.

INDEX MAP TO TABLES

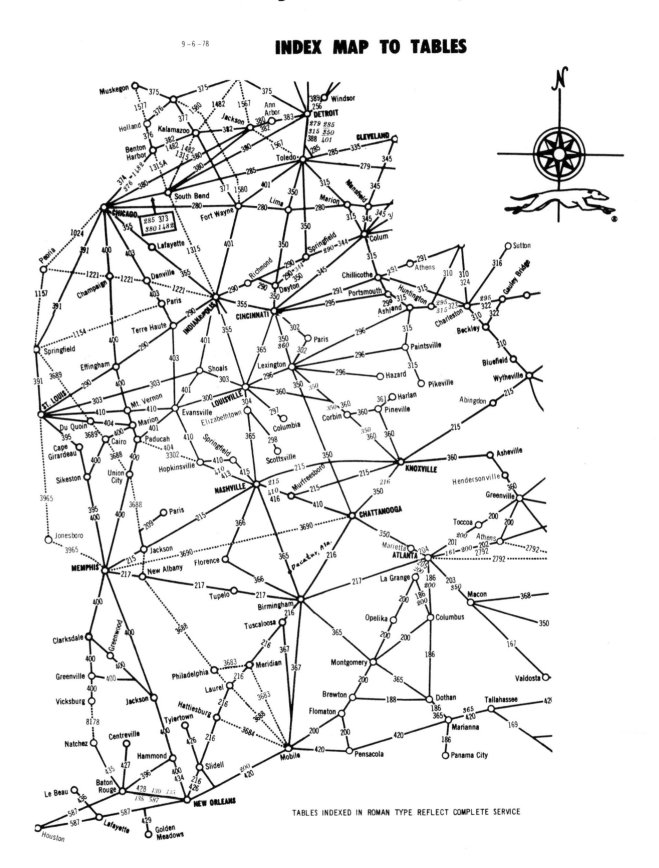

TABLES INDEXED IN ROMAN TYPE REFLECT COMPLETE SERVICE

TRAILWAYS.

NORTHEASTERN UNITED STATES

INDEX MAPS FOR LOCAL TABLES

———— *TRAILWAYS LINES*
··········· *Connecting Carriers*

Copyright and Drawn by Russell's Guides, Inc. 8 — 1 — 77

All Tables and Maps reprinted
in this chapter and in Appendix A
are reproduced with the express
written permission of RUSSELL'S
OFFICIAL NATIONAL MOTOR COACH GUIDE.

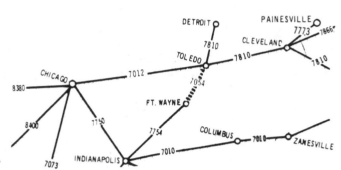

"The Empire Route"

7010

		READ UP				
		ALL SERVICE DAILY				
		Light Figures A.M.		Dark Figures P.M.		
Columbus............................Ar		2 40	8 35	2 20		8 45
London meal L		2 15	8 15			
London stop ....Ar		1 45	7 45	↑		↑
Springfield, Ohio.......(ET)......L		1 00	7 05	1 20		7 45
Richmond, Ind. (EST)........Lv		11 40	5 35	11 50		6 35
Richmond, Ind.................Ar		11 40	5 35	11 50		6 30
Indianapolis, Ind..............Lv		9 55	3 50	10 05		4 10

GOLDEN NUGGET ROUTE

7012   9-26-77

		READ UP				
Toledo, Ohio.......(ET)....Ar		•1150	6 20		12 50	5 50
Chicago, III. (CT)						
20 East Randolph St.........Lv		6 00	12 30 ←		7 00	12 01

GREYHOUND LINES

NEW YORK and WASHINGTON to DETROIT and CHICAGO *Via Philadelphia—Pittsburgh—Cleveland*

WESTBOUND—READ DOWN

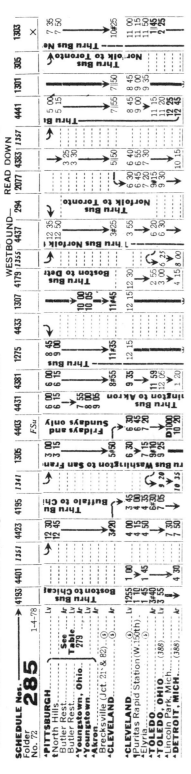

SCHEDULE Nos.
Folder No. 72 **285** 1-4-78

▲PITTSBURGH
†North Hills
Butler Rest.
Butler Rest.
▲Youngstown, Ohio
▲Youngstown
Akron
Brecksville (Jct. 21 & 82)
▲CLEVELAND
▲CLEVELAND
†Puritas Rapid Station (W.150th)
†Elyria
▲TOLEDO, OHIO
▲TOLEDO, OHIO
†Lincoln Park, Mich.
▲DETROIT, MICH.

SCHEDULE Nos.
Folder No. 72 **285** 1-4-78

▲DETROIT, MICH.
▲Lincoln Park, Mich.
▲TOLEDO, OHIO
▲TOLEDO, OHIO
†Elyria
†Puritas Rapid Station (W.150th)
▲CLEVELAND
Brecksville (Jct. 21 & 82)
Akron
▲Youngstown, Ohio
▲Youngstown, Ohio
†North Hills, Pa.
†PITTSBURGH

EASTBOUND—READ DOWN

ST. LOUIS—NEW YORK
Via Indianapolis—Columbus—Pittsburgh—Philadelphia

SCHEDULE Nos.
Folder No. 72 **290** 1-4-78

Chicago, Ill.
Indianapolis, Ind.
▲INDIANAPOLIS, IND.
Greenfield
Knightstown
Lewisville
Dublin
▲Cambridge City
Centerville
▲Eaton, Ohio
▲DAYTON
▲DAYTON
Fairborn
▲Springfield
▲COLUMBUS, OHIO

WESTBOUND—READ DOWN

SCHEDULE Nos.
Folder No. 72 **290** 1-4-78

▲COLUMBUS, OHIO
▲Springfield
Fairborn
▲DAYTON
▲DAYTON
▲Eaton, Ohio
Centerville
▲Cambridge City
Dublin
Lewisville
Knightstown
Greenfield
▲INDIANAPOLIS, IND.

- 71 -

GREYHOUND LINES

CHICAGO—INDIANAPOLIS—LOUISVILLE/CINCINNATI

SOUTHBOUND—READ DOWN

SCHEDULE Nos. Folder No. 77 **355** 1-4-78	4923	4915	4503	1169	4505	1173	4372	4925	4907	4931	1743 Sun	1133 FSS	1133 MTWT	1155	4909	1161	1137
CHICAGO, ILL. GL																	
▲Clark & Randolph Sts... (CT) Lv			7 00	7 25	10 45	10 45	1 00		2 15	2 45	3 00	5 15		5 15	8 00	11 30	11 30
t95th & Dan Ryan Expy...(373)			7 25		11 10				2 40	3 10					8 25	11 55	
▲**Hammond, Ind.** R			8 00			11 20			3 05	3 35	3 35						11 59
▲**Gary** R(373)			8 20		11 55	11 40	1 50		3 25	4 00	3 55				9 00		
▲Merrillville							2 10										
St. John																	
Cedar Lake (U.S. 41 & 133rd St.)			8 30							4 10							
Crown Point R			8 50							4 30							
▲Cedar Lake																	
Lowell			f							HS							
Lake Village			f														
Morocco			f							5 35							
Kentland (CT)			9 55							6 50							
▲Fowler (ET) Ar			11#10							7 15							
▲Fowler Lv			11 25							HS							
▲Oxford			11 40							f							
Templeton Cor.			f														
Otterbein			f														
West Lafayette (Purdue) Note 1			f														
▲**Lafayette**			12 10	10 55						8 05	7 05				11 59		
▲Frankfort			12 55							8 50							
▲Lebanon			1 20							9 15							
▲**INDIANAPOLIS** Ar			2#00	12#20		3#40	4#10		7#20	9 55	8 30	9#50		9#50	1#25	4#15	4#10

Thru Bus Chicago to Miami (1169) · Thru Bus Chicago to Richmond (4505) · Thru Bus Chicago to St. Petersburg (1173) · Thru Bus Chicago to Columbus (4925) · Thru Bus Chicago to Jacksonville Fridays, Saturdays, Sundays only (1133) · Thru Bus Chicago to Jacksonville (1155) · Thru Bus Chicago to Miami (1161) · Thru Bus Chicago to Jacksonville (1137)

SOUTHBOUND READ DOWN — NORTHBOUND READ UP

DETROIT—INDIANAPOLIS—EVANSVILLE—MEMPHIS

1403	1221	1743 Sun	5321	5329	1171 Fri	1741	1225	5319	1223	SCHEDULE Nos. Folder No. 80 **401** 1-4-78	5318	5320	5330	1406	1222	5326	5328 Fri	1742 Fri	1224	1220
4 30	2 15			8 40	6 30		5 10		12 30	Lv▲**DETROIT, MICH.** (388) GL Ar			8 35	8 35	10 55		4 05		8 30	1130	2 45
4 50	2 35			9 00	6 50					▲Lincoln Park			8 15	8 15	D1035						
5 10										▲Flat Rock									1040		
				9 40	7 35					▲Monroe, Mich.											
6 15	3 40			10 20	8 05		6 25		1 45	Ar▲**Toledo, Ohio** (388) Lv			7 10	7 10	9 30		2 45		7 15	1005	1 30
3 45	12 55			6 30			3 55		9 35	Lv Cleveland, Ohio (285) Ar					1 05		7 20		10 50		4 30
6 30	3 40			9 15			6 20		11 59	Ar Toledo, Ohio Lv					10 35		4 30		8 10		1 40
6 15	3 45			10 25	8 10		6 35		1 50	Lv▲**Toledo, Ohio** R Ar			6 45	7 05	9 25		1 55		6#40	1000	1 25
							6 50			▲Maumee R			6 30						D625		
							f			Waterville			f								
										Grand Rapids Jct. 1 Mile											
	4 34			11 14			7 35			▲Napoleon			5 50				1 00		5 40		12 27
	5 00			11 40			8 00			▲**Defiance**			5 25				12 35		5 15		11 59
	f			f			f			Antwerp, Ohio			f						f		f
	f			f			f			New Haven, Ind.			f								
	6#10			12#50			9#15		4#00	Ar▲**Fort Wayne** Lv			4 15		7 15		11 30		4 10		10 55
	6 30			1 20			9 30		4 20	Lv▲**Fort Wayne** Ar			3#55		6#50		11#10		4 05		10#35
							HS			Roanoke			HS								HS
	7 10			1 59			10 05			▲Huntington			3 15		6 10		10 30				9 50
	7 46			2 30			10 40			▲**Marion**			2 40		5 35		9 55				9 14
				3 07			11 10			Alexandria			2 02								8 47
	8 35			3 30			11 30			▲**Anderson**			1 40		4 45		9 05				8 25
										Pendleton (Jct. 67 & 38)½ Mile			f								
										Indiana State Ref.			HS								
										Fortville			f								
	9#45			4#40			12#40		6#40	Ar▲**INDIANAPOLIS, IND.** Lv			12 30		3 40		8 00		1 45		7 15

- 72 -

by no other type of bus ticket. It allows you to create your own versions of "holding patterns" in approaching a destination. Such routings would cost a small fortune to anyone using ordinary tickets.

Using a delayed-arrival bus riding technique, such as those described below, you can *always* avoid lodging costs. The "Greyhound Hotel" or "Trailways Motel" are always free to bus pass users.

It is necessary to become used to sleeping comfortably on a bus, but this comes naturally with making long return trips. And sleeping on a bus for free sure beats spending $10 - $20 per night for lodging. Especially if you do it five or six times a month, or more.

The 7 techniques detailed below were named by the bus pass users who discovered them, for ease of reference.

A. *"The Cleveland Snoozaround"*

This one is handy if you happen to find yourself in Detroit or Toledo late in the afternoon or evening.

Using Table 285 -- Leave Detroit at 9:15 p.m. and change at Toledo. Departure from Toledo is at 1:25 a.m. You arrive in Cleveland at 3:50 a.m. Leave Cleveland at 3:55 a.m., arriving in Toledo again at 6:20 a.m.

Using Table 401 -- Leave Toledo at 6:35 a.m., arriving in Ft. Wayne at 9:15 a.m. Then, as shown on Table 1390, take the A.B.C. bus to Decatur at 11:00 a.m., and arrive home at 11:40 a.m.

(Under normal conditions, it would be very risky to attempt to connect with a bus going in the opposite direction with only a five-minute window, as this itinerary calls for at Cleveland. However, long experience has shown that the westbound bus out of Cleveland almost invariably leaves substantially late. Normally, it is a good rule to never count on a bus leaving late. In this particular case, though, I have never seen the 3:55 a.m. bus leave even close to on time.)

Simply shown, the whole itinerary looks like this:

Lv.	Detroit	--	9:15 p.m.	
Ar.	Toledo	--	10:30 p.m.	
Lv.	Toledo	--	1:25 a.m.	Table 285
Ar.	Cleveland	--	3:50 a.m.	Greyhound
Lv.	Cleveland	--	3:55 a.m.	
Ar.	Toledo	--	6:20 a.m.	
Lv.	Toledo	--	6:35 a.m.	Table 401 - G.L.
Ar.	Ft. Wayne	--	9:15 a.m.	
Lv.	Ft. Wayne	--	11:00 a.m.	Table 1390 - ABC
Ar.	Decatur	--	11:40 a.m.	

This technique provides the passenger with 4 hours and 50 minutes of potential nighttime sleep, from the time he leaves Toledo until he returns to Toledo again from Cleveland. However, if that is not sufficient, he can generally sleep comfortably for up to 2 hours and 40 minutes more on the bus to Fort Wayne. That bus seldom has more than 8 or 10 passengers on it.

The remaining techniques in this section are shown in the "shorthand" used at the bottom of the previous page. This is a handy format to use in preparing your itineraries.

B.   *"The Pittsburgh Snoozaround"*

Lv.	Toledo	--	5:15 p.m.
Ar.	Cleveland	--	7:45 p.m.
Lv.	Cleveland	--	8:25 p.m.
Ar.	Pittsburgh	--	11:15 p.m.
Lv.	Pittsburgh	--	12:35 a.m.
Ar.	Toledo	--	6:20 a.m.

Table 285 - GL

* Lv.	Toledo	--	6:35 a.m.
Ar.	Ft. Wayne	--	9:15 a.m.

Table 401 - GL

Lv.	Ft. Wayne	--	11:00 a.m.
Ar.	Decatur	--	11:40 a.m.

Table 1390 - ABC

Overnight Sleep Time Available: 8 hrs. 35 min.

* Note that this technique is identical to the "Cleveland Snoozaround" from Toledo to Decatur on the return leg. (In fact, it is the same from Cleveland on; the bus from Pittsburgh is the same one that is boarded in Cleveland, in that method.)

The "Pittsburgh Snoozaround" is a return technique more commonly used when making deliveries in the Cleveland area. Toledo is shown at the beginning just to show that the method may be initiated from that point.

C.   *"The Cincinnati Trampoline"*

This one is used in the same manner as the "Cleveland Snoozaround", but is somewhat better in that the 3:55 a.m. bus out of Cleveland occasionally fails to connect with the Ft. Wayne bus due to lateness in departure. Further, the ideal sleeping hours aren't as badly disrupted, and there are more of them.

Lv.	Toledo	--	8:30 p.m.
Ar.	Cincinnati	--	1:20 a.m.
Lv.	Cincinnati	--	2:00 a.m.
Ar.	Toledo	--	6:20 a.m.

Table 350 - GL
(Not Illustrated)

The total overnight sleep time available is quite favorable: 9 hours 10 min. This technique concludes from Toledo on the same as the previous two methods.

D. *"The Toledo Backdoor"*

This technique is so named because it is usually used by drivers returning from the *west*, but they end up *arriving* from the *east* -- through the back door, so to speak.

Lv. Chicago -- 12:30 a.m.⎱
Ar. Toledo -- 6:20 a.m.⎰ Table 7012 - Tr

Overnight Sleep Time Available: 4 hrs. 50 min.

The trip is completed in the usual "Snoozaround" fashion. In this case, though, it is important to remember that you will be arriving at the Trailways Depot, which is about six blocks away from Greyhound, in Toledo. And you only have 15 minutes in which to make the transfer.

E. *"The Upper Midwest Zigzag"*

This is a long trip, offering considerably more time on the bus than usually would be desired simply for sleep. It is a good way to work on log or budget books, read, write letters, or compose the Great American Novel.

Lv. Detroit -- 6:45 p.m.⎱ Table 380 - GL
Ar. Chicago -- 11:40 p.m.⎰ (Not Illustrated)

Overnight Sleep Time Available: 10 hrs. 45 min.

The return is identical to the last leg of the "Toledo Backdoor". This technique is quite pleasant; it utilizes two of the nation's least-interrupted express schedules. It has only one fast station stop and a 15-minute coffee break en route to Chicago, and then proceeds nonstop from Chicago to Toledo. The 50-minute layover in Chicago makes the 2½-block transfer down Randolph Street quite easy.

F. *"The Indianapolis Dogleg"*

Lv. Chicago -- 11:30 p.m.⎱
Ar. Indpls. -- 4:10 a.m.⎰ Table 355 - GL
Lv. Indpls. -- 7:15 a.m.⎱
Ar. Ft. Wayne -- 10:35 a.m.⎰ Table 401 - GL

Overnight Sleep Time Available: 3 hrs. 40 min.

An alternative to the "Toledo Backdoor", this is far less desirable because of the lack of potential sleep time, and the long red-eye layover at Indy. However, it becomes quite useful if there's an outbreak of bad winter weather, because the schedules are not tight. It's particularly handy if the adverse weather conditions are concentrated in Ohio.

G.   *"The Columbus Ricochet"*

Notice that both Greyhound and Trailways have regular service between Indianapolis and Columbus, Ohio. For illustrative purposes, both Tables 7010 (Trailways) and part of the schedules of 290 have been reprinted in this chapter. In this instance, only one table provides a good rebound pattern: Table 290. Examination of Table 7010 will show that Trailways cannot be used in this case as a "holding approach" to Decatur because arrival in Columbus would be too late to allow sufficient time to return to Indy to catch the bus to Ft. Wayne.

Here's the method that works:

```
Lv. Indpls.    --   8:30 p.m.)
Ar. Columbus   --  12:40 a.m.}
Lv. Columbus   --   2:10 a.m.}   Table 290  - GL
Ar. Indpls.    --   6:20 a.m.)
```

Overnight Sleep Time Available: 8 hrs. 20 min.

The trip ends the same as the "Indianapolis Dogleg".

Still other special access methods certainly could be devised, but these have worked so well in the past for returns from all directions, further research has not been necessary.

Depending upon the location of your base of operations, one type of bus pass may be more advantageous than the other. Which one is best is determined entirely by the bus line you use the most in your travels.

For Decatur, the Greyhound *Ameripass* is best suited, while in many other areas, particularly in the southern states, the Trailways *Eaglepass* might be handier.

A series of Itinerary Plotting Exercises have been provided in Appendix B to enable you to sharpen your skills in advance.

4

GAMES BUS LINES PLAY
(A Survival Manual)

Shortly after I stepped off the plane onto the soil of Hawaii for the first time, in 1976, a friend greeted me by saying, "Welcome to Paradise!"

As I learned soon afterward, it rains in Paradise. Sometimes it rains hard, and sometimes it falls as a gentle mist -- but the inescapable fact remained: it *rains* in Paradise.

Like rain anywhere else, it ends sooner or later. But unlike more ordinary places, when the rain stops falling in Paradise, it frequently departs leaving a dazzling rainbow, and exotic tropical flowers and vegetation glisten and sparkle under brilliant sunshine.

And so it is also when one is a Road Rat. The "rain" falls in this job too. There are problems that arise now and then. But when the problems end, one is left with the realization that the world of the Road Rat is itself a sort of Paradise, composed of the magnificent vistas and wonderlands of all North America, to which he has complete access, all the time. Coming back into the reality of such a fantastic lifestyle after experiencing a problem makes the difficulty seem trifling and insignificant afterward. It is the contrast that makes one realize just how perfect his Paradise is -- to be able to find oneself again embracing the beauty of all America when the problem passes, instead of under fluorescent lights behind a desk in a sterile office.

In Hawaii, the rain is necessary to sustain the exotic vegetation.

To the Road Rat, the occasional irksome tribulations help him to appreciate all the more the incredibly unique position he is in.

Bus riding can be a real joy in this job, for reasons that are detailed on pages 60 thru 62. However, most of the "rain" you are likely to encounter usually has something to do with bus travel. The best way to avoid many of these problems is to develop an awareness of the pitfalls associated with riding busses regularly.

That's what *this* chapter is all about. (First the bad news -- then the good news.)

The bad news is... there are a number of "games" that bus lines play.

The bus lines have nearly all the **experience**, and they teach the rules slowly. The result is evidenced in inconvenience to their passengers in varying degrees. Learning the rules in advance can return much of the edge to the novice bus rider. Often, he can win, or at least settle for a draw.

In **fairness**, it must be said at the outset that the bus lines play very few of these games intentionally. Most of the time, the games are initiated as accidents of circumstance. This is inevitable in a large-scale operation that constantly involves huge volumes of people.

Sometimes, though, the intent is present.

Times such as those should be avoided by the bus companies, for that is their obligation to us.

Game #1 -- *ADMINISTER THE RUN-AROUND*

Bus lines depend on the public. Every day, they work directly with countless numbers of travellers. For this reason, it is understandable but unfortunate when even one bus line employee inconveniences a passenger when the action is uncalled for. Two instances are noteworthy here.

CASE I -- Early one morning, I found myself en route to a destination which had no Greyhound depot. My *Ameripass* had no coupons remaining. It had to be re-issued while I was outbound so that I could travel back out of my destination city on a competing bus line.

It was a very tight schedule; my E.T.A. showed no more than 90 minutes available between delivery of the unit and the next bus out. Should I miss that bus, I would incur a delay of nearly half a day. I had to get the ticket reissued quickly. The run would pass through only two *Ameripass*-issuing cities: Indianapolis and Little Rock, Ark.

I opted for Indy, to take advantage of the early-morning lack of line at the ticket window.

I found the window closed, and a sign indicated the agent would be out on break for 20 minutes.

Envisioning a 12-hour wait in Baytown, Texas, I asked a man standing nearby if he'd seen the agent.

"Why do you want to know?" he asked.

I quickly outlined the problem, whereupon he replied, "Nope. I haven't seen him."

Fortunately, by leaving immediately, I had my ticket reissued in Little

Rock, and arrived in Baytown with enough time to deliver and catch my bus, thanks to a very gracious dealer.

The next time I passed through the Indy Greyhound Depot, guess *who* the ticket agent on duty was(?) Yep.

CASE II --   In the Southwest, one afternoon, two ladies were sitting at a table in a depot restaurant, worriedly discussing the fact that they needed to catch the next bus to San Diego, but were unsure of the schedule. Clearly, they were new to bus travel, and needed assistance. Two bus drivers were sitting at the next table, and were listening to the conversation.

A minute later, the two ladies got up and left, still confused. As soon as they were out of earshot, one driver got up, smiled, and said to the other, "Well, I guess I'll go to San Diego!"

Disbelieving her ears, a waitress who had witnessed it all challenged the driver.

"You mean to say you're going to San Diego *now*, and you didn't even let those ladies *know*?!" she demanded.

Later on, relating the incident to me, the waitress said, "It's really criminal! These people are their company's bread and butter! They pay the drivers' salaries! Yet, some drivers treat them like cattle. It's so hard to believe!"

Solution to Game #1

Now understand, most drivers (probably over 98%) get along fabulously with people. Many are witty, and a few even provide their passengers with a running commentary of items of geographical and historical interest as they drive. It is rare to find a driver working for any bus line who isn't at the very least courteous, helpful and friendly. It is obvious that they take a genuine interest in people. The same can be said of a slightly lower percentage (probably around 90-95%) of ticket agents.

But just as one bad hitch-hiker can give the practice a bad name and spoil things for thousands of other hitch-hikers, the same is true here. A discourteous or thoughtless agent or driver will contact tens of thousands of people over the course of a year. This can result in poor public relations for the bus industry.

The solution to this game is greater sensitivity on the part of all bus line employees, who should use peer pressure and any other reasonable methods to ensure more courtesy on the part of those few who are not inclined to extend it.

Game #2 -- DELAY THE LUGGAGE

In many bus terminals across the land, signs are posted that read, "*If You Check Your Luggage at Bus Side, It Will Travel With You.*"

That should be corrected. Change the word, "will" to "may", and then add: "If You're Lucky."

CASE I -- Upon boarding an express bus from Jacksonville, Florida to New York, I checked my largest suitcase underneath the bus. Night fell, and under early morning starlight, I awoke to find that the bus had stopped in Raleigh, N.C., and baggage men were re-arranging the luggage. My suitcase was being transferred to another bus on the same schedule.

I disembarked and ordered the suitcase returned to my bus. (Port Authority Bus Terminal in New York has dozens of stalls. It is highly unlikely that two busses on the same schedule would even arrive at the same time, let alone park next to each other.)

The baggage man griped and groused, but the suitcase was moved back.

In Washington, D.C., I slept through the 10-minute stop, during which the suitcase was transferred successfully to another bus.

In New York, I waited three full hours for it to arrive, missing two of the three useful connections to Albany, and making the last with moments to spare. Instead of enjoying a planned 2½-hour visit with a friend, I was reduced to having only five minutes there during which I changed busses.

CASE II -- The trip from Reno to Boise seemed routine enough. It was back in 1975, when I still believed in the myth of efficient baggage handling by bus lines. The suitcase was checked through to Boise.

At Winnemucca, I transferred from the transcontinental New York Express to a northbound bus.

The suitcase didn't.

It probably visited the Port Authority Bus Terminal.

No one is sure. The only certain fact was that it took Greyhound 10 days to get it to Spokane, where I finally recovered it.

A loaf of genuine San Francisco sourdough bread (no preservatives added) had turned a sickly green.

Game #3 -- LOSE THE LUGGAGE

QUIZ: Which statement is *incorrect?*

   a. New York State is all one big city.
   b. Brand name gasoline is better than cut-rate gasoline.
   c. It is safe to check your luggage on the bus if you are only travelling a short distance.

ANSWER: _All_ of the above.

It is only 60 miles from Los Angeles to San Bernardino, California.

As a basic rule, nothing goes wrong in so short a distance, so I had developed the habit of checking most of my luggage over this, a typical last leg of many return trips to San Berdoo.

It was a great idea, in theory. As long as the bus arrived during the hours the depot was open, my belongings, as checked luggage, were entitled to reside in the security of the baggage room while I walked, unencumbered, to my office six blocks away, and picked up a new coach.

The effect was to save $1.00 per trip in coin locker fees, or $1.50 in cab fare to the office. Over a period of months, it was paying off handsomely.

It was a great system while it lasted.

Then, one evening in September, 1978, the plan failed.

In Los Angeles, I had checked three items (the maximum number allowed); a box, and two suitcases.

At San Bernardino, as I disembarked, I told the driver, "Be sure that all three items are taken off."

(Normally, that's a safe assumption. It must have been a premonition that caused me to say that!)

Upon returning 15 minutes later, I presented my claim checks to the baggage man. He found the box right away. But nothing else.

Moments later, I spotted one of the suitcases sitting unprotected, outside on the platform.

"What's that suitcase doing out there?" I demanded.

"Oh -- that one. Some girl told me she'd be back in a few minutes to pick it up," he replied.

Some *girl?* Great. *Who?* Why would some unknown girl be planning to come by for *my* suitcase?

To make matters worse, the claim tag had been removed. Worse yet, the other suitcase -- my main one -- was nowhere to be found. It contained 90% of my clothes, a calculator, and several stereo tapes, among other things.

"It must still be on the bus," the baggage man said.

Together, we determined that the next open depot the bus would reach would be Indio. It would be another hour before it arrived there.

We called the baggage room at the Indio depot and explained, describing the missing bag in great detail. We were assured that it would be intercepted, and sent right back to San Bernardino. Then I started out for Seattle, assuming that the suitcase would be waiting for me upon my return.

It wasn't.

On October 1, nine days after the fiasco, I filed a complete set of claim forms with Greyhound in San Bernardino.

"You should be hearing from San Francisco about this in a few days," the baggage man said.

He told me that several times more, over the ensuing weeks.

In December, I wrote to Greyhound Tower in Phoenix. The letter was forwarded to the claims office in San Francisco.

The Claims Adjuster responded immediately, and was most apologetic. He explained that *this was the first they knew* of the matter! He enclosed new claim forms to fill out.

Many people in the bus lines care. He was one of them.

It's a shame that those who care sometimes have to work with those who do not. It must be very frustrating.

As this book goes to press in mid-November, 1986, there is still no word about the missing suitcase.

It's been over 8 years now.

How to WIN Games 2 and 3

As you can see, one can never count on checking luggage safely. If only *one* baggage handler out of 50 is an incompetent dunderhead, he can spoil it for the other 49. So the best way to stay ahead in games involving luggage is to *AVOID CHECKING YOUR BAGGAGE AT ALL COSTS!! Always* take *everything* aboard with you, and put your items in the overhead luggage racks. If you carry several pieces with you, arrive at the depot early, and try to be first in line. That way, you'll probably find more than enough available space.

Finally, if you ever find that you *MUST* check some luggage, certain survival rules apply:

1. Remember that the limit of liability on *all* the luggage you check under one ticket is $250.00. Try to check only expendable items, valued at less than that total. Also, avoid checking items that are irreplaceable, regardless of their value.

2. Be sure that you check the location within the bins, of *all* checked luggage, *every* time the bin doors are opened. (Don't sleep too soundly if you have luggage underneath. *Never* allow anyone to *transfer* your bags to a different bus.

3. If you need to change busses en route, check your luggage *only to the change point.* Upon arrival there, either check the bags onto the next bus yourself, or carry them aboard.

4. Trust no one to do his job right. Leave nothing to chance.

Game #4 -- STRAND THE PASSENGER

Probably the most cruel of all the games played by bus lines on occasion is "Strand the Passenger." To fit the criteria, there must be a *willful* act on the part of an agent or driver, which is *designed* to cause a passenger to become stranded.

It must be an action that could have been prevented or avoided easily.

CASE I -- A Road Rat was en route home to San Bernardino one summer evening from Bakersfield via Barstow. His bus was due to arrive at Barstow at 9:50 p.m., but was running late. If it were to miss the connecting bus to San Berdoo at 11:10 p.m., the RV driver would face a wait of over five hours.

The bus arrived 30 minutes late. The Los Angeles bus still was in the station, 10 minutes late in departing. It was close, but he'd made it.

Alas, as the bus pulled in, the L.A. bus began backing out of its berth. Knowing the Road Rat's plight, the incoming driver pulled up directly behind the outbound bus, blocking the outbound bus from further backing.

Simultaneously, the arriving bus driver flashed his lights and beeped the horn, rapidly.

The L.A.-bound driver could not have mistaken his intentions.

Unfortunately, the L.A. bus had backed up just enough to squeeze past the bus parked in the berth to his left. He purposely ignored the signals of the incoming driver, and pulled out of the depot.

"I don't *believe* it!" the Road Rat exclaimed in despair.

"Believe it!" his driver replied, grimly.

In one final effort to stop the departing bus, he then followed the L.A.-bound coach out the drive and onto the street. Still no dice.

It was dawn when the Road Rat arrived home.

CASE II -- In late 1978, while using a Trailways *Eaglepass*, a Greyhound ticket agent in Los Angeles failed to mark the ticket properly for a fast late-night round trip to San Bernardino for me. After calling this to her attention, she replied, "The driver will mark it."

Mentally, I questioned this, but the bus to San Berdoo was about to leave.

In San Bernardino at 4:40 a.m., the driver of the bus I'd planned to return on told me that he couldn't accept the unvalidated ticket, so I had to delay my departure until 7:00, after the depots had opened.

CASE III -- A woman waited anxiously but patiently in a long line leading to the ticket windows in the Los Angeles Greyhound Depot. The departure of her bus was imminent -- and it was the only bus serving her destination that day. Learning of her problem, everyone in the line offered to allow her to go to the front.

Upon seeing this, the agents commanded her to keep her original position in line. She missed her bus.

How to WIN Game #4

Administrative personnel in the bus lines deplore intentional acts of inconvenience to passengers almost as much as the passengers themselves dislike having it happen to them. Always keep this in mind. If you are ever stranded intentionally, it is almost certain to be the fault of one individual -- and not the company as a whole.

Be cheerful and diplomatic when confronting individuals such as those described in this game. Nevertheless, know your rights. Be as firm as is necessary.

If you *still* get hung out to dry, report the incident directly to the corporate offices of the bus line involved, giving full particulars (date, time, name(s), bus number(s) (if applicable), etc.). (I've found the Greyhound folks in Phoenix to be very reasonable and helpful.)

HINT: Write to the headquarters of a bus line only when you have been affected substantially. This way, they will always respect your opinions, and frequently will assist you in redressing your grievances.

Here are the addresses:

GREYHOUND:

Greyhound Bus Lines, Inc.
Greyhound Tower
Phoenix, Arizona 85077
(602) 248-5000

Greyhound Bus Lines
222 First Avenue, SW
Calgary, Alberta, CANADA
(403) 265-9111

TRAILWAYS:

Trailways Lines, Inc.
13760 Noel Road
Dallas, Texas 75240
(214) 770-8500

Game #5 -- DISCOURAGE THE PASSENGER

We in the RV delivery business jokingly call ourselves Road Rats, but in actuality we are business people who comprise a substantial percentage of the clientele of bus lines, throughout this continent. There are many thousands of drivers in this field, and nearly all of us ride the bus frequently.

There are many ways by which the bus lines can improve service to their passengers in the *depots*. Many of these are presented here to give you an awareness of the overall conditions before you start -- *and* -- so that you can provide encouragement to the bus companies to make necessary changes and improvements.

The average full-time bus pass-equipped Road Rat spends over $3,000 annually for tickets. (Full-time RV drivers using one-way return tickets usually spend several thousand dollars more.) For all this expense, the bus lines owe us a strong upgrading of certain conditions within the depots, and then constant maintenance of these reasonable standards.

In addition, they owe this courtesy to the bus-riding public as a whole, which keeps them in business.

1. *Restaurant Prices*

In many locations, bus lines take unfair advantage of the fact that people have to eat. Most thru passengers disembarking for a scheduled meal stop will eat at the specified restaurant. (The "captive audience" concept.) Bus companies are well aware of this, and the majority of restaurants sell food for wildly inflated prices, even when compared with prices within comparable restaurants in the same communities.

Just as one example, a price of 30¢ per *strip* for bacon is a common going rate. That represents an *incredible* profit!

Increasing awareness of this by the public could eventually cost the bus lines sufficient numbers of passengers (turning to the airlines as a good economic alternative) that it could offset the excessive profiteering by depot restaurants.

A bus driver in Alabama recently commented privately on this issue:

"Imagine a family of four travelling from Birmingham to Los Angeles," he said. "By the time they reach L.A., which can take up to three days of constant travel, they will have spent so much money on depot food, it might actually have been cheaper for them to have flown."

Until recently, Greyhound maintained a system of "Post House" restaurants in many of its depots nationwide. Almost invariably, the food prices were vastly inflated. Until 1976, pink post cards were found in most of these restaurants, encouraging customer comment. One of the questions asked if the prices were considered to be: "low, average, reasonable, or high." in *that* order. Perhaps this was an indication that Greyhound Food Management was well aware that its prices were out of line. (Most customers undoubtedly would consider a *low* price to be "reasonable". It would be hard to imagine anyone thinking that reasonable prices would fall between "average" and "high".)

Today, Greyhound is phasing out its Post House restaurant chain, and replacing them with Burger King. This has already been accomplished in many cities. Whether or not this represents a real improvement is questionable, since fast-food restaurants found within terminals often charge substantially more than others of the same type which may be located in town, sometimes as close as 3 or 4 blocks from the depot.

Solution

Two things can be done. (1) Bus lines can become more responsive to the economic needs of its passengers -- and this should be directly encouraged by all bus travellers. (2) In the meantime... it takes a surprisingly short time to walk a block or two. In most cities, truly reasonably-priced cafes, restaurants, and even supermarkets can be found close to the depot. Be adventurous enough to seek food *outside* the depot. You'll see more, save more, and contribute to the effort to reduce depot food prices.

2. *Vending Machines*

A common sight in most depots, vending machines charge prices that vary widely, but as a rule they are seriously inflated. Occasionally (such as at Greyhound's brand-new depot in Buffalo, N.Y.), you may find prices that best could be described as *exorbitant*.

The identical can of Coca-Cola that you can get out of a pop machine at a service station for 50¢ is likely to cost you from 75¢ to even a dollar at a depot.

Depots frequently increase their profit margins on soda pop by purchasing quantities of "Brand X" soft drinks and dispensing it for the same prices they would charge for brand names like Coke and Pepsi.

Before leaving the subject of vending machines, let's visit the insult-to-injury department: change-making machines.

Most depot dollar bill changers will return only 95¢ for each dollar inserted -- despite the fact that most of the change gets spent on the high-priced food machines in the same establishment.

3. *Sale of Sundries*

Most large depots include a section which sells books, candy, magazines, postcards, etc.

As late as 1976, even the *kids* were being ripped off by Greyhound's newsstands. Just about anywhere else, kids could purchase comic books for the cover price, but the Post Houses were repricing these at between five and fifteen cents above the cover price. (By 1978, the comics themselves had achieved these inflated prices, and the practice seems to have ended.)

In some depots, there is a policy against allowing potential customers to browse through magazines. These shops must learn that people usually have to do some browsing in order to select the magazines they *want*. This would do wonders for public relations.

4. *Depot Rest Room Facilities*

According to law, public establishments such as depots must provide at least one free toilet per rest room.

All too often (most of the time), conditions prevail which would make its use undesireable or impossible, such as:

    a. The free one has no door.
    b. The free one lacks a door latch.
    c. No toilet paper.
    d. Broken seat.
    e. Unattended by custodians.
    f. Out of order.

The best way to correct this is to bring it to the attention of the terminal manager and/or ticket agent wherever you encounter such a situation. Access to a working free toilet is a legal *right*.

5. *Shower Facilities*

However modern our technology may be getting, being able
to take a shower will always be a basic need to the traveller.
Yet, as time goes on, less and less of these are available,
despite our technological advances.

The showers in the Greyhound/Amtrak Depot in New Orleans
are *constantly* out of order.

Showers are available at Houston's Greyhound Depot -- but
Trailways' *brand-new* terminal in that city does not provide
them.

Shower facilities in all depots serving cities of 250,000
population or larger would seem like a reasonable expectation.

6. *Coin Lockers*

Vancouver, B.C., Canada is one of the few remaining cities
having a depot (Greyhound) which offers coin locker storage
space for 25¢. This even includes the king-size ones that have
become almost extinct.

(That just proves that they can _do_ it for that price. Just
like Ma Bell's 10¢ local pay phone rate all over Louisiana
proves that they are ripping us off by charging as much as
a quarter elsewhere.)

The problem, however, isn't so much the 75¢ price of most
coin lockers, but the fact that some depots *have no* lockers.

In this case, if you have luggage you want to check within
the depot, take it to the baggage room or ticket agent. They
usually will put it in a secure place -- sometimes free of
charge, and sometimes for a fee of 50¢ per bag.

In most locations that charge, either the lockers or the
baggage room space is charged by the 24-hour day. In this case,
baggage room claim checks often will have a time stamped on
it (such as those issued at the Denver Bus Center). In that
case, be sure to check the item back *out* before the same time
the next day, or you will likely be charged for another day.

The biggest problem exists in relatively few places...

where they have *no facility at all* for checking luggage. This is
worthy of complaint.

> *SPECIAL ROAD RAT HINT:* If you carry a CB radio, use an antenna
> that will fit inside a coin locker, or
> expect some extra difficulty and/or
> expense from time to time.

7. *General Convenience*

For many months, Trailways actively has been working to generate
interest on the part of the public to lobby with their federal
representatives (Congress, etc.) in behalf of improved terminal
facilities in cities nationwide.

Therefore, it seems paradoxical that showers were not the only
omission by Trailways in their new Houston depot.

The new depot was built approximately a mile from Greyhound,
rather than in close proximity, which would have been more
convenient for transferring passengers.

Only one ticket agent was on duty when I observed it, serving
dozens of people. On that occasion, a waiting time of 15-20
minutes was required to reach the window.

Other depots share that problem. Frequently, especially in the
larger towns and cities, long lines of passengers must wait to see
only one or two agents, while other ticket windows remain closed
and unattended.

8. *Seat Space on Busses*

Although this final item doesn't concern depot facilities, it is
worthy of mention here.

Expect greater comfort south of the (Canadian) border than north
of it, particularly on Greyhound's busses. Greyhound uses the same
model coaches in both countries, but in Canada they cram in four
extra seats -- an extra row. (47, vs. 43 in the U.S.)

This greatly reduces passenger space and comfort. The seats
recline only slightly compared to the seats in the U.S.-based
busses.

Canadians should be entitled to equal comfort. All who travel in
Canada should call this to the attention of Greyhound's headquarters
in Calgary, Alberta, as well as in Phoenix, Arizona.

Game #6 -- MISS THE CONNECTION

This is a game which is almost always played unintentionally and often is due to adverse weather. Surprisingly, connections are generally made even under ungodly weather conditions -- professional bus drivers are excellent at maintaining schedules.

Most of the time, busses will wait up to 15 minutes beyond their scheduled departure time to connect with an incoming bus going in the same general direction. If a bus is running later than that, however, the continuing bus will usually delay its departure for up to 30 minutes *if* the dispatcher receives a message that connecting passengers are on their way in on the late bus.

Solution

If you find yourself riding a bus that you think is likely to be more than 10 minutes late for a connection, ask the driver if he thinks he will make up the time.

If he says he will, believe him -- he's usually right.

However, if he doesn't think he will connect, check with the dispatcher at the last terminal you contact before the one that has your connection. He can sometimes save the day for you by teletyping or phoning ahead and asking that your bus be held.

SUMMARY

Like any large industry, the bus lines have their problems. They employ tens of thousands of people, and it would be unrealistic to expect all of those myriads of employees to deal all the time with their millions of customers without an occasional conflict.

The important thing to remember is that the transportation industry involves countless human situations and conflicts daily. Most of those involved deal with each other in a magnificent manner, considering the magnitude of the operation.

This chapter has been included to prepare you for most of the types of situations you are likely to encounter. Hopefully, you will thus be able to avoid many of the pitfalls that befall novice bus travellers.

And after all of the "bad news" that has herein been described, here's some "good news". Recently, I discovered a remarkable bus line employee -- a girl who works evenings as a custodian at a Greyhound depot 'way up in the Pacific Northwest. If you are lucky enough to run across Debbie, you'll know it right away; her bright eyes and radiant smile cast a soft, warm glow over all of Seattle.

If you see her, say "Hi!" for me!

INTERLOCK: THE ULTIMATE TRIP!

Interlock is the heart of *The XANADU System*. It's potential is vast. Using it, the Road Rat can soar to misty heights of success undreamed of!

In Part IV, Chapter 1, it was demonstrated that though driving RV's only 330 days per year, a driver working for a manufacturer which pays *average* wages can earn *more* than $30,000 a year.

But in that example, the driver still was working for only *one* company.

Interlock is established when a driver begins working regularly for *two or more* companies.

If all RV manufacturers were located in one specific part of the continent, *Interlock* would be impossible. Fortunately, the manufacturers are situated all over the USA and Canada.

Some manufacturers serve only their own regions, and their market areas fall far short of overlapping the markets of more distant manufacturers.

For example, many of the southern California manufacturers ship only as far <u>east</u> as Denver. *And,* many of the Indiana manufacturers ship only as far <u>west</u> as Denver. No *Interlock* between the West Coast and Indiana could be achieved in a situation such as this. One could do equally well working for any *one* of them, exclusively, due to the 1,000-mile-plus gap.

There are three *effective* forms of *Interlock*:

1. *Partial Interlock --*

    <u>Example</u>: A Road Rat finds a company in Indiana that ships all the way to southern California on a regular basis, and he *also* gets hired by another company *there* that ships regularly to Denver, but no farther east.

    It takes 2 1/2 days to drive from Indiana to Los Angeles. Los Angeles to Denver takes another full day. The bus from Denver to northeastern Indiana takes still another 1 1/2 days.

    The driver could reasonably expect to take five days to make the complete round trip. However, during 3 1/2 of these days, he would be driving for one or the other company..

    This particular type of *Partial Interlock* yields 70% productive time. Payment per mile would depend entirely by the pay scales used by his employers.

2. *Regional Interlock --*

    This type of *Interlock* is established when one becomes employed by two companies whose marketing territories overlap completely.

Since experienced Road Rats easily can cover 1,000 miles per 24-hour day, the ideal situation is a *Regional Interlock* spanning at least 1,000 miles.

Working full-time for two widely-separated companies (when the driver routinely is sent back and forth from one region to the other) establishes *Regional Interlock*.

It is called *"Regional"* Interlock because the Road Rat seldom travels through parts of North America that are not on his normal corridor between companies.

(Road Rats with wanderlust who like to vary their scenery can take an occasional run elsewhere now and then for that purpose. However, he can expect some loss of income while he cushions back to one company or the other, on the bus. *Unless* he has established the *next* generation of *Interlock...*)

3. *Continental Interlock --*

The Road Rat who has *this* form of *Interlock* has the right to feel at home wherever he goes.

Continental Interlock is exceedingly rare; at this writing, I'm not sure that anyone has ever established it! It requires becoming a regular driver for *three or more* companies in three or more widely-separated regions.

For example, a Road Rat might become established with companies in Pennsylvania, Florida, Indiana, California, and Idaho... many of whose markets overlap each other. Through much complex planning, a driver with *Continental Interlock* could move continually across the land from one region to another. However, there are drawbacks to this:

(1) The *Interlock* would be a loose confederation. Unlike the driver with *Partial* or *Regional Interlock,* *this* driver's employers could never count on his services on a regular and predictable basis.

(2) Even *if* a network of employers could be established which would provide our friend with high-priority runs whenever he happened to drop in, this Road Rat probably would earn considerably *less* than one having *Regional Interlock*, and perhaps even less than one having *Partial Interlock*.

Reasons? The need to make unusual numbers of long distance phone calls to line up runs, and the down time involved in bus riding from dealerships to the nearest *Interlock* points. Depending upon how regularly his dispatchers could send him to dealerships close to other *Interlock* points, a driver with *Continental Interlock* might be able to spend between 60% and 90% of his time in productive driving.

Continental Interlock could be a lark, or a rat race, or something in between. If you'd like to try it, I wish you the best of luck. Your success at it will depend upon your ingenuity, skill, disposition of potential employers, and substantial luck.

To help you get a complete overview of the potential earnings of Road Rats at various Levels, the table below has been prepared to provide comparisons.

POTENTIAL EARNING POWER OF ROAD RATS

Road Rat Level	Type of Employment	Typical Daily Average Pay	Total Pay: 60 Days	Total Pay: 300 WD/yr.	Total Pay: 330 WD/yr.
I	T only	$ 38.45	$ 2,307	$11,535	$12,689
II	PI: T-t	$ 58.50	$ 3,510	$17,550	$19,305
III	RI: T-T	$ 79.20	$ 4,752	$23,760	$26,136
IV	PI: T-m	$ 83.70	$ 5,022	$25,110	$27,621
V	M only	$ 98.45	$ 5,907	$29,535	$32,489
VI	PI: M-t	$111.30	$ 6,678	$33,390	$36,729
VII	RI: T-M	$132.00	$ 7,920	$39,600	$43,560
VIII	PI: M-m	$136.50	$ 8,190	$40,950	$45,045
IX	RI: M-M	$184.80	$11,088	$55,440	$60,984
"X"	CI	*U N P R E D I C T A B L E*			

CI -- *Continental Interlock*
PI -- *Partial Interlock* (Type of company giving longest runs is capitalized.)
RI -- *Regional Interlock*
T or t -- Transporter Company (18¢/mile used in the calculations.)
M or m -- Manufacturer (30¢/mile used in the calculations.)

WD/yr. -- Working Days per Year

Making connections and/or returns using a bus pass is assumed.
For purposes of calculation, *Interlocks* are calculated using companies in the regions of Los Angeles, California and Elkhart, Indiana.

Gasoline cost of driving the units is assumed at 9¢/mile in the calculations.

Partial Interlocks assume Elkhart to L.A. runs, and L.A. to Denver runs, with bus returns from Denver to Elkhart, for purposes of calculation.

Distances used in the calculations: Denver to Elkhart: 1,250 miles
Elkhart to L.A.: 2,200 miles
L.A. to Denver: 1,050 miles

Note that the table provides a column of predicted earnings for a 60-day period, as well as for full-time drivers. This information should be particularly helpful to students and teachers looking for lucrative summer employment.

The 300-Working-Days column is for the benefit of those who would like to drive full time, but either spend many weekends at home, or take longer periods of vacation.

The 330-Working-Days column should be particularly useful for those who would like to enter the field full-time, and take only two or three weeks of vacation or holidays per year. With four or five days of down time due to breakdowns thrown in, 330 working days is a pretty realistic annual estimate for the steady worker.

"Road Rat Levels" in the table are progressive; a Level VI Road Rat could reasonably expect to earn more than a Level V Road Rat over the same period of time. Amounts of pay for each level are realistic estimates at the time of this printing, in early 1987 -- based on the assumption that the economy and RV market will remain stable.

Even though specific examples were used to derive rates of pay, they are realistic, typical situations, and the rates of pay should be similar wherever in the nation the driver happens to work.

However, since some companies *pay* more than others, a driver at a lower actual *level* could earn more than one at a close-by (on the chart) higher level, if his company (or companies) happened to pay substantially more.

The last level shown in the table (*Continental Interlock*), is depicted as Level "X", *rather* than the *tenth* level, because earnings in this complex category are so unpredictable as to make it impossible to classify by earning potential.

Any aspiring and enterprising RV driver, whether currently working or now planning to seek employment, should be able to earn *at least* $30,000 per year.

Those who are not yet working can make applications with *Interlock* in mind, and start right out on *at least* Level II. (Notice that Level II Road Rats can expect to earn at least $6,000/year more than those at Level I.)

Wherever you start, however, unless you manage to *begin* on Level IX, you can easily work your way up in a reasonably short period of time, using this, *The XANADU System,* to full advantage.

PART VI

THE EXPANDING HORIZON ...
ALTERNATE MEANS OF TRAVEL FOR PAY

The markets provided in Appendix A are specifically-designed
for the purpose of applying for work driving motorized RV's, as well as
the full range of *other* specialized vehicles normally *driven*.

While this book tells you just about all you need to know about
becoming an RV driver, and additionally provides lists of hundreds of potential employers, there are still other ways of finding work in this field.

1. *Dealer Pick-Ups   (DPU's)* --

   Every year, tens of thousands of new RV's are picked up directly
   at the factory by drivers working as employees of RV dealerships.
   Many dealerships are so large, they maintain their own driving
   staff. These drivers are paid by the *dealer* to travel to the factories whose lines he sells, and bring the units back to him. Pay
   scales vary, but many such drivers are paid as well as they would be
   if they worked directly for a manufacturer.

   Drivers working for dealerships near other RV manufacturers **may**
   even be able to set up a form of *Interlock*.

   NOTE: Some dealers send drivers to distant points, but most DPU's
   are done locally to within a few hundred miles of the dealership.
   A prospective Road Rat who wishes to go this route might do well
   to investigate to determine which situation best suits his needs.

   The DPU method has one important advantage: One who does not
   live near RV manufacturers, and who wants to return frequently to
   his present home, can often get into this field by working for a
   dealership in his home area.

2. *Independent Vehicle Transporter* --

   For an *investment* of several hundred to perhaps one thousand
   dollars or more, a person can set himself up as an independent
   vehicle transporter. For his investment, he will be officially
   registered as a transporter in the state in which he applies, have
   his own transporter license plate, and furnish his own insurance.
   He then works directly with manufacturers and/or dealers to contract
   for runs. On interstate trips, he has the normal requirements pertaining to reciprocity and buying permits.

   There is a lot of promise in this method. An enterprising Road
   Rat with a good head for business can have a truly unusual degree
   of independence, and earn very good money.

The last chapter explained why *Continental Interlock* was possible, but not necessarily practical. However, if one finds the concept of *Continental Interlock* intriguing, *this* is probably the best way to achieve it.

3. *Delivering Travel Trailers and Fifth Wheels --*

Many manufacturers of non-motorized RV's maintain a staff of drivers who deliver the vehicles by pulling them with a company-owned pick-up truck.

Nearly all of the manufacturers listed in Appendix C fabricate motorized coaches, but many of these make travel trailers and fifth wheels as well.

A driver making deliveries with a company pick-up truck would have the disadvantage of having to drive constantly, with no breaks as is provided coach drivers through (occasional) bus rides. However, a strong advantage is clear - one *never* has to buy a bus ticket. That produces substantial savings: well over $2,000/year.

Many drivers purchase *their own* Camper Special with fifth wheel assembly, and work independently or lease to a transporter company. There are many options to be considered when one gets into this area.

Summary

Many of the methods described in this chapter require a large investment. One of the great advantages of getting into this field is not having to invest *anything*.

If, for any reason, a driver wanted to change jobs on short notice, it would be far less complicated if he didn't have to worry about wasting part of his money (as in the case of being an independent vehicle transporter), or having a truck on his hands (complete with payments to make), for which he perhaps would have little or no use.

Comfort and lodging requirements are another major consideration in some of these methods. Pickup trucks used for delivering fifth wheels, for example, would not be equipped with a comfortable bed. Coach drivers never have lodging costs, because they sleep either in the RV's or in commercial busses. Lodging becomes a **very** real economic factor for a driver using a pick-up truck.

PART VII

MAXIMIZATION... FOR THOSE WHO LOVE TO FLY!

Throughout this book, the emphasis has been on *bus* travel for making return trips from runs... and you've been told that road rats who concentrate on *flying* back will have little money left over to show for their efforts.

There is a *VERY* important *exception* to this!

If you should become employed by a *manufacturer* which *pays well,* and which keeps you *constantly busy*... AND... *if* you really love to drive, and don't mind being constantly busy... you are an ideal candidate for using *Maximization.*

These days, most manufacturers pay quite well, and generally the pay for the miles you drive is based on the assumption that returns from longer trips will be by air. The company might not specify to you that *"x"* number of dollars is allotted for that purpose; rather, it simply is understood that your pay scale is as high as it is because the assumption is made that flights will be taken (whether or not you choose to do so. And most companies don't mind how you choose to return).

If you are used to driving, a three-day trip across the country is not excessively wearing, and on several occasions I have been called upon to take consecutive trips to California from Virginia. This has resulted in some 12,000-mile weeks: Drive to L.A. in three days, fly back overnight, and then repeat the process. (Note: Do *that* too often, and it *would* be very tiring. But on an occasional basis, especially in nice weather, it's not nearly as rough as it sounds.)

By 1985, most manufacturers were paying well enough that one could routinely expect to earn $1,000 clear (after expenses & return flight, but before taxes) for a 3,000-mile trip. As 1987 dawns, that is still a good average to work with.

So... in the above example, you would earn $2,000. (Two round trips.)

Why is this called *maximization?*

Simply because you are maximizing your driving opportunities, and earning your pay from that single company at the fastest rate safely possible. (By the way, take *four* days to cross the country, and you *still* make out very well! Set the pace that is best for *you.)*

MORE good news!

Examine the programs the various airlines have for their frequent fliers. Select the one you would be happiest with, and fly with *it* as often as possible on your return trips.

First thing you know... you'll find yourself taking *FREE* round trips all over the place, just as I have. (For example, I've flown free to such places as Mexico City, Cozumel, Haiti, and Guatemala.)

Frequent flier programs are getting better all the time. One of these days you could be touring Europe, or even more exotic shores... all as a result of being a road rat who employs... *Maximization.*

THE JOB MARKET: MANUFACTURERS AND TRANSPORTERS

This is the most important part of the book, since it tells you where the jobs can be found. It is divided into two sections. The first lists all of the manufacturers of recreational vehicles and other types of specialized vehicles throughout the United States and Canada. The second section lists all of the transporter companies for both nations. (If we missed any of either one, to your knowledge, please let us know, so that it can be included in the next edition. Meanwhile, this book lists over 850 potential employers for you to choose from!)

The first section includes special encoded information to help you learn more before you apply. It took many hundreds of hours of research, and hundreds more phone calls to obtain this, and still... a few were missed. Should you try a company which shows no ZIP code, or shows no code, this is a chancy one. But these are included because it is *possible* they might be useful to you. (By the next edition, we'll know more about them.)

Wherever possible, a company's special toll-free numbers have been included for your convenience. However, there are many companies that do not have these. If this is listed as "WATS", it is uncertain how much area it covers. One good only within its region (such as the Northwestern States, for example) is listed after the word, "Region". "Nation" refers to a number that can be called from everywhere except in its own state.

The last information given is the code. The first part shows what the company manufactures, as follows:

A -- Ambulances	S -- School Busses	R1 - Class A Motorhomes
E -- Emergency/Rescue Vehicles	U -- Custom Busses	R2 - Mini-Motorhomes
F -- Fire Trucks	V -- Beverage Trucks	R3 - Micro-minis
G -- Garbage Trucks	W -- Wreckers/Tow Tr.	R4 - Van Conversions
H -- Hearses/Funeral Cars	Y -- Bread Trucks	R5 - 5th-Wheel Travel
M -- Dump Trucks	X -- Other	Trailers
R -- Armored Cars		R6 - Travel Trailers

Next is a code showing the types of drivers used. This often is followed by a colon, then the *number* of drivers currently employed. The code:

A indicates the company's product is TRUCKED to the destination point.
B indicates there are drivers who TOW the company's trailers to destination.
C indicates the company's units are DRIVEN to the respective destinations.

    A-1 -- TRUCKED by company employees driving company trucks
    A-2 -- TRUCKED by independent contractors driving company trucks
    A-3 -- TRUCKED by independent contractors driving their own trucks
    B-1 -- TOWED by company drivers using company trucks
    B-2 -- TOWED by independent contractors driving company vehicles
    B-3 -- TOWED by independent contractors driving their own vehicles
    C-1 -- DRIVEN by company employees on payroll
    C-2 -- DRIVEN by independent contractors
     D -- Deliveries are handled by an outside transporter company

MANUFACTURERS of RECREATIONAL and SPECIALIZED VEHICLES

Some of the addresses and phone numbers used in this listing are from the 1986 30th Annual RV Business Directory published by TL Enterprises, Inc., Agoura, CA.

ALABAMA

BIRMINGHAM --

Pinson Truck Equip. Co.
7444 Pinson Valley Pkwy.
P.O. Box 9848
Birmingham, AL 35220
Region: (800) 633-8461
       (205) 681-2120
Bulk Feed Trailers
C-1:2

RED BAY --

Tiffin Motor Homes, Inc.
P.O. Box 596
Red Bay, AL 35582
Tel. (205) 356-8661
R1, R3
Uses: Driveaway of Red Bay

ARIZONA

PHOENIX --

Castle Mfg., Inc.
3702 W. Lower Buckeye Rd.
Phoenix, AZ 85001
Tel. (602) 269-0604
R5, R6

ARKANSAS

CONWAY --

Amer. Transp. Corp. (AmTran)
Highway 65 South
Conway, AR 72032
Tel. (501) 327-7761
Contact: Fran Marshall
Busses

FAYETTEVILLE --

Hackney Bros. Body Co.
P.O. Box 1846
2364 Armstrong Ave.
Fayetteville, AR 72702
Nation: (800) 334-2296
       (501) 443-2335
Contact: Donna Evans
Beverage Route Trucks
C-1:3

LITTLE ROCK --

Bridger's Coach Co.
P.O. Drawer 7356
Little Rock, AR 72207
WATS: (800) 468-1320
      (501) 945-1647
Contact: Robert Wagner
A,E,X   C-1:2

CALIFORNIA

ANAHEIM --

Taylor-Dunn Mfg. Corp.
P.O. Box 4240
Anaheim, CA 92803
Tel. (714) 956-4040
A,E,F,G,M A-1,A-3:3

BAKERSFIELD --

American Van Conversion
5601-A Rosedale Hwy.
Bakersfield, CA 93308
Tel. (805) 327-4134
R4

BAKERSFIELD --

El Kapitan Van Conv.
5455 Rosedale Hwy.
Bakersfield, CA 93308
Tel. (805) 324-4004
Contact: Gus Anton
R3, R4   C-1:4

CALIFORNIA (Cont'd.)

CARSON --

Revcon Enterprises
1400 Watson Center
Carson, CA 90745
Tel. (213) 518-6950
C-1:4

EL MONTE --

Leader Industries, Inc.
P.O Box 1248
El Monte, CA
Tel. (818) 575-0880
A

HAYWARD --

Gillig Corporation
25800 Clawiter Road
Hayward, CA 94545
Nation: (800) 468-2914
(415) 785-1500
S, & 30- and 40-foot
Transit Busses
C-1,C-2:5-10 D

HEMET --

Skyline - Nomad Div.
920 W. Mayberry
Hemet, CA 92343
Tel. (714) 658-7106
Contact: Mark Bissel
R6   D

LA PALMA --

Ultra Limos
6951 Walker Avenue
La Palma, CA
Tel. (714) 630-5571
Custom Limousines

LOS ANGELES --

Yeager & Sons
1512 E. Olympic
Los Angeles, CA 90021
Tel. (213) 680-2890

CORCORAN --

Starcraft
1190 Orange Ave.
P.O. Box 788
Corcoran, CA 93212
Region: (800) 222-1787
In CA: (800) 292-0556
(209) 992-2177
R6

FOWLER --

Jacobsen Trailer, Inc.
1128 E. South Ave.
Fowler, CA 93625
Tel. (209) 834-5971
Great variety of utili-
tarian trailers
C-1:1

HEMET --

Skyline - Leyton Div.
425 South Palm
Hemet, CA 92343
Tel. (714) 925-0414
R6   D
Uses: Transit Homes of
America

HOLLISTER --

Shelton Industries
1802 Shelton Drive
Hollister, CA 95023
Tel. (408) 637-8201
Contact: Jack Glass
R5,R6

LOS ANGELES --

Crown Coach Corp.
2428 E. 12th St.
Los Angeles, CA
Tel. (213) 489-5152
Busses

LOS BANOS --

Auto-Mate Rec. Prods., Inc.
150 W. "G" Street
Los Banos, CA 93635
Tel. (209) 826-1521
R5,R6

CORONA --

Six-Pac Industries
14296 E. 6th St.
Corona, CA 91719
Tel. (714) 737-8232
Contact: Harold Hamaker
C-2:2

GARDENA --

Landmark/National
Coach Corporation
130 W. Victoria Blvd.
Gardena, CA 90248
Region: (800) 682-4100
In CA: (800) 682-3100
(213) 538-3122
R4,R5; Shuttle Busses
Uses: RV Transport

HEMET --

Skyline - Limited Div.
335 South Lyon
Hemet, CA 92343
Tel. (714) 652-1980
R5   D
Uses: Transit Homes of
America

IRWINDALE --

Calif. Custom Design/
Red-E-Kamp
5257 N. Vincent Ave.
Irwindale, CA 91706
Tel. (213) 334-0376
R4

LOS ANGELES --

Panamco Corporation
2616 Hyperion
Los Angeles, CA
Tel. (213) 666-0906

LYNWOOD --

Fire-X Corporation
10857 Drury Lane
Lynwood, CA
Tel. (213) 636-9881

MIRA LOMA --

Calif. Custom Design/
  Red-E-Kamp
Mira Loma Space Center
Mira Loma, CA 91752
Tel. (714) 685-0151
Contact: Bill Richards
  at above phone.
C-2:5

OAKDALE --

P.E. Van Pelt, Inc.
P.O. Box 365
Oakdale, CA
Tel. (209) 847-0347
F

ONTARIO --

Hawkins Motor Coach
1610 S. Cucamonga
Ontario, CA 91761
In CA: (800) 128-1249
       (714) 947-2512
Contact: Jerry Hawkins or
  Angela Duits
R1   C-1:3

PARAMOUNT --

SSP Truck Equipment, Inc.
14001 S. Garfield
Paramount, CA
WATS: (800) 325-7057

PERRIS --

Travel Queen Motor Homes
975 Morgan Street
Perris, CA 92370
Nation: (800) 826-5964
In CA: (800) 826-3192
       (714) 943-4911
Contact: Katrina DeGermano
R1 & Custom   C-1:2-3

POMONA --

Lazy Daze, Inc.
4303 E. Mission Blvd.
Pomona, CA 91766
Tel. (714) 627-1219
R2

MORENO VALLEY --

West Sundial, Inc.
23846 Sunnymead Blvd.
Moreno Valley, CA 92388
Tel. (714) 242-1127 or
     (714) 242-1128
Contact: Mike Womack or
  Patsy Stahley
R4   C-1:2-3

OAKLAND --

L.N. Curtis & Sons, Inc.
4133 Broadway
Oakland, CA
Tel. (415) 655-5111
F

ORANGE --

Overland
1825 W. Collins
Orange, CA 92667
Tel. (714) 633-6264
R1,R2,R5,R6

PERRIS --

Coachmen Rec. Veh. Co.
P.O. Box 1823
Perris, CA 92370
Tel. (714) 943-2961

PLACENTIA --

Roll-A-Long Vans, Inc.
210 E. Crowther St.
Placentia, CA 92670
Tel. (714) 528-9600
Contact: Marlene Gasparovic
R4   C-2:2

RIVERSIDE --

Fleetwood Enterprises
3125 Myers St.
Riverside, CA 92523
Tel. (714) 351-3500
NOTE: Corporate HQ. Ask
them for location of
plant nearest you. There
are dozens of these. ALL RVs.

NEWARK --

Mobility Ind., Inc.
37555 Willow St.
Newark, CA 94560
Nation: (800) 523-2387
In CA: (800) 523-2386
        (415) 794-6441
C-1:1 A-2 D
Uses: Auto Driveaway

OAKLAND --

Roll-Rite Corp.
421 Pendleton Way
P.O. Box 2107
Oakland, CA
Tel. (415) 638-9305

PACOIMA --

Lance Camper Mfg. Corp.
10234 Glenoaks
Pacoima, CA 91331-1689
Tel. (818) 897-3155
R5

PERRIS --

National R.V., Inc.
3411 N. Perris Blvd.
Perris, CA 92370
Tel. (714) 943-6007
R1,R2,R3

PLACENTIA --

Saddleback R.V., Inc.
710 Hundley Way
Placentia, CA 92670
Tel. (714) 961-8900
R3

RIVERSIDE --

Komfort Industries, Inc.
7888 Lincoln Ave.
P.O. Box 4698
Nation: (800) 772-3030
        (714) 687-4040
R1,R5,R6

RIVERSIDE --
Six-Pac Industries, Inc.
4880 Feldspar St.
Riverside, CA 92509
Tel. (714) 681-1320
Contact: Harold Hamaker
B-2:2

SAN BERNARDINO --
Leisure Odyssey, Inc.
2362 S. Gardena Ave.
San Bernardino, CA 92408
Nation: (800) 826-9943
        (714) 796-8331
Contact: Dee Cox
R1,R2,R5 & Customized
C-2:6

SAN FERNANDO --
Fireball Mfg., Inc.
12087 N. Lopez Canyon Rd.
San Fernando, CA 91342
Tel. (818) 790-3900
Contact: Bill Durkee

SAN JOSE --
FMC Corp. - Ordnance Div.
1105 Coleman Ave., Box 1201
San Jose, CA
WATS: (800) 672-5715
      (800) 826-0860
      (800) 621-4500
R

SOUTH EL MONTE --
Isuzu Truck of America
1180 Durfee
S. El Monte, CA 91733
Nation: (800) 637-7228
        (818) 350-8980
Large Industrial Trucks

SOUTH SAN FRANCISCO --
McLellan Industries/
  McLellan Equipment, Inc.
251 Shaw Road
S. San Francisco, CA 94080
Nation: (800) 848-8449
In CA: (800) 843-8118
        (415) 873-8100
Contact: Scott McLellan
Specialized Trucks
C-1,C-2:2-4

RIVERSIDE --
Wolverine Western Corp.
3087 12th St.
Riverside, CA 92509
Tel. (714) 684-3800

SAN BERNARDINO --
Ranger Industries, Inc.
1050 E. Cooley Ave.
San Bernardino, CA 92408
Tel. (714) 796-6804
R3

SAN FRANCISCO --
Gladix Corp.
P.O. Drawer 1523
San Francisco, CA
Tel. (415) 668-5286
      (415) 957-0638
A

SAN LEANDRO --
G. Paoletti Co., Inc.
496 Hester St.
San Leandro, CA
Specialized Truck Bodies
DPUs, in general

SOUTH EL MONTE --
R & R Custom Coachworks, Inc.
1126 N. Santa Anita Avenue
S. El Monte, CA 91733
Tel. (213) 488-6109
R1,R2,R4, & Spec. Vehicles

SOUTHGATE --
New Horizon
10711 Sessler St.
Southgate, CA 90280
Tel. (213) 862-4218
R3,R5, & Custom
C-1,C-2:6-8   D

SACRAMENTO --
Van Camp Ind., Inc.
2264 Auburn Blvd.
Sacramento, CA 95821
Tel. (916) 925-VANS
Contact: Elizabeth
                Molina
R4   C-1:2-3

SAN FERNANDO --
Establishment Ind., Inc.
11949 Borden Avenue
San Fernando, CA 91340
Tel. (818) 365-6395
(You may call collect.)
R1,R2,R3   C-1 D
Mainly uses Transit Homes
of Amer.: (800) 227-9050

SAN JACINTO --
Skyline - Lindy Div.
39395 Esplanade
San Jacinto, CA 92383
Tel. (714) 654-7341
R2

SANTA FE SPRINGS --
C & O Mfg. Div. of
  Dempster Systems, Inc.
12927 Marquardt
Santa Fe Spgs., CA 90670
Tel. (213) 921-8652 or
Co. HQ: (615) 637-3711
G   D

SOUTH EL MONTE --
Vacation Enterprises
2656 Rosemead Blvd.
S. El Monte, CA 91733
Tel. (818) 442-4194

SUN VALLEY --
Contempo Campers, Inc.
9175 San Fernando Road
Sun Valley, CA 91353-2051
Nation: (800) 423-2263
In CA: (800) 253-5754
        (818) 768-2800
Contact: Yolanda Agnas
R4   C-1:7

CALIFORNIA (Cont'd.)

SUN VALLEY --

Elite Coach Corporation
8525 Telfair Avenue
Sun Valley, CA 91352
Tel. (818) 768-6806
R1

SUN VALLEY --

Excel Trailer Co., Inc.
11238 Peoria St.
Sun Valley, CA 91352
Tel. (818) 767-3363
R5,R6

SUN VALLEY --

Traveleze Ind., Inc.
11473 Penrose St.
Sun Valley, CA 91352
Tel. (818) 768-6330
Contact: Dick Porter
R5,R6   D

TORRANCE --

Toyota Motor Sales USA, Inc.
19001 S. Western Ave.
Torrance, CA 90509
Tel. (213) 618-4000
Specialty Vehicles

UPLAND --

Vehicle Systems
   Development Corp.
1265-67 West 9th St.
P.O. Box 356
Upland, CA
Spec. Purpose, & R

VALLEJO --

Gardner-Pacific Corp.
369 Kelly Road
Vallejo, CA 94589
Tel. (707) 252-8188
R3   D

WEST SACRAMENTO --

Beachcomber Vans, Inc.
3300 W. Capitol Ave.
W. Sacramento, CA 95691
Tel. (916) 372-6550
Contact: Don Wallace
A-1:1

WINTERS --

Six-Pac Industries, Inc.
1805 Railroad St.
Winters, CA 95694
Tel. (916) 795-4166
R5,R6

YUBA CITY --

Perris Valley Campers
655 Cooper Avenue
Yuba City, CA 95991
Tel. (916) 674-0440
Contact: Bob Nissen
R3,R5,R6 B-3:2

- -

COLORADO

BOULDER --

Aspen Coach Corporation
2907 55th Street
Boulder, CO 80301
Tel. (303) 444-4534
R5,R6

BRIGHTON --

Hallmark Mfg., Inc.
1150 Brighton Road
Brighton, CO 80601
Tel. (303) 659-5572
Contact: Craig Floreth
R5 & Custom-built C-2:2

COLORADO SPRINGS --

Harloff Mfg. Co., Inc.
752 Garden of the Gods
   Road
Colo. Spgs., CO 80907
Tel. (303) 598-5081

WHEATRIDGE --

Four Seasons Mfg., Inc.
10501 W. 48th Avenue
Wheatridge, CO 80033
Nation: (800) 843-6829
        (303) 425-5888
Contact: Robert Entrup
R3   A-1:2

WHEATRIDGE --

Van Dale Co.
7999 W. 48th Street
Wheatridge, CO 80033
Tel. (303) 423-8021
R4

- -

CONNECTICUT

MIDDLEFIELD --

Custom Craft Trailers, Inc.
34 Old Indian Trail Road
Middlefield, CT 06455
Tel. (203) 349-3001
Custom-Built Trailers

NEW BRITAIN --

Superior Metal Products, Inc.
75 Christian Lane
New Britain, CT
Tel. (203) 225-7654

DANBURY --

Phoenix Bus Sales
180 Old Brookfield Rd.
Danbury, CT
Tel. (203) 792-1484
Contact: Lee Riley

BRADENTON --

Miller Trailers, Inc.
P.O. Box 511
Bradenton, FL 33506
Tel. (813) 748-3900
Military Trailers

CRYSTAL RIVER --

Dimensions Mfg. & Dist.
Veteran's Drive
Crystal River, FL
Tel. (904) 795-5125
R4

FORT MYERS --

Happy Times, Inc.
16133 S. Tamiami Trail
Fort Myers, FL 33908
Tel. (813) 482-2700
R4   C-1:1

OCALA --

Emergency One, Inc.
P.O. Box 2710
Ocala, FL 32678
Request their National
     "800" number
(904) 237-1122
A,E,F,R

OLDSMAR --

Chariot Mfg. Co.
209 Pickney Street
Oldsmar, FL 33557
Tel. (813) 855-5801
Contact: Robert Hott
Util. & Custom Trailers

POMPANO BEACH --

Zimmer Motor Cars
777 S.W. 12th Avenue
Pompano Beach, FL 33069
Tel. (305) 943-7600
Exotic Cars

BRADENTON --

Stimus Conversions, Inc.
1209 44th Ave., E.
Bradenton, FL 34203
Tel. (813) 749-1079
Contact: Joe Boulmo
R4   C-1:24

DELAND --

Gustafson Industries
1315 Highway 92
Deland, FL 32724
Tel. (904) 738-2230
R4

JACKSONVILLE --

Sherrod Vans, Inc.
6464 Greenland Road
Jacksonville, FL 32223
WATS: (800) 824-6333
       (904) 268-3321
Contact: Gene Strickland,
Or: Dick Grey, at
       (904) 268-0227
R4 & Special RVs

OCALA --

Federal Motors, Inc.
3611 S.W. 20th St.
P.O. Box 5000
Ocala, FL 32678
(904) 237-6215
R, Trolleys, & Special

PINELLAS PARK --

Southern Veh. Prods., Inc.
P.O. Box 8000
Pinellas Park, FL 33565
Tel. (813) 576-9142
F

RIVIERA BEACH --

E.V.F., Inc.
7555 Garden Road
Riviera Beach, FL 33404
Nation: (800) 848-6652
        (305) 848-6652
E & Spec. Vehs.; R4

CORAL GABLES --

Emergency Vehicle
   Equipment, Inc.
5256 S.W. 8th St.
Coral Gables, FL
A

FORT LAUDERDALE --

Sprite North
   America, Inc.
211 S.W. 17th St.
Ft. Lauderdale, FL
   33315
Tel. (305) 765-1909

MIAMI LAKES --

Protective Materials
   Co., Inc.
5863 Miami Lakes Dr.
Miami Lakes, FL 33014
R   D
Uses: Knudsen Ent.

OCALA --

Mark III Industries
2035 N.W. 8th Ave.
P.O. Box 2525
Ocala, FL 32678
Tel. (904) 732-5878
R4   C-1:3   D

POMPANO BEACH --

Tip Top Toppers
1220 S.W. 12th Ave.
Pompano Bch., FL 33069
Tel. (305) 781-4635
R4

SANFORD --

Starline Ent., Inc.
P.O. Box 1937
Sanford, FL 32772-1937
Tel. (305) 323-0411
Contact: Phyllis Savoie
A,E   C-1:2-3

FLORIDA (Cont'd.)

TAMPA --

Roman Wheels South, Inc.
5890 Jetport Indust. Blvd.
Suite 515
Tampa, FL 33634
Tel. (813) 886-2184
Contact: Frank O'Loughlin
R4   C-2:6-7

VENICE --

Skillcraft Industries, Inc.
355 Center St.
Venice, FL 33595
Tel. (813) 493-8706
Transit Busses   C-1:1

WINTER PARK --

Wheeled Coach Ind./
   World Trans, Inc.
2778 N. Forsyth Road
Winter Park, FL 32792
Tel. (305) 677-7777
Contact: Bill McLaughlin
   or Donald E. Goff

A,S,U & Resort Busses
C-2:8

WINTER PARK --

Tropic Traveler
2626 N. Semoran Blvd.
Winter Park, FL 32792
Tel. (305) 671-2626
R4   C-2:8

- -

GEORGIA

COLUMBUS --

Centennial Body Division
   of Douglas & Lomason Co.
420   10th Avenue
Columbus, GA 31993
Nation: (800) 241-7541
        (404) 323-6446
Contact: Melvin Davis
V,R5,R6   C-1,C-2:10+

CORDELE --

Zimmer Motor Vans
2801   13th Ave. E
Cordele, GA 31015
Tel. (912) 273-5320
R4   C-2:?

DECATUR --

Cricket Camper Mfg. Co.
4689 Covington Highway
Decatur, GA 30035
Tel. (912) 423-5471
Contact: Jimmy Smith
R4 & Custom   C-2:10

FITZGERALD --

Coachmen Rec. Veh. of Ga.
P.O. Box 948
Fitzgerald, GA 31750
Tel. (912) 423-5471
Contact: Lawton Tinley
R5,R6   C-2:2

FORT VALLEY --

Blue Bird Body Co.
1 Wanderlodge Way
P.O. Box 937
Fort Valley, GA 31030
Tel. (912) 825-2021
Contact: Joyce Wilder
S,R1 & Transit Busses
C-1:25

LA GRANGE --

Southern Ambulance
   Builders, Inc.
833 New Franklin Road
P.O. Drawer 949
La Grange, GA 30241
Nation: (800) 241-2304
A, Other Spec. Vehs.

MARIETTA --

Tra-Tech Corp., Southeast
1451 Cobb Industrial Drive
Marietta, GA 30062
Tel. (404) 427-2500
R4

VALDOSTA --

Skyline Corp.
P.O. Drawer 70
Valdosta, GA 31603
Tel. (912) 242-9620
R6   D

- -

IDAHO

BOISE --

Fireball Ind. of Idaho, Inc.
4100 S. Eagleson Road
Boise, ID 83705
Tel. (208) 362-9314
R5,R6

CALDWELL --

Kit Mfg. Co.
P.O. Box 1240
Caldwell, ID 83606
WATS: (800) 521-4127
      (208) 454-9291

NAMPA --

King Mfg., Inc.
1808 Industrial Road
Nampa, ID 83651
Tel. (208) 466-8941
R5,R6

SUGAR CITY --

Teton Traveler Mfg. Co., Inc.
Route 1
Sugar City, ID 83448
(208) 356-7226

- -

ILLINOIS

ARLINGTON HEIGHTS --

BB Conversions, Inc.
1315 E. Davis St.
Arlington Heights, IL 60005
Tel. (312) 577-8267
Contact: Bill Black
R4   C-1:3

AURORA --

Doney Recreational Vans, Inc.
471 N.E. Industrial Drive
Aurora, IL 60504
Tel. (312) 892-7141
R4

CALUMET CITY --

Calumet Coach Co.
2150 E. Dolton Ave.
Calumet City, IL 60409
Tel. (312) 868-5070
A & Custom Vehicles

CHICAGO --

Brennan Equip. & Mfg., Inc.
2939 N. Pulaski Road
Chicago, IL 60641
Tel. (312) 283-6664
G

CHICAGO --

Navistar
401 N. Michigan Ave.
Chicago, IL
Nation: (800) 654-0797
Nation: Dealer Info.:
          (800) 233-9121

DOWNERS GROVE --

J.E. Hailey Co.
1530 Coral Berry Lane
Downers Grove, IL 60515
Tel. (312) 953-8400

DUNDEE --

Taskmaster Equip. Co., Inc.
25 Crescent Drive
Dundee, IL 60118
Tel. (312) 428-6890
F

FOX RIVER GROVE --

Executive Coach Corp.
1003 Route 22
Fox River Grove, IL 60021
(312) 639-0575
Display Units

FRANKFORT --

Paratech, Inc.
1025 Lambrecht Road
Frankfort, IL 60423
Nation: (800) 435-9358
          (815) 469-3911
E, & Rescue Vehicles

GALVA --

Galvan Conversions
1 Murray Hill Road
Galva, IL 61434
Tel. (309) 932-2998
R4

GALVA --

I.M.E. Division of Pearson
    Industries, Inc.
c/o P.O. Box Z
Galva, IL 61434
Nation: (800) 447-5684
          (309) 932-2181

GALVA --

La Spree Corp.
1 Murray Hill Road
Galva, IL 61434
Tel. (309) 932-2750
R1

GALVA --

Motoroam Industries of
    America, Inc.
R.R. #1
Galva, IL 61434
R1

KEWANEE --

Classic Coach Interiors
Burlington Ave. Indus. Park
Kewanee, IL 61443
Tel. (309) 852-4656
Contact: Karen Hufnagel
R4   C-2:3-4 Retirees

LYONS --

Hendrickson Mobile Equip.
8001 W. 47th St.
Lyons, IL
Tel. (312) 447-4600
Specialized Vehicles

MELROSE PARK --

W.S. Darley & Co.
2000 Anson Drive
Melrose Park, IL
Tel. (312) 345-8050
F

MOLINE --

Deere & Co.
John Deere Road
Moline, IL
Tel. (309) 752-8000

NORTH CHICAGO --

Liberty Coach
1400 Morrow Avenue
No. Chicago, IL 60064
Tel. (312) 578-4600
Custom Busses   C-1:1

ILLINOIS (Cont'd.)

MARENGO --
Barrett Industrial Trucks
240 N. Prospect Street
Marengo, IL 60152
Tel. (815) 568-6525
Specialized Trucks

STREATOR --
Vactor Division of
    Peabody Myers Corp.
1621 S. Illinois St.
Tel. (815) 672-3171
Contact: Barry Collins
Street Sweepers & Vacuum
    Trucks   C-2:5

WARRENSBURG --
Lazy N, Inc.
Highway 121
P.O. Box 157
Warrensburg, IL 62573
R1,R6, Trackless
    Trolleys, Utility
    Trailers

- -

INDIANA

ALBION --
Starline Vans
P.O. Box 95
Albion, IN 46701
Tel. (219) 636-3119
Contact: Bob Burton
R4   C-2:10 Retirees

ANDERSON --
5th Season R.V.s
R.R.#6, Box 184-A
Anderson, IN 46011
Tel. (317) 642-9870
Customized Vehicles

ANGOLA --
Angola Coach, Inc.
S.R. 127 North
P.O. Box 301
Angola, IN 46703
Tel. (219) 425-6507

BREMEN --
Bremen Motor Corp.
425 Industrial Drive
Bremen, IN
Tel. (219) 546-3791
A

BRISTOL --
Beach-Craft Motor Homes Corp.
19224 C.R. 8
Bristol, IN 46507
Nation: (800) 358-4093
        (219) 848-7611
Contact: John Steinberg
R1   C-1:?

BRISTOL --
Gerwin Vans, Inc.
807 S. Division
Bristol, IN 46507
Tel. (219) 848-7602
Contact: Tony Piwoszkin
R4   C-2:10

BRISTOL --
Granada Conversions, Inc.
11901 C.R. 8
Bristol, IN 46507
Tel. (219) 848-7446
Contact: Dean Myers (Pres.)
R4   C-2:5-10

BRISTOL --
International Vehicle Corp.
200 Legion Street
P.O. Box 424
Bristol, IN 46507
Tel. (219) 848-7686
R4

BRISTOL --
Merhow Industries, Inc.
19757 C.R. 8
Bristol, IN 46507
Tel. (219) 848-4445
Contact: Tom Holdeman
Horse Trailers B-1,B-2:3

BRISTOL --
Roman Wheels Midwest, Inc.
S.R. 15 South
P.O. Box 108
Bristol, IN 46507
Tel. (219) 848-7646
R4

BRISTOL --
Vehicle Concepts Corp.
Bristol Industrial Park
S.R. 15 North
Bristol, IN 46507
Tel. (219) 848-7494
R2,R4

DECATUR --
Fleetwood Motor Homes
    of Indiana
1410 Patterson St.
Decatur, IN 46733
Tel. (219) 728-2121
R1,R2

ELKHART --
American Travel Trailer Corp.
P.O. Box 1282
Elkhart, IN 46515
Tel. (219) 293-3576
R5

ELKHART --
Auto Form Corporation
28620 C.R. 20 West
Elkhart, IN 46517
Tel. (219) 295-2229
Contact: Anita Reaker
R2,R6   C-2:5-10

ELKHART --
Beach-Craft Motor Homes
    Corporation
52684 Route 8
Dexter Drive
Elkhart, IN 46514
Bookmobiles

ELKHART --
Bock Products, Inc.
1901 W. Hively
Elkhart, IN 46515
Tel. (219) 294-5581
W

ELKHART --
Chariot Vans
28582 Jamie Street
Elkhart, IN 46514
Nation: (800) 521-8733
         (219) 262-2624
         (219) 262-4667
Contact: John Wisolek
R3,R4   C-2:10
NOTE: Parent Company is
      Georgie Boy, in
      Edwardsburg, MI;
      Damon Ind. in Elkhart is
      their sister company.

ELKHART --
Country Cruiser, Inc.
2206 Toledo Road
Elkhart, IN 46516
Tel. (219) 522-7586
R4

ELKHART --
Delmar Motor Coach
53112 Faith Avenue
P.O. Box 1444
Elkhart, IN 46514
Tel. (219) 262-3526
Contact: Mike Russo
R4   C-1:1   D

ELKHART --
Elk Enterprises, Inc.
25771 Miner Road
Elkhart, IN 46514
Tel. (219) 264-0768
R4   D

ELKHART --
Esterel, Inc.
30338 C.R. 12
Elkhart, IN 46514
Tel. (219) 264-2126
R6   A-2

ELKHART --
Bonanza Travelers, Inc.
30034 C.R. 10
Elkhart, IN 46514
Tel. (219) 262-2693
Contact: Pete Puxta
R3,R5   C-2:2-3

ELKHART --
Citation Motor Coach
25786 Miner Road
P.O. Box 517
Elkhart, IN 46515
Contact: Ray Feinberg
R4   A-2
NOTE: Cricket Motor
      Homes, in Elkhart,
      is their parent
      company.

ELKHART --
Cricket Motor Homes
25786 Miner Road
P.O. Box 377
Elkhart, IN 46515
Tel. (219) 264-9669
R6

ELKHART --
Designer Coach/A & S Corp.
435 W. Harrison
Elkhart, IN 46516
Tel. (219) 293-8696
R4

ELKHART --
Esquire, Inc.
21861 Protecta Rd.
Elkhart, IN 46516
Tel. (219) 232-6168
R2,R3,R4,R5,R6

ELKHART --
Etnom Corp.
53664 C.R. 9 North
Elkhart, IN 46514
Tel. (219) 262-4411
Contact: Robert Makela
R4   C-2:4-5 "Kept busy!"

ELKHART --
Century Motor Coach
53387 Ada Drive
Elkhart, IN 46514
Tel. (219) 262-1511
Contact: Jim Maxey
A-2,B-2,D

ELKHART --
Coachmen Industries, Inc.
601 E. Beardsley Ave.
Elkhart, IN 46516
NOTE: Corporate HQ

ELKHART --
Coachmen Van Conversions
Box 50
Elkhart, IN 46515
Tel. (219) 262-3474
R4

ELKHART --
Damon Industries, Inc.
28719 Jamie Street
Elkhart, IN 46514
Tel. (219) 262-2624
Contact: Ron Ulrey
R2,R3,R5   D

ELKHART --
Destiny Vans, Inc.
2336 Primrose
Elkhart, IN 46516
Tel. (219) 293-5210
Contact: John Ranschaert
R4   C-1:3

ELKHART --
Estate Mfg., Inc.
22617 Pine Creek Road
Elkhart, IN 46516-9689
Tel. (219) 295-3682
R5,R6

ELKHART --
Fleetwing Travelers, Inc.
21141 Protecta Drive
Elkhart, IN 46516
Tel. (219) 295-5377
R5,R6

ELKHART --

Goshen Coach
52684 Dexter Drive, E.
Elkhart, IN 46514
Tel. (219) 262-0199

ELKHART --

Granville, Inc.
2200 Middlebury
P.O. Box 2088
Elkhart, IN 46515
Tel. (219) 294-6437
Contact: Terry Crothers
   at (219) 293-6166
R3,R4   D

ELKHART --

Hornet Industries, Inc.
24245 C.R. 6, East
Elkhart, IN 46514
Tel. (219) 262-2561
Contact: Jim Foltz
R5,R6   B-2:6

ELKHART --

Journey Motor Homes, Inc.
27365 County Road 6, W.
Elkhart, IN 46514
Tel. (219) 262-1523
Contact: Vickie Kidder
R1 & Custom Vehicles C-1:3

ELKHART --

Legacy Vans
22896 Pine Creek Road
Elkhart, IN 46516
Tel. (219) 293-7040
Contact: Keith Pletcher
R4   C-2:2

ELKHART --

Longview Van Corp.
1147 Center St.
Elkhart, IN 46516
Tel. (219) 295-4277
Contact: Don Long
R4   C-2:2-3

ELKHART --

Gladiator, Inc.
55131 C.R. 1
P.O. Box 2237
Elkhart, IN 46514
Nation: (800) 348-7400
        (219) 262-2633
Contact: Jim Shedd
R4   C-2:15-20

ELKHART --

Hart Conversions
53049 Faith Avenue
Elkhart, IN 46514
Tel. (219) 264-2497
Contact: Lynda Stackman
R4   C-2:2

ELKHART --

Imperial Industries, Inc.
21141 Protecta Drive
Elkhart, IN 46516
Tel. (219) 522-6059
R4

ELKHART --

Kellogg Mfg. Co.
808 South 9th Street
Elkhart, IN 46516
Eastern Half of USA:
    (800) 654-9277
    (219) 295-4194
Contact: James Noble
R4   C-2:3

ELKHART --

Leisure Editions, Inc.
Dexter Drive
Elkhart, IN 46514
Tel. (219) 262-3681
R4

ELKHART --

Luxury Cruiser, Inc.
52906 Dexter Drive
Elkhart, IN 56514
Tel. (219) 264-9671
Contact: Dave Reed
R4   C-2:5

ELKHART --

Grand Systems, Inc.
2123½ Middlebury St.
P.O. Box 37
Elkhart, IN 46515
Tel. (219) 534-2414
R4

ELKHART --

Honey RVs
1809 W. Hively Ave.
Elkhart, IN 46517
Tel. (219) 294-6411
Contact: Sam Germano
R1,R2   C-1:10

ELKHART --

Intercoach Corp.
2525 Warren Street
Elkhart, IN 46516
Tel. (219) 295-5613
R4

ELKHART --

Lands Design, Inc.
27861 Dexter Drive
Elkhart, IN 46514
Nation: (800) 348-7437
        (219) 262-2567
Contact: Midge Bruggner
        or Blaine Barnhill
R4   C-2:7

ELKHART --

Li'l Cat/Meander
28867 Paul Drive
Elkhart, IN 46514
Tel. (219) 264-0796
Contact: Margo Weeks
Concession & Arcade
   Trailers, Cargo Trlrs.

ELKHART --

Luxury Vans
52918 Lillian Ave.
Elkhart, IN 46514
Tel. (219) 264-0602
R4

ELKHART --

Marathon Homes Corp.
Pine Creek Industrial Park
P.O. Box 1302
Elkhart, IN 46515
Tel. (219) 294-6441
Contact: Joe Bozzuto
R2,R5,R6   C-2:1

ELKHART --

Premiere Editions, Inc.
27801 Dexter Drive
Elkhart, IN 46514
Tel. (219) 262-3681
R4

ELKHART --

Sandpiper Conversions, Inc.
108 S. Elkhart Avenue
Elkhart, IN 46516
Tel. (219) 294-7664
R4

ELKHART --

Signature Van Corp.
28591 U.S. 20, W.
Elkhart, IN 46514
Tel. (219) 295-2530
R4

ELKHART --

Skyline Corp. - Motorized Div.
2520 By-Pass Road
Elkhart, IN 46514
Nation: (800) 633-2831
        (219) 294-7457
R2,R4   D
Uses: Morgan Driveaway

ELKHART --

Sunrader, Inc.
22503 Pine Creek Road
P.O. Box 188
Elkhart, IN 46515
Tel. (219) 295-3181
R3   C-2:5

ELKHART --

Midway Truck & Coach, Inc.
29391 U.S. 33 West
P.O. Box 1931
Elkhart, IN 46515
Tel. (219) 294-3531
Contact: Chuck Tubbs
R4   C-2:8

ELKHART --

Quality Coaches
52743 Stephen Place
Elkhart, IN 46514
Tel. (219) 262-3649
Contact: Lori Wright
R4   C-2:2-3 (More during
                the summer)

ELKHART --

Santa Fe Vans
1801 Minnie St.
Elkhart, IN 46516
Tel. (219) 293-0585
Contact: Chuck Ornduff
R4   C-2:6

ELKHART --

Sportscoach Corp. of America
P.O. Box 609
Elkhart, IN 46515
Nation: (800) 457-7164
        (219) 522-6224
R1

ELKHART --

Skyline Corp. - Nomad Div.
401 C.R. 15, South
Elkhart, IN 46514
Tel. (219) 294-2573
R6

ELKHART --

T-Line Enterprises
22800 Pine Creek Road
Elkhart, IN 46516
Tel. (219) 293-6026
Contact: George Thomas
R4   C-2:3-5

ELKHART --

Park Homes, Inc.
21746 Buckingham Rd.
Elkhart, IN 46516
Tel. (219) 293-8547
R5,R6

ELKHART --

Ram Coach
52705 Thorne Drive
Elkhart, IN 46514
Nation: (800) 348-7437
        (219) 262-2689
Contact: Phyllis Miller
R4   C-2:5

ELKHART --

Seven-O-Seven Ind., Inc.
2625 Lowell St.
Elkhart, IN 46516
Tel. (219) 294-6151
Contact: Thomas Martin
R4   C-1:1

ELKHART --

Skyline - Leyton Pl. So.
411 C.R. 15, South
Elkhart, IN 46514
Tel. (219) 295-6182
R5,R6   D
Uses: Barrett Transport

ELKHART --

Sprinter Rec. Vehs., Inc.
29391 U.S. Route 33, W.
Elkhart, IN 46515
Tel. (219) 295-2422
R2   D
Uses: Caravan (Elkhart)

ELKHART --

Titan Motor Homes
P.O. Box 482
Highway 19, South
Elkhart, IN 46514
Tel. (219) 293-6581
R1,R2

INDIANA (Cont'd.)

ELKHART --

Trans-Aire International, Inc.
52652 Mobile Drive
P.O. Box 2178
Elkhart, IN 46515
Tel. (219) 262-3411
Contact: Mary Carothers,
     Personnel Director
R4   C-2:8

ELKHART --

Travel Line Enterprises, Inc.
25876 Miner Road
Elkhart, IN 46514
Tel. (219) 264-3127
Contact: Bill Davis
R6   B-3:18

ELKHART --

Van Patton Vans/VEMCO Builders
22865 Pine Creek Road
P.O. Box 1305
Elkhart, IN 46515
Tel. (219) 293-4527
Contact: Scott Defenaugh
R4   C-2:5

ELKHART --

Wedge Conversion Group
52904 C.R. 13
Elkhart, IN 46514
Tel. (219) 264-0684
Contact: Bea Kirchner
R4   C-2:4-5   D

FORT WAYNE --

E-Vans, Inc.
515 Coliseum Blvd.
Fort Wayne, IN 46808
Tel. (219) 747-7452
    (219) 747-6865
Contact: Mickey Tomlin
R4   C-2:6

GOSHEN --

Casa Villa, Inc.
33 E. Industrial Park
P.O. Box 581
Goshen, IN 46526
Tel. (219) 642-3121
R6

ELKHART --

Travel Craft, Inc.
1135 Kent Street
P.O. Box 1687
Elkhart, IN 46514
Tel. (219) 262-4561
Contact: Junior Fiorentino
R1,R2,R4   C-2:10

ELKHART --

Travel Units, Inc.
P.O. Box 1833
Elkhart, IN 46515
Tel. (219) 293-8785
Contact: Production Mgr.
R5,R6

ELKHART --

VIC Vans
29449 U.S. Route 33, West
P.O. Box 1912
Elkhart, IN 46515
Tel. (219) 293-2925
R4   D

ELKHART --

Yellowstone, Inc.
28163 C.R. 20, West
P.O. Box 1128
Elkhart, IN 46515
Tel. (219) 293-9551
Contact: Jeanine Hall
R1,R2,R5,R6   A-1,C-1:6

FORT WAYNE --

Special Trucks, Inc.
5040 Hoevel Road
Fort Wayne, IN 46806
Tel. (219) 447-5572
Contact: Tom Clifford
Special Purpose Trucks
C-2:6-7
NOTE: See listing for
satellite plant in
Springfield, Ohio.
Tel. (513) 324-3657

ELKHART --

Travel Innovations, Inc.
30372 C.R. 12, West
Elkhart, IN 46514
Tel. (219) 262-4474
Contact: Brian Pritchard
R4   C-2:2   D
NOTE: Also known as
Gemini Van Conversions.

ELKHART --

U.S. Conversions, Inc.
27861 Dexter Drive
Elkhart, IN 46515
Tel. (219) 293-2925
R4

ELKHART --

V.I.P. Vans
55210 C.R. 3
Elkhart, IN 46514
Tel. (219) 293-0651
R4

ETNA GREEN --

Mallard Coach Co., Inc.
200 Tower Street
Etna Green, IN 46254
Tel. (219) 858-2531
Contact: Marv Miller
R1,R2,R5,R6   D

GOSHEN --

Advantage Division of
    Rockwood, Inc.
P.O. Box 461
Goshen, IN 46526
Tel. (219) 534-2694
R4   D

GOSHEN --

Contemporary Coach Corp.
64654 U.S. Highway 33
Box 512
Goshen, IN 46526
Tel. (219) 533-4161
Contact: Merv Bender
R4   C-2:5

INDIANA (Cont'd.)

GOSHEN --

Elkhart Traveler Corp.
2211 W. Wilden Avenue
Goshen, IN 46526
Tel. (219) 533-9527
R5,R6

GOSHEN --

Kropf Mfg. Co., Inc.
58647 S.R. 15
P.O. Box 30
Goshen, IN 46526
Tel. (219) 533-2171
Contact: Don Kropf
R5,R6   B-2:5

GOSHEN --

R.C. Industries, Inc.
16968 C.R. 38
P.O. Box 147
Goshen, IN 46526
Tel. (219) 534-3521
R5,R6

GOSHEN --

Shasta Industries
Box 728
Goshen, IN 46526
Nation: (800) 348-7477
        (219) 534-2651
Contact: Steve, for all
        Driver Information
R1,R2,R3,R5,R6

GOSHEN --

Turtle Top, Inc.
118 W. Lafayette Street
Goshen, IN 46526
Tel. (219) 533-4116
R2,R4

HUNTINGTON --

Sportsmobile, Inc.
250 Court Street
Huntington, IN 46750
Tel. (219) 356-5435
R4

GOSHEN --

Fan Coach Co., Inc.
P.O. Box 482
Goshen, IN 46526
Tel. (219) 534-3594
R5,R6

GOSHEN --

Newcomer Industries, Inc.
P.O. Box 806
16651 Go-Re-Co Drive
Goshen, IN 46526
Tel. (219) 534-3415
Contact: David Cuthbert
R5,R6   B-2:5

GOSHEN --

Rockwood, Inc.
3010 College Avenue
Goshen, IN 46526
Tel. (219) 534-3645
R4

GOSHEN --

Starcraft
2703 College Avenue
Goshen, IN 46526
Tel. (219) 533-1105
R4   A-1:10   C-2:16

GOSHEN --

Van American, Inc.
2766 E. College Ave.
Goshen, IN 46526
Tel. (219) 534-1418
R1,R2,R4

KOKOMO --

Panda Vans, Inc.
S.R. 19 & U.S. 35
Kokomo, IN 46901
Tel. (317) 457-6781
R4   C-1:2   D:Ocnly.

GOSHEN --

K & S Conversions
521 E. Lincoln
Goshen, IN 46526
Tel. (219) 534-3637
Contact: Bob Wilson, Jr.
R4   A-2,B-2,C-2
        Total of 12 Drivers

GOSHEN --

Paramount Industries, Inc.
64722 C.R. 27
P.O. Box 813
Goshen, IN 46526
Tel. (219) 534-3617
R4, Hearses, Spec. Veh.

GOSHEN --

Royal Diamond, Inc.
64654 U.S. Route 33
Goshen, IN 46526
Tel. (219) 642-4353
R6

GOSHEN --

Tour-Master Van Div. of
    Cargo Master
P.O. Box 724
Goshen, IN 46526
Tel. (219) 534-2451
Contact: John Caple
M,R4, Parcel Delivery
    Vans   B-1, C-2
    Total of 8 Drivers

GRANGER --

Heritage RV, Ltd.
13065 Anderson Road
Granger, IN 46530
Tel. (219) 272-8990
R1,R2,R5

LOGANSPORT --

Universal Fire
    Apparatus Co.
P.O. Box 178
Logansport, IN 46947
Tel. (219) 753-3223
Contact: Matt Franklin
F   C-1:1

INDIANA (Cont'd.)

MIDDLEBURY --

Coachmen Rec. Vehicle Co.
P.O. Box 30
Middlebury, IN 46540
Tel. (219) 825-5821
Various RVs

MIDDLEBURY --

Valley Vans, Inc.
11920 C.R. 14
Middlebury, IN 46540
Tel. (219) 825-9411
R4

MILLERSBURG --

Carriage, Inc.
P.O. Box 246
Millersburg, IN 46543
Nation: (800) 348-2214
        (219) 642-3622
Contact: Personnel Dept.
R4,R5,R6   B-1,C-1,C-2
15 Drivers Total.

MISHAWAKA --

R.B.R. Corporation
13301 Chippewa Blvd.
Mishawaka, IN 46545
Tel. (219) 256-0273
R3

NAPPANEE --

Franklin Coach Co.
South Oakland Avenue
P.O. Box 152
Nappanee, IN 46550
Tel. (219) 773-4106
R6

NAPPANEE --

Mallard Coach (Pl. 2, Bldg. 1)
354 N. Delaware Street
Nappanee, IN 46550
Tel. (219) 773-2471
R5,R6   D
Uses: Dallas Moser
        Transport

MIDDLEBURY --

Jayco, Inc.
58075 S.R. 13, S.
Middlebury, IN 46540
Tel. (219) 825-5861
R2,R4,R5,R6

MILFORD --

Barth, Inc.
S.R. 15, South
P.O. Box 768
Milford, IN 46542
Nation: (800) 348-5088
        (219) 658-9401
Contact: Mary Miller
R1 & Custom   C-2:2-3

MILLERSBURG --

Rockwood, Inc.
201 Elm Street
P.O. Box 85
Millersburg, IN 46543
Tel. (219) 642-3313
R1,R2,R4

MISHAWAKA --

Sun-Land Express RV, Inc.
1320 S. Merrifield
Mishawaka, IN 46544
Tel. (219) 256-6797
Contact: Personnel Dir.
R3, Custom Trlrs.   C-2:6

NAPPANEE --

Gulf Stream Coach, Inc.
P.O. Box 1005
Nappanee, IN 46550
Nation: (800) 348-4401
In IN: (800) 552-3308
        (219) 773-7761
Contact: Frank Kaufman
R1,R2,R3,R5,R6

NAPPANEE --

Mallard Coach (Pl. 2, Bldg. 2)
656 N. Delaware Street
Nappanee, IN 46550
Tel. (219) 773-2471
R6   D
Uses: Dallas Moser
        Transport

MIDDLEBURY --

Travelmaster Rec. Veh.
Box 1188
Middlebury, IN 46540
Nation: (800) 624-4610
        (219) 825-8223
Contact: Jim Miller at
    Sportscoach in Elkhart
NOTE: Co. plans move to
    Elkhart early in
    1987.
R1,R2,R3,R5,R6
A-1,A-3,B-1,B-3,C-1,D
25 Drivers Total.

MISHAWAKA --

Mondich Conversions
55955 Hoosier
Mishawaka, IN 46545
Tel. (219) 255-4432

MITCHELL --

Carpenter Body Works
P.O. Box 128
Mitchell, IN 47446
Tel. (812) 849-3131
S

NAPPANEE --

Mallard Coach (Plant #1)
26535 U.S. Route 6, E.
Nappanee, IN 46550
Tel. (219) 773-2471
R2   D
Uses: Dallas Moser
        Transport

NAPPANEE --

Newman Industries, Inc.
335 N. Delaware Street
Nappanee, IN 46550
Tel. (219) 773-7791
Contact: Glenn Troyer
R1,R2,R5,R6
B-1,C-1,C-2,D (12-15
Drivers Move 25 Units
per Week.)

INDIANA (Cont'd.)

NEW PARIS --

Terravan Mini Motorhomes
67895 Industrial Drive
New Paris, IN 46553
Tel. (219) 831-2940
R2

TIPTON --

FMC Corporation -- Fire
    Apparatus Division
516 Dearborn Street
Tipton, IN
Nation: (800) 621-4500
F

WAKARUSA --

Aviator Van Conversions
P.O. Box 757
Wakarusa, IN 46573
Nation: (800) 532-0810
      (219) 862-2121
R4

WAKARUSA --

Utilimaster Corporation
65266 S.R. 19
Wakarusa, IN 46573
Nation: (800) 582-3454
      (219) 862-4561

RICHMOND --

Vanco Industries, Inc.
755 Round Barn Road, S.
Richmond, IN 47374
Tel. (317) 966-1733
R4

TOPEKA --

Starcraft
536 Michigan Street
Topeka, IN 46571
Tel. (219) 593-2550
R6   B-1:30   B-3:20

WAKARUSA --

Holiday Rambler Corp.
65528 S.R. 19
Wakarusa, IN 46573
Tel. (219) 862-7211
R1,R2,R4,R5,R6

WINAMAC --

Braun Corporation
1014 S. Monticello
Winamac, IN 46996
Tel. (219) 946-6157
Contact: William R. Roth
R4   C-1:Up to 10

RICHMOND --

Wayne Corporation
Industries Road
P.O. Box 1447
Richmond, IN 47375
Tel. (317) 962-7511
S   C-2 (Drivers
fqtly. tow their cars.)

VALPARAISO --

Classy Chassis
1000 Axe Avenue
Valparaiso, IN 46383
Tel. (219) 462-5536
Contact: Curt Kennelly
        (Owner)
R4   A-1:1

WAKARUSA --

Marauder Travelers, Inc.
200 Industrial Parkway
Wakarusa, IN 46573
Tel. (219) 862-4541
R5,R6

- -

IOWA

ALTON --

Service Trucks, Inc.
P.O. Box 399
202 10th Street
Alton, IA 51003
Specialized Trucks

GRANGER --

Granger Industries
1913 Main
Granger, IA 50109
Tel. (515) 999-2390
      (515) 999-2224
R4

COMANCHE --

Compliment Vans
1924 Washington Blvd.
Comanche, IA 52730
Tel. (319) 259-83911
R4   C-2:6

HUMBOLDT --

Dodgen Ind./Born Free, Inc.
Hwy. 169, N., P.O. Box B
Humboldt, IA 50548
Tel. (515) 332-3755
Contact: Herb Nelson
R2, Mobile Veterin. Clinics
C-1,C-2   3 Drivers, Total

FOREST CITY --

Winnebago Industries, Inc.
P.O. Box 152
Forest City, IA 50436
Nation: (800) 248-1309
In IA: (800) 247-4646
      (515) 582-6858
Contact: Dave Slette

HUMESTON --

K & S Mfg., Inc.
319 Fletcher Street
Humeston, IA 50123
Tel. (515) 877-6551
R5,R6

MONTICELLO --

DMR Van Conversions, Inc.
200 South Cedar
Monticello, IA 52310
Tel. (319) 465-5620
Contact: Marilyn Schneiderman
R4   C-1:2

MOUNT PLEASANT --

Blue Bird - Midwest
Highway 34 West
Mount Pleasant, IA
(319) 385-2231
S

TRIPOLI --

Fabricated Products Co.
R.R. #1, P.O. Box 251
Tripoli, IA 50676
R5,R6

POCAHONTAS --

E.R. Buske Mfg. Co., Inc.
P.O. Box 129
Pocahontas, IA 50574
(712) 335-3585
Contact: John De Wall
W   C-2:4

- -

KANSAS

CHANUTE --

Nu-Wa Industries, Inc.
P.O. Box 808
4002 Ross Lane
Chanute, KS 66720
Tel. (316) 431-2088
R5,R6   A-1:9

HUTCHINSON --

Collins Industries, Inc.
Air Base Industrial Tract
RFD #2
Hutchinson, KS 67504
Tel. (316) 663-5551
H,S, Limousines, Transit
  Busses, Other Special-
  ized Vehicles. C-1:3

McPHERSON --

Kit Mfg. Co. - RV Division
1000 Kit Blvd.
P.O. Box 586
McPherson, KS 67460
Nation: (800) 835-2058
        (316) 241-4320

OSWEGO --

Coons Mfg., Inc.
2300 W. 4th Street
P.O. Box 489
Oswego, KS 67356
Tel. (316) 795-2191
Contact: Beverly Stewart
U,R2, & Secialty Vehicles
C-2:6

CHANUTE --

Rawhide Custom Covers, Inc.
Route 1, W. 21st Street
Chanute, KS 66720
Tel. (316) 431-3990
Contact: Gary Taylor or
         Jerry Whitworth
R5,R6   B-1:4

INDEPENDENCE --

Hackney & Sons, Midwest
300 Hackney Avenue
Independence, KS 67301
Nation: (800) 835-0660
        (316) 331-6600
Contact: Mike Coltharp
V, & Beverage Trailers
C-1:4

McPHERSON --

Western Turtle Top
201 North C.R. 319
McPherson, KS 67460
Tel. (316) 241-4360
Contact: Gordon Reimer
R4   C-2:6-7

RUSSELL --

King of the Road
538 Front Street
Russell, KS 67665
Nation: (800) 255-0521
        (913) 483-2138
R2,R5,R6

COLUMBUS --

Cameo Industries, Inc.
236 W. Pine
Columbus, KS 66725
Tel. (316) 429-3000
R5,R6

INDEPENDENCE --

Mobile Traveler, Inc.
P.O. Box 268
Junction City, KS 66441
Nation: (800) 332-0283
        (913) 238-7176
Contact: Jack Barron
R1,R2,R5, & Specialty
  Vehicles. B-3,C-1
Total of 20 Drivers.

MINNEAPOLIS --

El Dorado RV, Inc.
1200 W. 10th Street
P.O. Box 266
Minneapolis, KS 67467
Nation: (800) 255-7212
Nation: (800) 654-6545
In KS: (800) 826-4441
        (913) 392-2171
Contact: Gary Plush
R1,R2, & Transit Busses
C-1:48-60

KANSAS (Cont'd.)

SALINA --

Lorenson Industries, Inc.
461 East Avenue A
Salina, KS 67401
Tel. (913) 823-6036
Specialty Vehicles

SMITH CENTER --

Peterson Industries
R.R. 2, Box 95
Smith Center, KS 66967
Tel. (913) 282-6692
Contact: Vaughn Peterson
R5,R6   C-1:2

WICHITA --

Ketch-All, Inc.
1006 E. Waterman
Wichita, KS
Tel. (316) 262-7316

WELLINGTON --

Mayflower Travel Trailer
19 Industrial Avenue
Wellington, KS 67152
Tel. (316) 326-5973
Contact: Bob De Jarnett
R5,R6   A-1:1   C-2:5

- -

KENTUCKY

COVINGTON --

A.F.C.O., Inc.
1549 Kellogg
Covington, KY
Tel. (606) 261-3585

LOUISVILLE --

Koach Krafters/AmeriKraft Corp.
5202 Crittenden Drive
Louisville, KY 40213
Nation: (800) 626-1565
        (502) 364-1000
Contact: Jim Fraley
A-1 and C-1   (Total of 3 Drivers)

Product Line:
  Racing/NASCAR Trailers
  Mobile Medical Units
  Special Trailers, & R4

- -

LOUISIANA

DELHI --

Starcraft
Illinois Avenue
P.O. Box 277
Delhi, LA 71232
Nation: (800) 826-4820
        (318) 878-2433
R6

MINDEN --

Clement Industries, Inc.
P.O. Box 914
Minden, LA 71058
Tel. (318) 377-2776

- -

MARYLAND

GAITHERSBURG --

Protective Materials Co.,
   Inc./Fargo International
7914 Queenair Drive
Gaithersburg, MD 20879
Tel. (301) 921-6380
Survey Vans, Arson Vans,
& Crime Labs

WOODSBORO --

Eastern Turtle Top
10822-B Woodsboro Road
Woodsboro, MD 21798

GLYNDON --

Sherrod Vans Northeast, Inc.
P.O. Box 218
Glyndon, MD 21071
Tel. (301) 833-2800
Contact: Kellie Aker
R4   A-2 Occasionally
C-2 Mostly (3)

Special Vehicles
Tel. (301) 845-8070
Contact: Steve Augustine   2 Drivers

HAMSTEAD --

Mid-Atlantic Universal
   Motor Coach
Rear 1900 Hanover Pike
Hamstead, MD
Tel. (301) 374-5000

MARYLAND (Cont'd.)

WOODSBORO --

Eastern Mobility
#4 Council Drive
Woodsboro, MD 21798

Tel. (301) 845-4188
Handicapped Units

- -

MASSACHUSETTS

LYNNFIELD --

Eastern Technologies, Ltd.
7 Kimball Lane
Lynnfield, MA 01940
Tel. (617) 246-5000
Contact: Ann Marie Klowers
Mfrs. of:
Fire Trucks, Water Trucks,
Crash/Rescue/Fire Trucks,
Runway Foam Trucks, Water
Trucks, Gasoline Trucks,
Aircraft Service Trucks,
Lube Trucks, and Refuelers
of the following: AV-Gas,
MO-Gas, and Jet Fuel. Also
mfrs. Large Trailers.
A-2,A-3,C-2
Total of 10-15 Drivers.

NORTH ANDOVER --

Eastern Technologies, Ltd.
2350 Turnpike Street
North Andover, MA
Tel. (617) 683-2441
NOTE: Call Lynfield (their
corporate HQ) about work.
All mfg. is done here.

SPRINGFIELD --

Hodge Mfg. Co., Inc.
55-57 Fisk Avenue
Springfield, MA 01107
Tel. (413) 781-68

G

PITTSFIELD --

Lenco Industries, Inc.
442 Merrill Road
Pittsfield, MA 01201
Tel. (413) 443-7359

SPRINGFIELD --

Eastern School Bus Sales
2257 Main Street
Springfield, MA 01104
Tel. (413) 734-0838
Contact: Peter Picknelly
S (Distribution Center)

WALTHAM --

New England Transit Sales
131 Linden Street
Waltham, MA 02154
Tel. (717) 894-9877
Contact: George Logen

WOODVILLE --

Farrar Co., Inc.
Winter Street
P.O. Box 58
Woodville, MA 01784
Tel. (617) 435-3431
F: Custom-Built
C-2:2-3

MIDDLEBORO --

Maxim, Inc.
Abbey Lane
Middleboro, MA 02346
Tel. (617) 947-4802

F (NOTE: Subsidiary of
Eastern Technologies,
Ltd., Lynnfield, Mass.)

- -

MICHIGAN

ALMONT --

Almont Welding Works, Inc.
4091 Van Dyke Road
Almont, MI 48003
Tel. (313) 798-8512
F   CPU

BAY CITY --

Marcan Industries, Inc.
808 Woodside Avenue
P.O. Box 1062
Bay City, MI 48706
Tel. (517) 892-8586
F, Customized Trucks,
S: Refurbishing

BENTON HARBOR --

Carl Heald, Inc.
Dept. YSO
Benton Harbor, MI 49022
Tel. (616) 849-3400
S

BROOKLYN --

Endesco, Inc.
P.O. Drawer 739
Brooklyn, MI
Tel. (517) 592-5115
W

BROWN CITY --

Frank Industries, Inc.
3950 Burnsline Road
Brown City, MI 48416
Tel. (313) 346-2771
R1,R4, & Spec. Vehs.

CASSOPOLIS --

Juno Industries, Inc.
67320 Cassopolis Road
Cassopolis, MI 49031
Tel. (616) 699-5302
R2,R5,R6

CENTREVILLE --

Viking Recreational Vehicles
Box 549
Centreville, MI 49032
Tel. (219) 825-8242
     (616) 467-6321

DETROIT --

Cadillac Motor Car Division
2860 Clark Avenue
Detroit, MI
Tel. (313) 554-6132

DETROIT --

General Motors Corp.
3044 W. Grand Blvd.
Detroit, MI
Tel. (313) 556-5000

EDWARDSBURG --

Georgie Boy
P.O. Drawer "H"
Edwardsburg, MI 49112
Nation: (800) 521-8733
        (616) 663-3415
Contact: Charlie Chew
R1   D

EDWARDSBURG --

Trophy Travelers, Inc.
19875 Highway M-205
Edwardsburg, MI 49112
Tel. (219) 264-4911
R2,R5,R6

FLINT --

Buick Motor Division
902 E. Hamilton
Flint, MI
Tel. (313) 236-5000

CONSTANTINE --

Cabriolet Div. of CTR, Inc.
67351 U.S. Hwy. 131, South
P.O. Box 337
Constantine, MI 49042-0337
Tel. (616) 435-7714
     (616) 435-7360
Contact: Ken Gingerich
R5, Horse Vehicles
A-2, B-2:1

DETROIT --

Chrysler Corp. - Truck Div.
P.O. Box 1919
Detroit, MI 48288
Tel. (313) 497-1000

DETROIT --

Tusco Products
3030 E. Woodbridge Ave.
Detroit, MI 48207
Tel. (313) 259-1012
S

EDWARDSBURG --

L.E.R. Industries, Inc.
19475 Hwy. U.S. 12, East
Edwardsburg, MI 49112
Tel. (616) 641-7763
Contact: Gary Rivers
R4   C-1,C-2,D
Uses 5 or 6 Drivers.

ESCANABA --

Hilltop Camper, Inc.
2905 N. Lincoln Road
Escanaba, MI 49829
Tel. (906) 786-7986
R4 is mfd. here. They also
Distribute R1,R2,R3,R5,R6.

GRAND RAPIDS --

Landau Motor Homes
4675 40th Street
Grand Rapids, MI 49508
Tel. (616) 957-3491
Contact: Gary White (Pres.)
R1   C-1

DEARBORN --

Ford Motor Company
American Road
Dearborn, MI
Tel. (313) 322-3000

DETROIT --

Ford Motor Co. - RV Div.
300 Renaissance Center
P.O. Box 43306
Detroit, MI 48243
Tel. (313) 446-3813
Contact: Bob Bricker
Chassis Cabs

DRYDEN --

Champion Home Builders Co.
5573 North Street
Dryden, MI 48428
Tel. (313) 796-2211
Med.-Duty Transit Busses,
R1,R2

EDWARDSBURG --

Cargo-Tec
19875 M-205
Edwardsburg, MI 49112
Tel. (616) 641-2222
Contact: Ken Gard
Custom Trailers
A-2,B-2   4 Drivers

FARMINGTON --

Prestige Vans
36681 Heatherton
Farmington, MI 48024
Tel. (313) 478-0467
R4

IMLAY CITY --

Trans-Van/Champion RV
275 Graham Road
P.O. Box 7
Imlay City, MI 48444
R1,R2

MICHIGAN (Cont'd.)

KALAMAZOO --

Kalamazoo Mfg. Co.
1827 Reed Blvd.
Kalamazoo, MI 49001
Tel. (616) 349-9723
A-3

MARCELLUS --

Cree Coaches
R.R. #1, Route M-40, N.
Marcellus, MI 49067
Tel. (616) 646-5131
Contact: Joe Shreiner
R5,R6   A-1,B-1
         (2 Drivers)

MOUNT CLEMENS --

PSI Mobile Products, Inc.
25 Eldridge Street
Mt. Clemens, MI 48043
Nation: (800) 222-3133
        (313) 468-4200
Contact: Hendron Ray
Mobile Health Clinics,
Patrol Wagons, Offices,
Laboratories, Classrooms,
Display Units, Banks,
Stores-on-Wheels, Fire
Trucks, A/V Vans, &
Service Centers.   D

LANSING --

Oldsmobile Division
920 Townsend Street
Lansing, MI
Tel. (517) 377-5000

MOUNT CLEMENS --

Fire Trucks, Inc. (F.T.I.)
164 Grand Street
Mt. Clemens, MI 48043
Nation: (800) 222-3133
        (313) 468-0801
Contact: Hendren Ray
A,E,F & Rebuilding of
Fire Trucks for municipal-
ities, also.
Delivery Methods:
  85% via Flatbed Truck
  14% via Driving (C-1:3)
  1% via Rail

NOTE: Fire Trucks, Inc., London Coach, and
PSI Mobile Products, Inc. have two main
things in common: they are all owned by
the same person, and one can reach all
three through the same WATS line. Otherwise, these are three completely independent companies.

LIVONIA --

AAR Brooks & Perkins
Advanced Structures Div.
12633 Inkster Road
Livonia, MI
Tel. (313) 522-2000
Airport Trucks & Veh. to
Military, Commercial, &
Industrial specs.

MOUNT CLEMENS --

London Coach
25 Eldridge Street
Mt. Clemens, MI 48043
Nation: (800) 222-3133
        (313) 468-0710
Contact: Hendren Ray or
         Sue Kozlowski
Exotic Automobiles:
  London Taxis -- for
    personal or livery
    use, and
  London Sterlings --
    Limousines
C-1:1   C-2:2

PONTIAC --

Gen. Motors Truck & Bus Group
31 Judson Street
Pontiac, MI 48057
Tel. (313) 456-5000

PONTIAC --

Vixen Motor Company
1 Silverdome Indus. Park
Pontiac, MI 48057
Tel. (313) 335-9800
R1

PONTIAC --

Pontiac Motor Division
1 Pontiac Plaza
Pontiac, MI 48057
Tel. (313) 857-5000

ROMEO --

Sun Hawk, Inc.
67780 Van Dyke
Romeo, MI 48065
Nation: (800) 772-7755
        (313) 752-3547
Contact: Jim Becker or
         Sharon Lattanzi
R4   C-2:4

PONTIAC --

Tra-Tech Midwest
3801 Industrial Drive
Pontiac, MI 48057
Tel. (313) 852-2620

ROMEO --

Van Epoch, Inc.
15055 32-Mile Road
Romeo, MI 48065
Tel. (313) 752-3518
R4

MICHIGAN (Cont'd.)

SOUTHFIELD --

American Motors Corp.
27777 Franklin Road
Southfield, MI
Tel. (313) 827-1000

STURGIS --

Universal Motor Coach
810 Broadus Street
Sturgis, MI 49091
Nation: (800) 882-4145
(616) 651-4765
Contact: Todd Hurley
or Tim Brandys
R4   C-2:6

UNION --

Tara Products, Inc.
North Route M-40
Union, MI 49130
Tel. (616) 641-5935
Trailers

WARREN --

Volkswagen of America, Inc.
2721 Parkview Blvd.
Warren, MI
Tel. (313) 362-6000

SOUTHFIELD --

General Trailer Mfg. &
Distribution, Inc.
19000 West 8-Mile Road
Southfield, MI 48075
Tel. (313) 354-0980

THREE RIVERS --

Sands Industries, Inc.
52161 U.S. Route 131
Three Rivers, MI 49093
Tel. (616) 273-8441
R4

VANDALIA --

Bivouac Automotive Corp.
17321 Route M-60, East
P.O. Box 279
Vandalia, MI 49095
Tel. (616) 476-9794
Contact: Cora Nuss
R4   C-2:8

WHITE PIGEON --

Centurian-Lehman
P.O. Box 715
White Pigeon, MI 49091
Tel. (616) 483-9691
R4

STURGIS --

Magnum Motor Coach, Ltd.
21397 U.S. Route 12, W.
Sturgis, MI 49091
Tel. (616) 651-1698
R4, & Pickup Conversions,
Light-Duty Trucks, and
Heavy-Duty Tow Vehicles
for the RV Industry.
A-3 D

TROY --

The Budd Company
3155 W. Big Beaver Road
Troy, MI
(313) 643-3500

WARREN --

Chevrolet Motor Division
30007 Van Dyke Avenue
Room 228-04
Warren, MI 48090
Tel. (313) 492-5400
Specialized Vehicles

WHITE PIGEON --

Country Sales, Inc.
71049 U.S. Route 131, S.
P.O. Box 635
White Pigeon, MI 49099
Tel. (616) 483-9695
Contact: Frank Reynolds
R4   B-3, C-2
(5 Drivers)

- -

MINNESOTA

BACKUS --

Scamp Travel Trailers
P.O. Box 2
Backus, MN 56435
Nation: (800) 346-4962
In MN: (800) 432-3749
(218) 947-4932
Contact: Duane Eveland
R2,R5,R6 A-2,B-2,C-2
(5 Drivers)

LUVERNE --

Luverne Fire Apparatus Company, Inc.
P.O. Box 437, 308 E. Maple
Luverne, MN 56156

BLOOMINGTON --

Wakefield Coach
9010 Pillsbury Ave., S.
Bloomington, MN 55420
Tel. (612) 888-8451
Bus Conversions

FOREST LAKE --

Waldoch Crafts, Inc.
13821 Lake Drive
Forest Lake, MN 55025
Nation: (800) 328-9259
(612) 464-3215
Contact: Todd Bjerknes
R2,R4, & Specialty Vehs.

Tel. (507) 283-4485
Contact: Steve Reedy
E,F   C-2:2

MINNESOTA (Cont'd.)

NORTH BRANCH --

General Safety Equip. Corp.
550 Eighth Avenue
North Branch, MN 55056
Tel. (612) 674-4804
Contact: Kevin Kirvida
F   C-1:3-4

ROSEAU --

Polaris Industries, Inc.
Highway 89
Roseau, MN
Tel. (218) 463-2312
Utility Vehicles

SAINT PAUL --

Kajo, Inc.
3276 Fanum Road
St. Paul, MN 55110
Tel. (612) 481-9299
Contact: Carol Kohler
R3   C-1:1

SAINT PAUL --

Road Rescue, Inc.   Nation: (800) 328-3804   Mfrs.: A,E, & Mobile Medical Clinics,
1133 Rankin Street   In MN: (800) 652-0208   Mobile Libraries, Mobile
St. Paul, MN 55116   (612) 699-5583   Recording Studios, Mobile
                           Contact: Scott Huestin   Dental Labs, etc. C-1:Varies

- -

MISSISSIPPI

KOSCIUSCO --

Sheller-Globe Corporation
Kosciusco Plant
Hamilton Building
Kosciusco, MS
Tel. (601) 289-1231

TISHOMINGO --

Heil Preferred Systems
P.O. Box 49
Tishomingo, MS
Tel. (601) 438-7801
G

- -

MISSOURI

BELTON --

Smitty's Van Interiors, Inc.
401 Commercial
P.O. Box 407
Tel. (816) 331-3007
Contact: Paul Smith
R4   C-2:2

CONCORDIA --

Spacecraft Motor Homes, Inc.
Route 1, Box 93
Concordia, MO 64020
Tel. (816) 463-7520
W,R1,R5,R6

KANSAS CITY --

Aero Leisure Ind., Inc.
1601 W. 25th St.
Kansas City, MO 64108
Tel. (816) 842-3611
Contact: Julie Fox
R4   C-2:2-3

KANSAS CITY --

Hesse Corporation
6700 St. John Avenue
Kansas City, MO 64125
Nation: (800) 821-5562
In MO: (800) 892-8715
        (816) 483-7808
Contact: Sue Duncan
V   C-1:2-3   D

NORTH KANSAS CITY --

The Van Scene
315 E. 18th Avenue
N. Kansas City, MO 64116
Tel. (816) 842-2389
Contact: Bill or Judy Bailey
R4

WESTPHALIA --

Play-Mor Trailers, Inc.
Highway 63, South
Westphalia, MO 65085
Tel. (314) 455-2387
R5,R6

- -

MONTANA

HELENA --

Superior Fire Apparatus Co.
Joslyn & Leslie Streets
Helena, MT 59601

Inside MT: (800) 222-0093
           (406) 442-0745
F   C-1:3

NEBRASKA

DAKOTA CITY --

The Broyhill Company   Tel. (402) 987-3412
N. Market Square   G
Dakota City, NE

- -

NEW HAMPSHIRE

DOVER --

Bayhead Products Corp.
1 Washington Street
Dover, NH

Tel. (603) 742-3000
G

SEABROOK --

Protective Materials Co., Inc.
Folly Mill Road
Seabrook, NH 03874   Mfrs.: Bomb Trailers, Arson
                                   Vans, Crime Labs, &
Tel. (603) 474-5523   Specialty Armored Vehs.

- -

NEW JERSEY

ELIZABETH --

William Bal Corporation
945 Newark Avenue
Elizabeth, NJ 07208
Tel. (201) 354-9625

MONTVALE --

Mercedes-Benz of N. America
1 Mercedes Drive
Montvale, NJ
Tel. (201) 573-0600

POINT PLEASANT --

Coast Cap Mfg.
3145 Route 88
Point Pleasant, NJ 08742

HAMMONTON --

Custom Sales & Service, Inc.
1 2nd Road & 11th Street
Hammonton, NJ 08037
Nation: (800) 257-7855
In NJ: (800) 322-8089
        (609) 561-6900
Pizza Delivery Trucks,
Food Modules, Refrigerated
and Heated Trucks.

Tel. (201) 295-2447
Concession Trailers,
Portable Booths

HAWTHORNE --

Trilectron Ind., Inc.
300 Ninth Avenue
Hawthorne, NJ
Tel. (201) 423-4005

PENNSAUKEN --

Merican Curtis, Inc.
7815 Airport Highway
Pennsauken, NJ

Tel. (609) 665-8484
F

- -

NEW YORK

BETHPAGE --

Grumman Corporation
1111 Stewart Avenue
Bethpage, NY
Tel. (516) 575-0574
Busses, Route Trucks

EAST SYRACUSE --

Sanford Fire Apparatus Corp.
P.O. Box 430
East Syracuse, NY
Tel. (315) 437-2516 or
     (315) 445-0512
F

BROOKLYN --

Franklin Body & Equip. Corp.
1025 Dean Street
Brooklyn, NY
Tel. (718) 789-5400
A,W

ELMIRA --

Empire Bus Sales
756 Baldwin St.
P.O. Box 1238
Elmira, NY 14902
Tel. (607) 732-3472
S   C-1:3-4 C-2:3-5
Uses Retired People

DEER PARK --

Garsite Products, Inc.
10 Grand Blvd.
P.O. Box 4289
Deer Park, NY 11729
Tel. (516) 667-1010
Contact: Wayne Turi
Aircraft Refueling
Trucks, Oil Trucks,
Liquid Handling Trucks.
C-2:2-3

ELMIRA --

La France Equipment Corp.
P.O. Box 333
Elmira, NY 14902
Tel. (607) 733-5511
Contact: Dave Farr or
John Berry
Fire Trucks mfd. here for
export only. They are driven
to ports at N.Y. City,
Baltimore, & Fla.   C-1:3

GLENS FALLS --

V.W. Weeks & Sons
Sweet Road
Glens Falls, NY
Tel. (518) 792-0075
Contact: Don Weeks
S Distributor

LANCASTER --

Young Fire Equipment Corp.
204 Cemetery Road
Lancaster, NY
Tel. (716) 684-8400
F

HAMBURG --

South Camp RV, Inc.
So. 5026 S.W. Blvd.
Hamburg, NY 14075
Tel. (716) 649-4600
R4

NEW YORK CITY --

Autoxport, Inc.
180 Broadway
New York City, NY
Tel. (212) 349-1168
Long-Wheelbase Limos

NEW YORK CITY --

Dover Corporation
277 Park Avenue
New York City, NY
Tel. (212) 826-7160
W

NEW YORK CITY --

Silo International, Inc.
30 East 42nd Street
New York City, NY
Tel. (212) 682-4331

NEW YORK CITY --

Thyssen-Bornemisza, Inc.
1211 Ave. of the Americas
New York City, NY
Tel. (212) 556-8500
Busses, Mini-Busses

NYACK --

Rockland Fire Equip. Co, Inc.
(Tri-County Police Supply Co.)
76-78 S. Franklin St.
P.O. Box 830
Nyack, NY 10960
Nation: (800) 227-1523
In NY: (800) 334-3523
(914) 358-1939
F,E

ONEONTA --

Medical Coaches, Inc.
Box 129
Hemlock Road
Oneonta, NY 13820
Tel. (607) 432-1333
Contact: Leonard Marsh
Custom Mobile Vehicles,
incl.: Bookmobiles, Mobile
X-Ray Units, Computer Units.
C-2:4-5

SUFFERN --

Econo Truck Body & Equip.
Foot of Ramapo Avenue
P.O. Box 329
Suffern, NY
Tel. (914) 357-2510

TARRYTOWN --

Wayne Bus & Truck Equip.
109 Central Avenue
Tarrytown, NY 10591
Tel. (914) 631-1116

WEST BABYLON --

Custom Trailer Builders
and Suppliers, Inc.
119 Lamar Street
West Babylon, NY
G

WEST LEBANON --

Samson Hydraulics, Inc.
U.S. Route 20
W. Lebanon, NY
Tel. (518) 794-7100
Truck Trailers

WYANDANCH --

Weld-Built Body Co., Inc.
278 Long Island Avenue
Wyandanch, NY
Nation: (800) 645-9055
(516) 643-9700
Truck Bodies

NORTH CAROLINA

BELMONT --

Catawba Coach Co., Inc.
103 E. Henry Street
Belmont, NC 28012
Tel. (704) 827-3001
R2

CHARLOTTE --

Equipment & Supply, Inc.
P.O. Box 30187
Charlotte, NC
Tel. (704) 537-0248
Airport Trucks

GREENSBORO --

Southern Coach
406 Pine Street
P.O. Box 20906
Greensboro, NC 27420
Tel. (919) 378-0567
R4

NORTH CAROLINA (Cont'd.)

HIGH POINT --

Thomas Built Busses/LP
1408 Courtesy Road
P.O. Box 2450
High Point, NC 27261
Tel. (919) 889-4871
Busses

WILSON --

Hackney Bros. Body Co.
P.O. Box 2728
Wilson, NC 27894
Nation: (800) 334-2296
        (919) 237-8171
Contact: W.T. Wray
Refrigerated Trucks for
Beer, Ice Cream, Etc.
C-1:6

NORTH WILKESBORO --

Corporate Coach
P.O. Box 1959
North Wilkesboro, NC 28659
Tel. (919) 378-0567
R4

WINSTON-SALEM --

Famco/Forsyth, Inc.
Drawer A
216 Junia Avenue
Winston-Salem, NC
(919) 721-1500
Airport Trailers

WASHINGTON --

Hackney & Sons, Inc.
400 Hackney Avenue
Washington, NC 27889
Nation: (800) 334-0711
In NC: (800) 682-8520
        (919) 946-6521
Contact: Mrs. Chipman
V, & Beverage Trailers
B-1, C-1, D No. of
Drivers Varies: 7-25.

- -

OHIO

AMLIN --

Sutphen Corporation
7000 Columbus-Marysville Rd.
Amlin, OH
Tel. (614) 889-1005
F

CANTON --

Canton Trailer Co.
1701 Gambrinus Ave., S.W.
Canton, OH 44706
Tel. (216) 477-0353
Special Trailers, and
Concession Stands. C-1:1

CINCINNATI --

Torbeck Industries
657 N. Wayne
Cincinnati, OH
Tel. (513) 367-0080
Truck Trailers & Airport
Vehicles

CLEVELAND --

HMC Fabricating
10147 Brecksville Road
Cleveland, OH
Tel. (216) 526-2420
A

BELLEVUE --

The Klein Steel Co.
1941 Carl Street
Bellevue, OH
Tel. (419) 483-3840
Truck Trailers

CINCINNATI --

Ellis & Watts Co.
P.O. Box 44010
Cincinnati, OH 45244
Tel. (513) 752-9000
Contact: Dave Meyer
Mobile Medical Units,
Spec. Units for Gov't. D

CINCINNATI --

Truck Cab Mfrs., Inc.
2420 Anderson Ferry Road
Cincinnati, OH 45238
Tel. (513) 922-1300
Custom Trucks

COLUMBUS --

The Chase Foundry & Mfg. Co.
2800 Parsons Avenue
Columbus, OH
Tel. (614) 444-1189
Truck Trailers

BOWERSTON --

Nolan Company
P.O. Drawer 201
601 Boyce Drive
Bowerston, OH
Tel. (614) 269-2771
F

CINCINNATI --

Hess & Eisenhardt Mfg.
8959 Blue Ash Avenue
Cincinnati, OH
Tel. (513) 791-8888

CLEVELAND --

Atlas Car Div. of
    Marmon Transmotive
1100-1144 Ivanhoe Road
Cleveland, OH
Tel. (216) 761-7663
Truck Trailers

COLUMBUS --

Horton Ambulance Co.
500 Industrial Mile
Columbus, OH
Tel. (614) 272-8181
A

OHIO (Cont'd.)

COLUMBUS --

Van Masters
1529 Alum Creek Drive
Columbus, OH 43209
Tel. (614) 253-0627
R4

CRIDERSVILLE --

United Fire Apparatus Corp.
204 S. Gay Street
Cridersville, OH
Tel. (419) 645-4083
F

DAYTON --

Springfield Equip. Co.
Wright Brothers Station
P.O. Box 523
Dayton, OH
Tel. (513) 228-8001
A

GALION --

Peabody Galion Division of
    Peabody International Corp.
500 Sherman Street
P.O. Box 607
Galion, OH
Tel. (419) 468-2120
G

JACKSON CENTER --

Airstream, Inc.
419 West Pike Street
Jackson Center, OH 45334
Tel. (513) 596-6111
Contact: Charlotte
                Hildebrandt
H,R1,R6 & Comm'l. Units
C-1:3 (Full-time)

LIMA --

Superior-Lima Div. of
    Sheller-Globe Corp.
1200 E. Kibby
Lima, OH
Tel. (816) 463-7520
H, Busses

NEW CARLISLE --

Kaffenbarger Welding &
    Truck Equipment
10100 Ballentine
New Carlisle, OH 45344
Tel. (513) 845-3804
Airport Vehicles &
Accessory Trucks

NORTH JACKSON --

Spacecraft Factory RV Sales
9180 Mahoning Avenue
P.O. Box 417
North Jackson, OH 44451
Tel. (216) 538-3108
R1,R5,R6

NORTH LIMA --

Lawless Industries
P.O. Box 1520
North Lima, OH
Tel. (216) 549-3946
Truck Trailers

OAKWOOD --

Braun
104 N. 4th Street
Oakwood, OH 45873
Tel. (419) 594-3391
A (Major Mfr.!)

RANDOLPH --

Randolph Coach, Inc.
1547 Hartville at Route 224
Randolph, OH 44265
Tel. (216) 325-9948
Specialized Vehicles

SPRINGFIELD --

Special Trucks, Inc.
235 Ogden Road
Springfield, OH
Tel. (513) 324-3657

Special-Purpose Trucks.
See Listing in Fort
Wayne, Indiana.

TOLEDO --

City Fire Equipment Co.
680 Bassett Street
Toledo, OH 43605
Tel. (419) 729-0602
F

WARREN --

Contempo Vans
5232 Tod Avenue, S.W.
Warren, OH 44481-9745
Nation: (800) 321-5534
            (216) 399-8334
R4

WASHINGTONVILLE --

Go-Tag-A-Long Trailer
    Mfg., Inc.
240 High Street
Washingtonville, OH 44490
Tel. (216) 427-2475
Contact: Robert Steensen
R6   B-3:3

- -

OKLAHOMA

McALESTER --

C.R.S. Company
P.O. Box 323
McAlester, OK 74502
Tel. (918) 426-5005
A,E,H,W

MIAMI --

Newell Coach Corp.
P.O. Box 1185, Hwy. 66, N.
Miami, OK 74355
Tel. (918) 542-3344
R1   C-1:2

OKLAHOMA CITY --

Boardman Steel Co.
P.O. Box 26088
Oklahoma City, OK
Tel. (405) 634-5434
F

OKLAHOMA (Cont'd.)

OKLAHOMA CITY --

Kinsey Enterprises
1218 N.W. 8th St., Suite A
Oklahoma City, OK 73106
Tel. (405) 232-9437
Specialized Vehicles

TULSA --

Crane Carrier Co.
1925 N. Sheridan
P.O. Box 582891
Tulsa, OK 74158
Tel. (918) 836-1651
G, & Mixer Trucks

- -

OREGON

BEND --

Beaver Coaches, Inc.
20545 Murray Road
P.O. Box 6089
Bend, OR 97708
Nation: (800) 423-2837
         (503) 389-1144
R1   C-1:9

CORNELIUS --

Western States Fire
   Apparatus
1389 Baseline Street
Cornelius, OR 97113
Tel. (503) 357-2163
F   C-1:1

JUNCTION CITY --

Country Camper, Inc.
135 E. First Street
Junction City, OR 97448
Nation: (800) 547-8015
In OR: (800) 452-8015
        (503) 998-3720
Contact: Bob Lee, Pres.
R1   C-1:4

JUNCTION CITY --

Monaco Motor Homes, Inc.
325 E. First St.
P.O. Box 345
Junction City, OR 97448

Nation: (800) 228-2831
        (503) 998-3336
R1   C-2:3-4

JUNCTION CITY --

Roadmaster, Ltd.
325 E. First St.
Junction City, OR 97448
Nation: (800) 228-6689
        (503) 998-3434
R1

McMINNVILLE --

Skyline Corporation -
   Leyton-Nomad Division
750 Booth Bend Road
McMinnville, OR 97128
Tel. (503) 472-3181
R5,R6   B-1

MILWAUKIE --

Komfort Industries of Oregon
3701 S.E. Naef Road
Milwaukie, OR 97268
Nation: (800) 228-8357
In OR: (800) 824-2589
        (503) 653-0931
R5,R6

MOUNT ANGEL --

Coachmen Rec. Veh. of Oregon
Box 1109
Mount Angel, OR 97362
Tel. (503) 845-2226

MOUNT ANGEL --

Shasta of Oregon
200 Industrial Way
Mt. Angel, OR 97362
Tel. (503) 845-9254

PORTLAND --

Northern Lite Mfg., Inc.
7410 S.E. Johnson Creek Blvd.
Portland, OR 97206
Tel. (503) 777-5826
R5,R6

SPRINGFIELD --

Collins Campers, Inc.
697 N. 34th Street
Springfield, OR 97478
Tel. (503) 746-7212
R5

WOODBURN --

Conestoga Mfg. Co.
13201 Wilco Hwy., N.E.
P.O. Box 496
Woodburn, OR 97071
Tel. (503) 634-2235
R5   1 Driver

- -

PENNSYLVANIA

ALLENTOWN --

Mack Trucks, Inc.
2100 Mack Blvd., P.O. Box M
Allentown, PA 18105-5000
Tel. (215) 439-3011
F, Many Others

BOYERTOWN --

Boyertown Auto Body Works
Third and Walnut Streets
Boyertown, PA 19512
Nation: (800) 523-0256
In PA: (800) 362-7979
        (215) 367-2091

Contact: Dale Smith, David
         Webb, or Keith Yoder
Trackless Trolleys, Army
Vehicles, & Parcel Vans
C-2:2-3   D

PENNSYLVANIA (Cont'd.)

BROOKVILLE --

TI-Brook, Inc.
McKinley Street
Box 300
Brookville, PA
Tel. (814) 849-2342

CONSHOHOCKEN --

Criminal Research Prods., Inc.
P.O. Box 408
Conshohocken, PA 19428
Tel. (215) 828-5326
Mobile Crime Labs
4 Drivers

IRWIN --

Serro Travel Trailer Co.
Arona Road
Irwin, PA 15642
Tel. (412) 863-3407
Contact: Ed Sova
R6   C-1:2-3

LIONVILLE --

National Foam System, Inc.
150 Gordon Drive
Lionville, PA 19533
Tel. (215) 363-1400
F

SOMERSET --

J & J Truck Bodies
733 S. Center Avenue
Box 735
Somerset, PA 15501
Tel. (814) 443-2671
Contact: Emily Barbuschak
D,G   A-2:9-10

BUTLER --

Watt Camper
709 W. Old Route 422
Butler, PA 16001
Tel. (412) 287-5493
R5,R6

ELIZABETHVILLE --

Swab Wagon Co., Inc.
1 Chestnut Avenue
Elizabethville, PA 17023
Tel. (717) 362-8137
Custom Truck Bodies &
A,F,R

LEOLA --

Shasta of Pennsylvania
P.O. Box 40
40 Hess Road
Leola, PA 17540
Nation: (800) 831-3123
In PA: (800) SHA-STA1
        (717) 656-2511
Contact: Greg Lewis
R5,R6   D

MANCHESTER --

Quigley Motor Co., Inc.
88 South Main Street
Manchester, PA 17345
Nation: (800) 233-9358
In PA: (800) 632-9016
        (717) 266-5631
Contact: William Quigley,
         Jr., Pres. & Owner
R4   C-2:1 Full-time
       C-2:1 Part-time

VALLEY FORGE --

Douglass Super Top, Inc.
Route 363
P.O. Box 701
Valley Forge, PA 19482
Tel. (215) 666-9100
Contact: Jack Donovan
R4   C-2:4 Retirees

CHRISTIANA --

Chateau Recreational Vehs.
48-52 Mill Street
Christiana, PA 17509
Tel. (215) 593-6921
R5,R6   C-2:1 Retiree

HAMBURG --

Hahn Fire Apparatus
400 S. 3rd Street
Hamburg, PA 19526
Tel. (215) 562-7591
F C-1:1 entitled, "Fire
   Delivery Engineer"

LEOLA --

Skyline Corp. -
   Nomad/Leyton Division
77 Horseshoe Road
Leola, PA 17540
Tel. (717) 656-2111
R5,R6

MIDDLEBURG --

Citair, Inc.
R.D. 3, Box 38
Middleburg, PA 17842
Tel. (717) 837-1663
Contact: Cris Rhoades
R5,R6   A-2:10

YORK --

Pitman Mfg. Co., Inc.
P.O. Box 446
951 Elm Street
York, PA 17403
Tel. (717) 843-9841
Utility & Construction
Co. Truck Bodies,
w/Hydraulic Equipment

- -

RHODE ISLAND

WOONSOCKET --

Janell Truck Bodies
840 Cumberland Hill Road
Woonsocket, RI 02895

Tel. (401) 762-6363
Contact: Rocky
Mfrs.: Truck Bodies

Drivers typically return in
cars towed behind trucks.

SOUTH CAROLINA

PIEDMONT --

Travelier Industries, Inc.
I-85 at Highway 153
P.O. Box 1130
Piedmont, SC 29673
Tel. (803) 269-4551
Contact: Sid Freeman
A-2, and Trailered by
Independent Contractors.
    (2 Drivers)

ROCK HILL --

Interstate Van Conversions
1701 W. Main Street
Rock Hill, SC 29730
Tel. (803) 324-8111
Contact: Bob Sarn, Owner
R4   C-2:2 Retirees

- -

SOUTH DAKOTA

FAULKTON --

Classic Vans
206 Ninth Avenue, N.
Box 508
Faulkton, SD 57438
Tel. (605) 598-4437
R4

FLANDREAU --

Viking Industries, Inc.
R.R. 3, Box 10-A
Flandreau, SD 57028
Tel. (605) 997-2427
Contact: Dick Julson
H,R4   C-2:4-5

- -

TENNESSEE

CHATTANOOGA --

Choo-Choo Customs, Inc.
7801 Lee Highway
Chattanooga, TN 37421
Nation: (800) 251-7832
        (615) 899-5382
R4

OOLTEWAH --

Century Wrecker Corp.
8503 Hilltop Drive
P.O. Box 120
Ooltewah, TN
Tel. (615) 238-4171
W

LAKE CITY --

Trail Manor, Inc.
304 Church Street
P.O. Box 130
Lake City, TN 37769
Tel. (615) 457-1142

SHELBYVILLE --

First Ambulance Center of Tennessee
334½ Cannon Blvd.
P.O. Box 172
Shelbyville, TN
Nation: (800) 251-3166
        (615) 684-3033
A

NASHVILLE --

Jakes Mfg. Co., Inc.
2725 Felicia Avenue
Nashville, TN
Tel. (615) 322-1300

- -

TEXAS

AMARILLO --

American Equipment &
    Trailer, Inc.
P.O. Drawer 32109
Amarillo, TX
Tel. (806) 383-8831
Truck Bodies: All Types

BROWNSVILLE --

Eagle International, Inc.
2045 Les Mauldin Blvd.
Brownsville, TX
Tel. (512) 541-3111
Inter-City Busses

BURLESON --

Komfort Industries of
    Texas, Inc.
545 E. Renfro Street
Burleson, TX 76028
Nation: (800) 527-5521
In TX: (800) 772-8014
        (817) 295-0441
R5,R6

TEXAS (Cont'd.)

DALLAS --

Ivory Coach
P.O. Box 53519
Dallas, TX 75253
Tel. (214) 286-1970
Contact: Don Potter
R4   C-2:6

FORT WORTH --

Hobbs Trailers
4800 Blue Mound Road
Fort Worth, TX
Tel. (817) 625-2181

GRAND PRAIRIE --

Sargent-Sowell, Inc.
1185   108th Street
Grand Prairie, TX 75050
Nation: (800) 527-2450
        (214) 647-1525
F (Fire Vehicles: Mini-
   Pumpers on 1- and 2-ton
   Truck Bodies)

HOUSTON --

Frazer, Inc.
P.O. Box 741369
Houston, TX
Tel. (713) 772-5511
A

LONGVIEW --

Coachmen Rec. Vehs. of Texas
P.O. Box 13209
Longview, TX 75602
Tel. (214) 758-6509

MANSFIELD --

Skyline Corporation
606 S. 2nd Avenue
Mansfield, TX 76063
Tel. (817) 477-3161
R5,R6

DALLAS --

The LTV Corporation
P.O. Box 225003
Dallas, TX
Tel. (214) 266-2011
A

FORT WORTH --

Tra-Tech Corporation
R. 1, Box 28-D
Fort Worth, TX 76179
Nation: (800) 433-7680
Nation: (800) 433-7681
        (817) 232-4900
Contact: Lyle Brown
R4   C-2:20   D

GRANDVIEW --

Bentley Corp./Good Times Vans
P.O. Drawer 464
Grandview, TX 76050
Tel. (817) 866-2611
Contact: Roy Burklow
R4   A-1, C-1 (12-15)

LONGVIEW --

Capacity of Texas, Inc.
P.O. Box 7848
Longview, TX 75607
Tel. (214) 757-4626

LONGVIEW --

Fun Coach - Texas
P.O. Box 13209
210 Estes Drive
Longview, TX 75602
Tel. (214) 758-5763
R5,R6

MARSHALL --

Premiere Editions - South
1402 Commerce St.
Marshall, TX 75670
Tel. (214) 938-5614
Contact: John Cearnal, G.M.
C-2:3
NOTE: Related companies are
Lands Design, Inc. & Ram
Coach -- in Elkhart, IN.

DALLAS --

Tetradyne Corporation
4674 Olin Road
Dallas, TX 75244
Tel. (214) 991-4501
Money & Security
Transport Trucks & Vans;
R

GARLAND --

Merry Miler, Inc.
3137 National Circle
Garland, TX 75041
Tel. (214) 271-4402
Contact: Donald Thompson
R4   C-2:2

HOUSTON --

Ardco Industries, Inc.
322 Riley Road
Houston, TX

KERENS --

Casita Enterprises, Inc.
Highway 31, W., Box 309
Kerens, TX 75144
Tel. (214) 396-7461

MANSFIELD --

Classic Mfg.
208 N. Sentry
P.O. Box 390
Mansfield, TX 76063
Tel. (817) 473-0201
R4

NACOGDOCHES --

Travco/Foretravel, Inc.
1221 NW Stallings Drive
Nacogdoches, TX 75961
Tel. (409) 564-8367
R1, Special Vehicles

TEXAS (Cont'd.)

PLAINVIEW --
Emco Mfg. Co.
P.O. Drawer 1210
Plainview, TX
Tel. (806) 293-8331
G

PONDER --
Sherrod Vans of Texas, Inc.
FM Road 2449 & Florence Rd.
Ponder, TX 76259
Tel. (817) 479-2771
R4

RICHARDSON --
Roadrunner Vans, Inc.
809-819 S. Sherman
Richardson, TX 75081
Tel. (214) 783-8155
R4, & Special Vehs.

SAN ANTONIO --
Executive Armoring Corp.
4836 Whirlwind
San Antonio, TX 78217
Tel. (512) 654-3905
Custom Limousines

SAN ANTONIO --
Grizzly Mat'l. Handling Co.
7522 Reindeer Trail
San Antonio, TX 78238
Tel. (512) 680-BEAR
Airport Trucks

SAN ANTONIO --
Pak-Mor Mfg. Co.
P.O. Box 14147
San Antonio, TX
Tel. (512) 923-4317
G

- -

UTAH

SALT LAKE CITY --
Custom Van of Utah, Inc.
3665 S. 300 W.
Salt Lake City, UT 84115
Tel. (801) 266-1552   R4

- -

VIRGINIA

BUENA VISTA --
Blue Bird - East
Highway 501
Buena Vista, VA
Tel. (703) 261-7411

VIENNA --
Melody Coach Ind., Inc.
2830 Gallows Road
Vienna, VA 22180
Tel. (703) 560-6200
R4,R6

McLEAN --
Van Conversions by Kogon
1524 Springhill Road
McLean, VA 22102
Nation: (800) 368-3636
        (703) 821-6950
Contact: Jeff Kogon or
         Allen Makvandi
R4   C-1:5

ROANOKE --
Grumman Emergency
   Products, Inc.
1723 Siebel Drive
Roanoke, VA
Tel. (703) 982-6666

- -

WASHINGTON

EVERETT --
Morgan Brothers
3225 Cedar Street
Everett, WA
Tel. (206) 252-3163
Airport Trucks

SEATTLE --
Alaskan Outdoorsman, Inc.
6410 S. 143rd Street
Seattle, WA 98168
Tel. (206) 243-2271
R4   C-1:1

SEATTLE --
Chef's Campers, Inc.
1425 N.W. Ballard Way
Seattle, WA 98107
Tel. (206) 783-2700
Contact: Jay Sternoff
R4, & Special Vehicles
C-1:3

YAKIMA --
Chinook
1052 E. Lincoln
Yakima, WA 98901
Region: (800) 874-1277
In WA: (800) 422-5094
Contact: Gene Rossman
R4   C-2:6

YAKIMA --
Trail Wagons, Inc.
1100 E. Lincoln Ave.
Yakima, WA 98907
Region: (800) 541-4909
In WA: (800) 572-9232
R4

YAKIMA --
Western Rec. Vehs., Inc.
P.O. Box 9547
Yakima, WA 98909
Tel. (509) 457-4133
Contact: Scott Doyle
R5,R6 A-1,B-1 (8-10)

VANCOUVER --

Automotive Services, Inc.   Nation: (800) 426-5012
2001 W. Fourth Plain Blvd.   In WA: (800) 843-4564
Vancouver, WA 98660   (206) 693-5835   R4

- -

WISCONSIN

APPLETON --

Pierce Mfg. Co.
P.O. Box 2017
Appleton, WI 54911
Tel. (414) 731-5251

E,F, & Utility Vehicles

CHILTON --

MANORette, Inc.
311 E. Main
Chilton, WI 53014
Tel. (414) 849-2713

R2,R6

CLINTONVILLE --

FWD Corp./Seagrave
    Fire Apparatus, Inc.
107 E. 12th Street
Clintonville, WI
Tel. (715) 823-2141

F, Airport Vehicles

EAU CLAIRE --

Northwestern Motor Co.
(Div. of Page Arjet Corp.)
1123 Starr Avenue
Eau Claire, WI 54703

Tel. (715) 835-3151
Airport Trucks

ELROY --

Elite Heritage Motors Corp.
1 Heritage Lane
Elroy, WI
Tel. (608) 462-8100
Commercial Automobiles

KENOSHA --

Pirsch, Peter & Sons Co.
1308 35th Street
Kenosha, WI
Tel. (414) 658-8141

F

LAKE GENEVA --

Geneva Luxury Motor Vans/
    C.T.I., Inc.
910 Madison Street
P.O. Box 87
Lake Geneva, WI 53147
R4

LAKE GENEVA --

Geneva Luxury Motor Vans/
    C.T.I., Inc.
1055 Carey Street
Lake Geneva, WI 53147
R4

MARION --

Marion Body Works, Inc.
P.O. Box 555
Marion, WI

A,F, Mini-Pumpers, &
    Tankers

MILWAUKEE --

Custom Craft Vans, Inc.
960 W. Armour Ave.
Milwaukee, WI 53221
Tel. (414) 744-8118
Contact: Larry Scott
R4   C-1:3-5

MILWAUKEE --

Excalibur Automobile Corp.
1735 S. 106th St.
Milwaukee, WI
Tel. (414) 771-7171
Exotic Cars

MILWAUKEE --

Milwaukee Truck Co. Div.
    of Gleason Corp.
P.O. Box 343
Milwaukee, WI 53201
Tel. (414) 271-8357

MONROE --

Monroe Truck Equipment, Inc.
1020 3rd Avenue
Monroe, WI
Tel. (608) 328-8127
F

OSHKOSH --

Leach Co.
2737 Harrison St.
Oshkosh, WI 54901
Tel. (414) 231-2770
G

OSHKOSH --

Oshkosh Truck Corp.
P.O. Box 2566
Oshkosh, WI
Tel. (414) 235-9150
F

VALDERS --

A & J Vans, Inc.
333 Washington St.
Valders, WI 54245
Tel. (414) 775-9333
Contact: John Kupsh
R4

WYOMING

MILLS --

Teton Homes
P.O. Box 2349   Tel. (307) 235-1525
Mills, WY 82644   R5,R6

ALBERTA

LETHBRIDGE --

Scamper Canada, Ltd.
3504 9th Avenue, N.
Lethbridge, AB   T1H 5E6
Tel. (403) 329-0307
Contact: Brian Clifford,
          Sales Manager
R5,R6   C-2:2-4

RED DEER --

Travelaire Trailer
Red Deer, AB
Tel. (403) 347-6641

- -

BRITISH COLUMBIA

ARMSTRONG --

Big Foot Industries
R.R. 3, C-65 Pallisades
Armstrong, BC VOE 1BO
Tel. (604) 546-8741
R5,R6   B-2:2

WINFIELD --

Vanguard Mfg.
P.O. Box 280
Winfield, BC VOH 2CO
Tel. (604) 766-2811
R1,R2 & Special Vehicles

OLIVER --

General Coach Division
   of Citair, Inc.
P.O. Box 700
9th Street, East
Oliver, BC VOH 1TO
Tel. (604) 498-3471
Contact: Wayne Atkinson
R2,R3,R5   C-2:12

PENTICTON --

Okanagan Mfrs., Ltd.
316 Dawson Avenue
Penticton, BC V2A 3N6
Tel. (604) 493-1535
R2,R3,R4,R5   C-1:1

- -

MANITOBA

BRANDON --

R.V. Services
Brandon, MB
R7A 5Y8
Tel. (204) 725-1453
R4 & Special Vehicles

SELKIRK --

Vantasy, Ltd.
P.O. Box 246
850 Greenwood Avenue
Selkirk, MB R1A 2B2
Tel. (204) 785-8502
R4

WINKLER --

Triple-E Canada, Ltd.
P.O. Box 1230
301 Roblin Blvd.
Winkler, MB ROG 2XO
Tel. (204) 325-4361
R1,R2,R4

- -

ONTARIO

BURLINGTON --

ABI Leisure
P.O. Box 1520, Station B
Burlington, ON L1P 4C5
Tel. (416) 336-2494
R6

COBOURG --

MacDonald Conversion
   Industries, Inc.
300 White Street
P.O. Box 700
Cobourg, ON K9A 4R5
Tel. (416) 372-3302
A,S,R2,R4

GUELPH --

Triple-E Canada, Ltd.
530 Governors Road
Guelph, ON N1K 1E3
Tel. (519) 836-4333
R4   C-2:3   D

KITCHENER --

Home & Park Motor Homes
75 Ardelt Place
Kitchener, ON N2C 2C8
Tel. (519) 745-1169
Contact: Ted Fitzgerald
Mfrs.: Camper Vans

HENSALL --

General Coach Division
   of Citair, Ltd.
73 Mill Street
Hensall, ON NOM 1XO
Tel. (519) 262-2600
Contact: Bill Solden
R1,R2,R6   C-2:10-12

Drivers:
A-1:2 (60% of Deliveries)
C-1:3 (40% of Deliveries)

ONTARIO (Cont'd.)

LINDSAY --

Fleetwood Canada, Ltd.
70 Mt. Hope Street
Lindsay, ON   K9V 5G4
Tel. (705) 324-0095
Contact: William Wood
R1,R5,R6   A-2,A-3,D

MISSISSAUGUA --

Ontario Bus Industries, Inc.
5395 Maingate Drive
Mississaugua, ON
Tel. (416) 625-9510
Busses

WOODSTOCK --

Timberjack, Inc.
P.O. Box 160
925 Devonshire
Woodstock, ON
Tel. (519) 537-6271

LISTOWEL --

Starcraft Recreational
   Products, Ltd.
801 Tremaine Ave., S.
Listowel, ON   N4W 3G9
Tel. (519) 291-1391
Contact: Shirley Hutton
NOTE: Driver Opportunity
   for students!
"Sometimes it's hard to
find a student to drive."
R4

MISSISSAUGUA --

A.H.A. Mfg. Co., Ltd.
5309 Maingate Drive
Mississaugua, ON
Tel. (416) 625-6860
H

STRATHROY --

Glendale Rec. Vehicles
145 Queen Street
Strathroy, ON   N7G 3J6
Tel. (519) 245-1600
R2,R5,R6   C-1:2

- -

QUEBEC

SAINT CLAIR --

Provost Car, Inc.
35 Gagnon Blvd.
Saint Clair, PQ   G0R 2V0
Tel. (418) 883-3391
Contact: Gaetan Roy,
        Sales Coordinator
R1   C-1:2

TRANSPORTER COMPANIES of the U.S.A. and CANADA

AUTO CARAVAN

Agent for North American Transportation Co.

40 N. Van Brunt Street
Englewood, NJ 07631

Company has many locations and terminals throughout the continent. All driver applications and hiring are processed through this headquarters office.

Prospective drivers should call:

Nation: (800) 221-0566
(201) 568-8100

ALWAYS TRANSIT

28730 Phillips Street
Elkhart, IN 46514

Tel. (219) 264-5575

AUTO DRIVEAWAY
-- NATIONAL HEADQUARTERS --

310 S. Michigan Ave.
Chicago, IL 60604

Nation: (800) 346-CARS
(312) 341-1900

KEY: ADC - Auto Driveaway Co.
D/S - Driveaway Service

ARIZONA --

Phoenix	3737 E. Indian School Road, Suite 201 Maury Spear	85018	(602) 952-0339
Tucson	4420 E. Speedway, Suite 201 Ken & Helen Zettle	85712	(602) 323-7659

CALIFORNIA --

Anaheim	1011 E. Kenwood Avenue Jim Aschenbrenner and his son, J.R.	92805	(714) 956-9471
Chico	4950 Cohasset Stage, P.O. Box 62	95927	(916) 893-0527
Chino	11962 Central Avenue, P.O. Box 1577	91710	(714) 628-8941
Fresno	3705 N. Clovis Ave., Suite 106 Al Dennis	93727	(209) 292-2500
Long Beach	2735 E. Carson Street (Lakewood) Mary Alcott	90712	(213) 421-0313
Los Angeles	4800 Melrose Avenue Bob Aschenbrenner	90029	(213) 666-6100
Sacramento	3333 Watt Avenue, Suite 110 Judy Hansen	95821	(916) 486-4277
San Diego	ADC -- 3960 Park Blvd. Arlette Stein	92103	(619) 295-8006
	D/S -- 3585 Adams Ave. Veronique Stein	92116	(619) 280-5454
San Francisco	833 Market St., Suite 412 Clive & Claudia Walker	94103	(415) 777-3740
San Jose	742 N. First St. Jim Henke	95112	(408) 288-7507

AUTO DRIVEAWAY (Cont'd.)

COLORADO --

Denver	5777 E. Evans Avenue, Suite 101 Ted Joens	80222	(303) 757-1211

FLORIDA --

Ft. Lauderdale	1322 E. Commercial Blvd. John Muller	33334	(305) 771-4059
Fort Myers	17568 Rockefeller Circle, S.E.	33912	(813) 267-7070
Hollywood	2520 E. Hallandale Beach Blvd. (Hallandale) Barry Halpern	33009	(305) 456-2277
Jacksonville	405 Carmichael Ave., Suite 230 Fred Dunbar	32207	(904) 398-4400
Miami Beach	6742 Collins Avenue Tony Basco	33141	(305) 861-4441
Orlando	One Purlieu Place (Driggs Dr.), #124 Eddie Reiss (NOTE: In Winter Park)	32792	(305) 678-7000
Palm Beach	ADC -- 3923 Lake Worth Road (Lake Worth) Ina & Rick Schwartz	33461	(305) 439-7060
	D/S -- 1306 Broadway (Riviera Beach) John Jeffs	33404	(305) 848-3432
St. Petersburg	300 31st Street, Suite 123 Charlie Kard	33713	(813) 327-2111
Sarasota	3800 S. Tamiami Trail, Suite 206	33579	(813) 366-9446
Tampa	Direct Line to St. Petersburg (No office)		(813) 228-9595

GEORGIA --

Atlanta	805 Peachtree St., N.E., Suite 179 Mitty Jacobs, Lenny Mates	30308	(404) 881-1688

HAWAII --

Honolulu	414 Kuwill Street Lyle Okuda	96817	(808) 536-8668

IDAHO --

Boise	5303 Chinden Blvd. Charles & Wanda Smith	83714	(208) 376-7816

ILLINOIS --

Chicago	310 S. Michigan Avenue, Suite 1401	60604	(312) 393-3600

INDIANA --

Indianapolis	2555 East 55th Place, Room 207 Wayne Moss	46220	(317) 259-7060

IOWA --

Forest City	Crystal Lake Blacktop, P.O. Box 366	50436	(515) 582-4432

KANSAS --

Kansas City	7930 State Line Road, #203 (Prairie Village) Sharie Bell	66208	(913) 381-2125
Wichita	3330 W. Douglas Len Henrickson	67203	(316) 945-2882

AUTO DRIVEAWAY (Cont'd.)

KENTUCKY --

Louisville	1250 Bardstown Road, Suite 100 Gene Joiner	40204	(502) 456-4990

LOUISIANA --

New Orleans	201 Kent Avenue, Suite 106 (Metairie) Don & Joanne Vickrey	70001	(502) 885-9292

MARYLAND --

Baltimore	1124 E. 25th Street Chuck Fuller	21218	(301) 366-8869

MASSACHUSETTS --

Boston	566 Commonwealth Avenue Morry Levine, Ed Fisher	02215	(617) 267-4836

MICHIGAN --

Detroit	ADC -- 22476 Grand River Avenue Harold Long	48219	(313) 532-3800
	D/S -- 4710 Horger (Dearborn)	48126	(313) 584-5000
Grand Rapids	7520 Main Street (Jenison) -- Jim Frye	49428	(616) 457-1130
Imlay City	585 N. Main Street	48444	(313) 724-6279
Kalamazoo	1330 Healy Street	49001	(616) 344-2158

MINNESOTA --

Minneapolis	6950 France Avenue, South, Galleria Offices, Suite 109 (Edina) Grant & Melva Wilmert	55435	(612) 926-0262

MISSOURI --

St. Louis	1401 South Brentwood, Suite 404 Jane Wohl	63144	(313) 961-3400

NEBRASKA --

Omaha	11414 West Center Road, Terrace Plaza, Suite 315 Bud O'Brien	68144	(402) 333-8220

NEVADA --

Las Vegas	3305 W. Spring Mountain Rd., Suite 60 Sharon & Lee Webb	89102	(702) 873-9110

NEW JERSEY --

Elizabeth	519 Pennsylvania Avenue John Manganelli	07201	(201) 352-3800
Metro NY	519 Pennsylvania Avenue (TRUCKING DIVISION)	07201	(201) 351-2225

NEW MEXICO --

Albuquerque	3320 Second Street, N.W. Jack Reid	87107	(505) 345-4317

NEW YORK --

Buffalo	599 Niagara Falls Blvd. (Amherst) Gloria Gibson	14226	(716) 833-8500

AUTO DRIVEAWAY (Cont'd.)

NEW YORK (Cont'd.) --

New York City	ADC -- 264 W. 35th Street, Suite 500 Amy Villafane	10001	(212) 967-2344
	D/S -- 37-11 Prince Street, Suite B (Flushing) Mailing Address: P.O. Box 1504, Flushing 11354 Don Clarkin, Mike Brown		(718) 262-3800
Rochester	2815 Monroe Avenue Bill Dintruff	14618	(716) 442-3150
Syracuse	116 Maple Drive, P.O. Box 247 (Fayetteville) Bob Waters, Maureen De Santis	13066	(315) 445-0809

NORTH CAROLINA --

Greensboro	216 Commerce Place Joan & Ken Schneiderman	27401	(919) 272-2153

OHIO --

Akron	3457 Akron-Cleveland Rd. (Cuyahoga Falls) Mailing Add.: P.O. Box 1119, Cuyahoga Falls	44223 44223	(216) 929-1677
Cincinnati	5721 Cheviot Road, Room 5 Mary Hinkle	45247	(513) 385-6654
Cleveland	5100 W. 164th Street Frank O'Neil	44142	(216) 676-4800
Columbus	4256 N. High Street Bill Huber	43214	(614) 261-8170

OKLAHOMA --

Oklahoma City	2218 N.W. 39th Street Bill Parker	73112	(405) 525-5622

OREGON --

Portland	2836 N.E. Sandy Blvd. Franz Ridgway	97232	(503) 238-5515

PENNSYLVANIA --

Philadelphia	225 S. 15th Street	19102	(215) 735-6685
Pittsburgh	214 E. Main Street (Carnegie) Don Addlespurger	15106	(412) 276-6922
Reading	1500 N. 9th St. (Rear) (Pro-Driver Div.)	19603	(215) 376-7300

RHODE ISLAND --

Providence	428 Smith Street, Suite 6 -- Barry Cook	02908	(401) 351-9696

SOUTH CAROLINA --

Columbia	721 King Street Bernie Malone	29205	(803) 799-5800

TENNESSEE --

Memphis	3141 Carrier, P.O. Box 161070 Bailey Barry, David Matthews	38116	(901) 345-3360
Nashville	333 Gallatin Road, Suite 13 (Madison) Al Morris	37115	(615) 244-8000

TEXAS --

Beaumont	1290 Lindbergh Drive, Suite 4	77707	(409) 842-3606

AUTO DRIVEAWAY (Cont'd.)

TEXAS (Cont'd.) --

Dallas	6222 North Central Expwy. (at Dyer), Suite 206 Ed Wood	75206	(214) 691-2125
El Paso	2159 Mills Lee & Dot Smith	79901	(915) 533-7000
Fort Worth	106 W. 5th Street, Suite 902	76102	(817) 332-1880
Houston	603 W. Tidwell Gary Smith	77091	(713) 692-3433
Irving	D/S -- 1425 W. Pioneer Drive Jim Williams	75061	(214) 254-2227
San Antonio	105 N. Alamo, Room 501 Tom Williams	78205	(512) 226-1676

UTAH --

Salt Lake City	3965 South 200 East		(801) 262-3662
	Mailing Add.: P.O. Box 7632, Murray	84107	

VIRGINIA --

Richmond	4905 Radford Avenue, Box 105 Mac Perkinson	23230	(804) 353-9390

WASHINGTON --

Auburn	3635 C Street, N.E.	98002	(206) 735-3800
Seattle	13470 Empire Way South Rich Mather	98178	(206) 235-0880
Spokane	W. 933 Third Avenue, Suite 203 Sue Leckie	99204	(509) 747-8900

WASHINGTON, D.C. --

	1408 N. Fillmore, Suite 2 Bernie Wright	22201	(703) 524-7300

WISCONSIN --

Milwaukee	9039-A W. National Avenue Charlie Kalashian	53227	(414) 327-5252
Milton	961 Storrs Lake Road	53563	(608) 868-4777

CANADA

ALBERTA --

Calgary	2707 Centre Avenue, S.E. Flo Sabin	T2A 2L4	(403) 273-7271

BRITISH COLUMBIA --

Vancouver	211 W. 1st Street Archie Lockhart	V7M 1C9	(604) 985-0936

MANITOBA --

Winnipeg	115 Clarke Street, Suite 108 Nick Logan	R3L 1W7	(204) 452-9442

NEWFOUNDLAND --

St. John's	229 Kenmount Road Larry Feltham	A1B 3P9	(709) 753-2886

AUTO DRIVEAWAY (Cont'd.)

NOVA SCOTIA --

Halifax	6155 North Street, Suite 408 Gerry Giovannetti	B3K 1P2	(902) 455-1880

ONTARIO --

Toronto	505 Eglinton Avenue, West Paul & Cora Segal	M5N 1B1	(416) 481-9194

QUEBEC --

Montréal	1117 St. Catherine West, Suite 606 John Paquette	H3B 1H9	(514) 844-1033

INTERNATIONAL
(Overseas)

ENGLAND --	29 Market Place, Mildenhall, Suffolk	1P28 1H9	(0638) 717132

* * * * *

BARRETT MOBILE HOME TRANSPORT

-- NATIONAL HEADQUARTERS --

2910 University Drive, S.
Box 2586
Fargo, ND 58108

Tel. (701) 237-5352

-- OFFICE in ELKHART, IN --

56960 Elk Park Drive
P.O. Box 1893
Elkhart, IN 46515

-- DISPATCH OFFICES THROUGHOUT the U.S.A. --

State		Town or City		Phone
ALABAMA	- - -	Gardendale	- -	(205) 631-6224
ARIZONA	- - -	Phoenix	- -	(602) 254-7077
CALIFORNIA	- - -	Riverside	- -	(714) 688-2210
CALIFORNIA	- - -	Woodland	- -	(916) 666-5568
IDAHO	- - -	Boise	- -	(208) 342-3806
KANSAS	- - -	Newton	- -	(316) 283-3480
MISSOURI	- - -	Springfield	- -	(417) 831-6822
NORTH CAROLINA	- - -	Mooresville	- -	(704) 663-7750
OREGON	- - -	Woodburn	- -	(503) 981-7939
PENNSYLVANIA	- - -	Akron	- -	(717) 859-2080
TEXAS	- - -	Longview	- -	(214) 759-6590
TEXAS	- - -	Waco	- -	(817) 772-9782
UTAH	- - -	West Jordan	- -	(801) 569-8330

DALLAS MOSER TRANSPORT

-- NATIONAL HEADQUARTERS --

26297 U.S. 6, East
Nappanee, IN 46550

Tel. (219) 773-4181

Contact: Dallas Moser II

-- BRANCH OFFICES --

P.O. Box 6
Paxinos, PA 17860

Tel. (717) 644-0262

Contact: Keith

P.O. Box 87
Decatur, IN 46733

Tel. (219) 728-2452

Contact: Roger Hill

* * * * *

DRIVEAWAY OF RED BAY

P.O. Box 596
Red Bay, AL 35582

Tel. (205) 356-8661

Contact: Jack Bostwick

28 Drivers

GORDON CONTINENTAL

1069 Lincolnway W., Box 13
Chambersburg, PA 17201

Nation: (800) 247-4516
(717) 267-1952

* * * * *

HORIZON

66402 S.R. 19
Wakarusa, IN 46573

Tel. (219) 862-4278

Contact: Marion Schrock

J.T.L. DRIVEAWAY

2200 Middlebury Street
Elkhart, IN 46516

Tel. (219) 293-6166

Contact: Terry Crothers

35 Drivers

* * * * *

KNUDSON ENTERPRISES

P.O. Box 7161
McLean, VA 22106

Tel. (703) 241-0920

LADD TRANSIT SERVICE

Box 716
Williamsburg, IN 47393

Tel. (317) 966-0815

Drivers: 50 during summer
20 rest of year

* * * * *

LUNDIN'S DRIVEBACK, LTD.

Drivers work out
of Woodstock and
Trenton. ALL trips
are assigned by
Frank, from Trenton.

R.R. #1
Trenton, ON K8V 5P4
CANADA

Tel. (416) 372-3302

Contact: Frank Yateman,
Dispatcher

Numbers of Drivers;

In Trenton: Around 50
In Woodstock: Varies: 5-10

MAY RIVER CORPORATION

HOME OFFICE ---

BRANCH ---

3033 Hartley Road
Suite 5
Jacksonville, FL 32217
Tel. (904) 268-0227
Contact: Dick Grey
35 Drivers

P.O. Box 1124
1125 Avenue B
Denton, TX 76201
Tel. (817) 382-7307
Contact: James Baldwin
8 Drivers

MORGAN DRIVEAWAY

-- NATIONAL HEADQUARTERS --

PHYSICAL ADDRESS ---

MAILING ADDRESS ---

28651 U.S. Route 20
Elkhart, IN 46514
Nation: (800) 348-7565
(219) 295-2200

P.O. Box 1168
Elkhart, IN 46515
Nation: (800) 348-7565
(219) 295-2200

MAJOR BRANCH ---

P.O. Box 1405
Greer, SC 29652
Nation: (800) 845-6115

Morgan is one of the giants of the transporter industry, having branches and
terminals throughout North America.
Prospective drivers should contact one of
these offices to obtain full information
regarding activity in their region of
interest.

* * * * *

TRANSFER DRIVERS, INC.

NATIONAL HEADQUARTERS ---

REGIONAL OFFICE ---

10920 E. McKinley Highway
Osceola, IN 46561

Nation: (800) 535-4895
Nation: (800) 348-7013
(219) 674-6985
Contact: Phil Matire or
Larry Skallerup

1336 S.W. 12th Avenue
Ocala, FL 32674

Nation: (800) 325-7243
(904) 351-5831
Contact: Wanda Richardson or
Renee Tindale

50 Drivers used here

T.D.I. is another of the larger
transporter companies in existence,
having 30 terminals. ALL coordina-
tion of driver hiring, activity,
and dispatching is done through
the two offices listed above.

* * * * *

TRANSIT HOMES of AMERICA

-- NATIONAL HEADQUARTERS --

P.O. Box 5155
Boise, ID 83705
Nation: (800) 345-0323
(208) 362-8640

Larry Kling, President

Key: If a city is shown in parentheses, the Terminal is in a suburb of that city. See address for the exact location.

Key: Sometimes a Terminal has more than one number. These are shown with a slash between the numbers. *e.g.,* 40/85

-- TERMINALS --

ARKANSAS --

Little Rock	Terminal #45 Raymond Cheatham	12901 Route I-30	72209	(501) 455-3686

ARIZONA --

Kingman	Terminal #32 Helen Kash	4405 Charles Avenue	86401	(602) 757-3338 or (602) 757-3038
Phoenix	Terminal #55 Carla Newton	4110 E. Elwood	85040	(602) 437-0393 or Nation: (800) 522-0393
Tucson	Terminal #68 Frances Berno	6651 S. Avenida Don Fernando 85746		(602) 578-0146

CALIFORNIA --

Auburn	Terminal #70 Willi Shaw	3223 Period St., N.E., Suite 1-D	98002	(206) 939-5029

FLORIDA --

Lake City	Terminal #3 Keith Kingery	3213 Defender Avenue	32055	(904) 755-3405 or (904) 752-6691
Lakeland	Terminal #33 Shirley Colvin	6730 Newman Circle, E.	33803	(813) 644-6879
Naples	Terminal #31 LeAnn Pajcic	Lot 39, Southwind Village	33942	(813) 643-1838
Panama City	Terminal #2 Linda Hicks	Rt. 1, Box 818-R Shamrock Street	32404	(904) 784-1943 (904) 784-8149

IDAHO --

Boise   (SEE ALSO NATIONAL HQ. INFORMATION AT TOP OF PAGE)

	Terminal #13 Wayne Kringen	Transit Homes of America CENTRAL DISPATCH 5305 South Diamond	Nation: (800) 343-0323 (208) 362-8646 83705
	Terminal #10 Marcie Stewart	5007½ Overland Road	83705	(208) 342-5007 or Nation: (800) 344-5007
Idaho Falls	Terminal #51 Karen Ellis	2940 Sawtooth	83401	(208) 522-3848

INDIANA --

Elkhart	Terminal #75 Lou Hall, Nancy Wheeler	29449 U.S. Highway 33	46516	(219) 294-4620

ILLINOIS --

Rockford	Terminal #15 Sharon Williams	3323 Lapey Street	61109	(815) 399-1110

KANSAS --

Burton	Terminal #76 Doris Redinger	c/o Coachman Mobile Home Park, Lot #33	67020	(316) 463-2565 *(Temporary No.)*

LOUISIANA --

Denham Springs	Terminal #96 Connie Walker	7990 Belmont Street	70726	(504) 664-8046

MISSISSIPPI --

Gautier	Terminal #86 Dixie Mattison	c/o Jeff's Mobile Home Service	39553	(601) 497-3099 *(Temporary No.)*
Richland	Terminal #56 Rebecca Brock	111 Jaybird Lane	39218	(601) 939-2012 or (601) 939-5299

MONTANA --

Billings	Terminal #15 Tim Pomeroy	P.O. Box 31136	59107	(406) 256-6305
Kalispell	Terminal #25 Fern Martin	535 Plentywood Drive	59901	(406) 752-2163 or (406) 752-2060

NEBRASKA --

Hastings	Terminal #61 Ron Foelgner	P.O. Box 255 1103 E. South Street	68901	(402) 463-6247

NEW MEXICO --

Farmington	Terminal #41 E.V. Isabel	P.O. Box 21 1650 San Juan Blvd.	87401	(505) 327-4104

NORTH CAROLINA --

Salisbury	Terminal #53 Jean Kurfees	Route 9, Box 442 Goodby Road	28144	(704) 278-9238
Silver City	Terminal #63 Elaine Etheridge	802 W. 5th Street	27344	(919) 742-2199

OKLAHOMA --

Claremore	Terminal #66 Susan Gerhart	2800 S. U.S. Highway 66	74107	(918) 341-0828

OREGON --

Bend	Terminal #12 John & Madeline Nelson	335 Roosevelt, S.E., #34	97702	(503) 389-3435
Coos Bay	Terminal #71 Jerri Statham	2004 Shasta	97420	(503) 269-1743
Grants Pass	Terminal #11 Larry Bisonette	2110 Dawn Drive	97123	(503) 476-0783
La Grande	Terminal #30 Mark W. Laurance	1609 Albany St., Suite 5	97850	(503) 963-9070
Portland	Terminal #60 Sue Richardson	5545 S.E. West Fork	97206	(503) 771-9456

OREGON (Cont'd.) --

Salem	Terminal #40/85 Judy Downer	5635 Ridge Drive, N.E.	97303	(503) 390-3903 & Nation: (800) 227-9050
Springfield	Terminal #20 Henriette L. Brewer	2049 Inland Way	97477	(503) 747-0046
Woodburn	Terminal #90/91 Lona Husk	1365 N. Pacific Highway	97071	National WATS: (800) 982-3105

SOUTH DAKOTA --

Ramona	Terminal #52 Barbara Hart	East 3rd St., Box 162	57054	(605) 482-8233 or (605) 482-8289

TENNESSEE --

Clarksville	Terminal #23 Beulah Coones	466 Lafayette Road	37042	(615) 648-8601

TEXAS --

Arlington	Terminal #26 Marilyn Santo	6509 Sunshine Valley Dr.	76016	(817) 483-9947 or (817) 572-1766
(Austin)	Terminal #6 Frankie Wallace	16800 Fagerquist Dale Valley, TX	78617	(512) 247-4887
Sulphur Spgs.	Terminal #9 Barbara Grantham	Route 1, Box 221-A	75482	(214) 885-3021 (Temporary No.)
Waco	Terminal #36 Margaret Stewart	2425 University Park Dr.	76706	(817) 753-4765

UTAH --

Cedar Hills	Terminal #35 John Vandorn	4309 West Oak Road	84062	(801) 292-9351

VIRGINIA --

Danville	Terminal #46 Bill Stewart	Route 1, Box 2454	24541	(804) 822-0000 & Nation: (800) 822-2043

WASHINGTON --

Marysville	Terminal #5 Sandra Turman	3915 152nd, N.E.	98270	(206) 659-6259
Pasco	Terminal #50 Sue Sabo	130 Meeker Road	99301	(509) 545-6465 or (509) 545-6445
(Spokane)	Terminal #95 Pat Pike	P.O. Box 1027, 402 E. 18th Airway Heights, WA	99001	(509) 244-5155

WYOMING --

Cheyenne	Terminal #42 Dee Van Goethen	1531 Otto Road	82007	(307) 778-7778 or (307) 638-4116
Glen Rock	Terminal #78 Sandy Bohart	Lot 48, Sage Hills P.O. Box 1505	82637	(307) 436-5736
Rock Springs	Terminal #22 Joe & Kam De Salvo	1643 Elk Street P.O. Box 1892	82902	(307) 362-1746 or (307) 382-6551

SPECIAL THANKS... To Gena Sliman, who generously and cheerfully provided all of the above Transit Homes of America data over the phone, even though her workday ended only two minutes after the call started. Without her thoughtful assistance just before this book's deadline, only the National Headquarters would have been listed.

ITINERARY PLOTTING EXERCISES

These problems are provided to give you some practical experience in plotting itineraries, as explained in Part IV, Chapter 3. The problems given here are just as realistic as any you will ever encounter in the field, with just one exception: the data provided all involve only one bus line.

Under actual field conditions, you should be sure to check *all* applicable schedules against each other (Greyhound, Trailways, etc.) and then compile your itinerary from the ones which fit together best to either (1) get you back as soon as possible, or (2) get you back at the most opportune arrival time. Whichever is best.

Nevertheless, you will have enough choices to make, given the tables and information that *are* provided in this appendix, to enable you to practice this skill before you actually go out on the road.

The problems all can be solved using the tables on the following pages, as well as the map on page 87. You will not necessarily have to use all the tables in order to find the best solutions. Which ones you use are up to you.

All schedules in this appendix are taken from the September, 1978 edition of the Russell's Guide, when Daylight Savings Time was in effect in most states. Table 1390 is not reprinted, so that information is provided below:

A.B.C. COACH LINES
1390

	Read Down				Read Up	
EASTERN	10 00	Lv	Fort Wayne	Ar	5	00
STANDARD	10 40		Decatur		4	28
TIME	**12 42**	Ar	Richmond	Lv	2	30

The regional Greyhound Lines Map on page 87 should be used in conjunction with the Tables in this appendix to construct your itineraries. Note also that Table 290 is reprinted above Table 400, instead of numerical order, in order to best utilize page space. Set up your itineraries in the style used in Part IV, Chapter 3.

The correct solutions to these problems are provided immediately after the tables.

Problem #1

You have just taken a run from your base in Decatur, Indiana which is assigned to a dealer in Metairie (pronounced: Mĕt´-ĕr-y), Louisiana, an immediate suburb of New Orleans which is served by frequently-running New Orleans city busses. Your projected E.T.A. has you arriving at the dealership on Wednesday at 4:00 p.m.

Assume that you want to return directly (rather than use a nighttime holding pattern) to Decatur, using the A.B.C. bus from Fort Wayne. If you have much extra time to kill in order to accomplish this, you prefer to spend it enjoying the sights, and perhaps nightlife, of New Orleans.

Plot an itinerary for your most ideal return.

Problem #2

Suppose that you have just delivered a coach in New Orleans at 8:00 a.m. on a Monday. Can you intercept the A.B.C. bus out of Fort Wayne on Tuesday morning? If so, prepare such an itinerary. And if not, is there any way that you can reach Decatur by bus before 5:00 p.m. on Tuesday afternoon?

Problem #3

What is the best way to reach Decatur, Indiana by bus before noon on Friday, if you deliver a coach in Decatur, Alabama at noon on Thursday?

CHATTANOOGA—BIRMINGHAM—NEW ORLEANS

GREYHOUND LINES

READ DOWN — SCHEDULE Nos. — READ UP

Folder No. 68 — **216** — 9-6-78

1167	3961	3965	3973	3971	5051	1185	1175	Stations	3960	5046	3972	3966	1150	1154	3974	3970
5 00			10 45	7 00		4 45	2 00	Lv Detroit, Mich......(ET)(365)...Ar	8 10				4 00	6 30	9 50	6 10
6 35			12 15	8 20		6 35	1 15	Toledo, Ohio	6 25				2 40	8 20		4 50
10 10			3 35	11 40		9 10	5 55	Dayton, Ohio	3 05				9 55	1 25	3 40	1 30
6 30			11 15	6 45		5 10	1 30	Cleveland, Ohio	7 40				2 55	5 40	7 55	
9 40			2 30	10 30		8 25	5 15	Columbus, Ohio	4 15				11 30	2 20	4 30	
12 40			5 00	1 15		10 50	8 15	Cincinnati, Ohio	10 15				8 15	11 30	1 45	10 30
3 25			7 45	3 35		1 15	10 45	Louisville, Ky. (ET)	10 35				5 35	7 55	11 15	6 50
7 15			10 45	6 40		1 35		Nashville, Tenn. (CT)	5 30				12 40	3 00	4 55	1 30
11#00			2 30	11 50		7 55	5‖20	Ar Birmingham, Ala. Lv	1 45				8 10	11 00	1 10	8 20
11 30	7 15		3 30	12 45	10 15	8 45	6 00	Lv **BIRMINGHAM, ALA.** Ar	9 50	1 20	2#50		7‖15	10#30	12 40	7‖15
12 01	7 45		4 00	1 15	10 45	9 15	6 30	Bessemer	9 20	12 50			6 45	10 00		6 45
	f							Bucksville		f						
								Rock Castle Road Jct.								
	8 20							Brookwood	8 45							
	8 35							Peterson	8 30							
								Coaling								
1 00	9 00		5 00	2 15	11 45	10 15	7 30	Ar **Tuscaloosa** Lv	8 05	11 50			1 35	5 45	9 00 11 25	5 45
1 05	9 05		5 05		10 20	7 40	7 40	Lv **Tuscaloosa** Ar	8 00	11 30			1 30	5 40	8 55 11 25	5 40
1 40	9 45		5 45	3 00	11 00	8 20		Eutaw	7 20		12 50		5 00	8 15	10 45	5 00
								Boligee								
			6 10	3 25	11 30	8 45		Epes					12 25	4 35	7 50	4 35
			6 25	3 40	11 40	9 00		Livingston					12 10	4 20	7 35	4 20
			6 40	3 55	11 45	9 15		York					11 55	4 05	7 20	4 05
			f					Cuba, Ala.								
								Kewanee, Miss.								
			f					Toomsuba								
2#45			7‖20	4‖35		12‖35	9#55	Ar **Meridian** Lv	11 15				3 35	6 50	9 35	3 35
3 00			7 50	5 05		1 05	10 10	Lv **Meridian** Ar	10‖50	10 25			3#20	6‖25	9#20	3#20
				5 35			10 35	Enterprise								
								Pachuta					f			
			f					Vossburg Road Jct. (1½ Mi.)					f			
			f					Stafford Springs					f			
			f					Heidelberg Jct. (2 Mi.)					f			
			f					Sandersville					f			
4 10			8 55	6 30		2 15	11 30	**Laurel**	9 30	9 18			2 10	4 55	8 10	2 10
				6 42			11 42	Ellisville	9 18						7 58	
								Moselle Road Jct. (¼ Mi.)								
								Eastabuchie								
4 55			9 40	7 25		3#00	12‖25	Ar **Hattiesburg** Lv	8 40				1 25	4 10	7 20	1 25
4 55			9 45	7 30		3 20	12 55	Lv **Hattiesburg** Ar	8#25				12‖55	3#55	6‖50	1 25
5 30				8 05		3 50	1 30	Purvis	7 50							
5 50				8 25		4 20	1 50	Lumberton	7 30						6 15	
								Poplarville							5 55	12 35
						4 55		Jct. Hwys. 26 & 43, Miss.	HS							
						5 35		Bogalusa, La.	6 00							
						HS		Covington	6 15							
						6 25		Mandeville	HS							
								Metairie, La.	5 35							
								McNeil, Miss.								
6 25			(L)11 00	9 00		2 25		Picayune, Miss.					11 40	2 35	5 25	12 05
								Pearl River, La.					f			
								St. Joe								
I6 45			11 25	9 30		3 00		**Slidell**					11 05	2 05	4 55	11 35
								NEW ORLEANS, LA.								
D			D	D		D		Ar Basin & Canal Sts. Lv								
7 40			12 15	10 20		6 45	3 50	Ar **Greyhound Terminal** Lv	5 15				10 15	1 15	4 05	10 45

Thru Bus Cleveland to New Orleans · *Thru Bus Birmingham to Demopolis* · *Thru Bus Cleveland to New Orleans* · *Thru Bus Thomasville to Birmingham* · *Thru Bus New Orleans to Atlanta* · *Thru Bus New Orleans to Nashville* · *Thru Bus New Orleans to Detroit* · *Thru Bus New Orleans to Knoxville*

For Complete Service See Table 426

PITTSBURGH LIMA CHICAGO

READ DOWN — *For Express Service See Table 285* — READ UP

Folder No. 72 — **280** — 9-6-78

43L9 NLC	4333	4373	4375	Stations	4368	4332 NLC	4372	4374
✕								
✦3 15	7 15			Lv **PITTSBURGH, PA.** (ET) Ar	12 55	11 10		
✦4 20	8 20			East Liverpool, Ohio	11 50	10 05		
✦4 45	8 45			Lisbon	11 25	9 40		
k f	f			Minerva				
5 05	9 05			Salem	11 05	9 20		
5 30	9 30			Alliance	10 40	8 55		
6#00	10 00			Ar **Canton** Lv	10 10	8 25		
6 20	10 10			Lv **Canton** Ar	9#55	8 20		
	10‖35			Ar Rest Stop Lv	7 55			
	11 05			Lv Rest Stop Ar	7‖25			
6 45	11 10			Massillon	9 30	7 20		
HS	HS			Dalton	HS			
7 15	11 40			Ar **Wooster** Lv	9 00	6 50		
7 20	h1145			Lv **Wooster** Ar	8 55	6 45		
8 05	12 30			Ar **Mansfield** Lv	8 10	6 00		
	h1235			Lv **Mansfield** Ar		5 55		
	1 05			Galion		5 05		
	2 05			Ar **Marion, Ohio** Lv		4 35		
	12 50	7 45		Lv Columbus, Ohio (315) Ar	5 45	1040		
	1 25	8 20		Lv Delaware, Ohio Ar	5 10	1005		
	2 05	8 55		Ar Marion, Ohio Lv	4 35	9 30		
	2 15	9 00		Lv **Marion, Ohio** Ar	4 25	9 30		
	f	f		Kenton	f	f		
	3#25	10 10		Ar **Lima** Lv	3 15	8 20		
	3 45	10 15		Lv **Lima** Ar	3#00	8 15		
	f	f		Elida	f	f		
	4 10	10 45		Delphos	2 35	7 45		
	4 30	11 05		Van Wert, Ohio (ET)	2 15	7 25		
	4‖25	11‖00		Ar **Fort Wayne, Ind.** (EST) Lv	12 20	5 30		
	5 20	11 30	7 00	Lv **Fort Wayne** Ar	11‖55	5‖00	10 10	
	5 55		7 35	Columbia City	11 20			9 10
	6 20	12 30	8 00	Warsaw	10 55	4 00		9 10
	6 55		8 35	Plymouth (EST)	10 20			8 35
	fhs		fhs	Hamlet (CDT)	(S)			(S)
	7 55	1 55	9 35	Valparaiso	9 20	2 35		7 35
		2 25		Merrillville		2 05		
	C 35	2 45	1015	**Gary**	8 40	1 45		6 55
	W855		1035	Hammond, Ind. (CDT)	8 20			6 35
				CHICAGO, ILL.				
	D915		1055	95th & Dan Ryan Expy. (CT) Lv	7 55			
	9 45	3 35	1125	Ar **Greyhound Terminal** Lv	7 30	1255	6 00	

Thru Bus Columbus to Chicago · *Thru Bus Chicago to Columbus*

MIAMI / ST. PETERSBURG — JACKSONVILLE—ATLANTA—CINCINNATI—DETROIT

READ DOWN

Folder No. 76 — **350** — 9-6-78

SCHEDULE Nos.	3970	4894	1236	344	4884	SES	4874	4862	2002	1230	1116	SES	2006	1114	1156	SES	4892	1110	2024	SES	4872	346
									×		×								ESu MaH			ESuH
New Orleans, La. (CT)(216) Lv										5 15	5 15		10 15				1 15	4 05				
Birmingham, Ala. (365)			12 01							6 00	6 00		9 00				11 00	1 10				7 00
Memphis, Tenn. (215)			1 15							5 15	5 15		8 15					1 20				11 15
Nashville, Tenn. (CT)(365)			6 25							10 15	10 15		1 10				3 30	6 15				
Louisville, Ky. (ET)			11 30								3 05		6 10				8 40	11 45			1 45	5 20
Cincinnati, Ohio Ar			1#30								5 15		8#15				11‖30	1#45			4 00	7 25
^CINCINNATI, OHIO Lv				12 25	2 00					5 55		8 45	8 40	9 00			12 05	2 25			4 30	9 30
^Sharonville (I-75 & Sharon Rd.)												f					12 25	2 45			4 50	9 50
Reading												f										
Sharonville												f										
Mason																						
Lebanon												9 45										
^Middletown R										6 05	6 40						12 55				5‖45	10 45
^Dayton Ar				1 30	3 05					6 05	7#10	10 30	9 55				1 25	3 40			6 15	10 45
^Dayton R Lv				1 35	3 10					6 10	7 45		10 00				1 35	3 45			6 35	10 50
⊠Vandalia R											8 00										f	
Ginghamsburg											8 20										6 55	11 20
Troy											8 40										7 15	11 40
^Piqua											8 40										7 35	
^Sidney											9 10						3 10				8 05	
^Wapakoneta											9 35						e3 35				8 25	*1245
^Lima											10 00										8 50	
^Bluffton													10 25				4 10					
^Fairborn													10 50				4 35					
^Springfield													11 20				5 05					
Urbana																	f					
West Liberty													11 50				5 35					
^Bellefontaine													12 25				6 10					
Kenton																	f					
Dunkirk																	f					
Arlington																	f					
^Findlay (Post House I-75) Ar				3#40	5#15					8‖15	10#25		1#05				4#00	6‖50			9#15	1#30
^Findlay (Post House I-75) Lv				3 55	5 30					8 45	10 40		1 30				4 15	7 25			9 30	1 45
^Bowling Green										9 20	11 15		2 05								10 05	
^Maumee																						
^Toledo Ar				4 50	6 25					9 55	12 05		2 40				5 10	8 20			10 40	2 40
^Toledo, Ohio Lv				4 55	6 30					10 00	12 10		2 45				5 15	8 25			10 45	2 45
^Monroe, Mich.					7 05					10 35	12 45										11 20	
^Flat Rock					7 30						1 10											
^Lincoln Park											1 30							9 25				
Taylor																		f				f
^DETROIT, MICH. GL Ar				6‖10	8 10					11 25	1 55		4 00				6 30	9 50			12 10	4#05

(For Complete Service See Table 388)

DETROIT—CINCINNATI—ATLANTA—JACKSONVILLE — ST. PETERSBURG / MIAMI

READ DOWN

Folder No. 76 — **350** — 9-6-78

SCHEDULE Nos.	4837	4915	1171	1169	1113	4547	4839	345	4955 Fri	1115	1403	1157	347	1133	1155	1111	1165
																	×
Toronto, Ont. (EDT)(389) ECG Lv	6 30								7 30	8 30		12 30				2 30	
Detroit, Mich. (ET) ECG Ar	12 30								1‖20	2 00		5‖55				8 40	
^DETROIT, MICH. GL Lv	3 45		6 30				11 45	2 00		2 45	4 45	7 00	7 00			10 45	
^Lincoln Park	4 05		6 50				12 05			3 05	5 05		7 20			11 05	
Flat Rock										5 25							
Monroe, Mich.				7 35						5 50	5 50						
^Toledo, Ohio Ar	5 10		8 05				1 10			4 10	6 30	8 15	8 25			12 10	
^Toledo Lv	5 15		8 10				1 15			4 15	6 35	8 20	8 30			12 15	
^Maumee										4 35							
^Bowling Green			8 45				1 50			5 05							
^Findlay (Post House I-75) Ar	6‖25		9#20				2#25	☎15		5‖40	7#30	☎15	9#40			1#10	
^Findlay (Post House I-75) Lv	7 00		9 35				2 45			6 10	7 45		9 55			1 25	
Arlington			f							f							
Dunkirk			f							f							
Kenton			10 15							6 50							
^Bellefontaine			10 50							7 25							
West Liberty			f							f							
Urbana			11 20							7 55							
^Springfield			11 50							8 25							
^Fairborn			12 15														
^Bluffton	7 25						3 10										
^Lima	7 50						3 35					*1040					
^Wapakoneta	8 15						4 00										
^Sidney	8 45						4 30										
^Piqua	9 05						4 50										
Troy	9 25						5 10										
Ginghamsburg R																	
⊠Vandalia R	9 45						5 25										
^Dayton Ar	10 05						5 45			9 05	11 35	12 15				3 30	
^Dayton Lv	10 10						5 55			9 10	11 40	12 20				3 35	6 15
^Middletown	10 40						6 25			9 40							
Lebanon																	
Mason																	
Reading R																	
Sharonville R	11 10							6 55		10 10						4‖40	
^Sharonville (I-75 & Sharon Rd.)			1 40														
^CINCINNATI, OHIO Ar R	11 30		2#00				7‖25	7 15		10#30	12#45		1#25			4‖40	7#20

(For Complete Service See Table 388)

Column notes (vertical "Thru Bus" legends):
- 4915: Thru Bus ...olis to Knoxville
- 1113: Thru Bus to St. Petersburg
- 345: Thru Bus Toronto to Miami
- 4955: Thru Bus Detroit to Miami
- 1403: Thru Bus Detroit to Los Angeles
- 1157: Thru Bus Detroit to Panama City
- 1155: Thru Bus Detroit to Miami
- 1111: Thru Bus Detroit to Miami — Daily except Sundays & Holidays
- 1165: Thru Bus Dayton to Birmingham

TALLAHASSEE—BIRMINGHAM—CINCINNATI

READ DOWN

SCHEDULE Nos. →
Folder **365** No. 78   9-6-78

SCHEDULE Nos. →

	1154	1156	1158	1406	4812	1162	1234	1164	4538	4980	1166	1168	1170	1172	1150	1152
Mobile, Ala. (367) Lv			7 00									5 40				3 00
Selma			10 50								7 15	9 45				5 40
Birmingham, Ala. Ar			12 55								9 55	12 25				8 35
New Orleans, La. (216) Lv	1 15		4 05				10 45						5 15		10 15	
Hattiesburg, Miss.	4 10		7 20				1 25						8 40		1 25	
Meridian, Miss.	6 50		9 35				3 35						11 15		3 35	
Tuscaloosa, Ala.	9 00		11 25				5 45				8 05	11 50	1 35		5 45	
Birmingham Ar	10#30		12 40				7 15				9 50	1 20	2 50		7‖15	
▲BIRMINGHAM, ALA. Lv	11 00		1 10				8 20				12 01	1 45	6 00		8 10	9 00
Gardendale Jct.							f				f	f				
Warrior							f				f	f				
Garden City							f				f	f				
Hanceville							f				f	f				
▲Cullman	11 55						9 20				1 10		6 55		9 05	
Falkville							9 53				1 43				9 33	
Hartselle							10 10				2 00				9 50	
▲Decatur	L1240						10#35				2#25				10 15	
▲Athens Ar	1 05						10 55				2 45				10 15	
▲Athens, Ala. Lv	1 05						11 22				3 10					
▲Ardmore, Ala.							f				f					
Elkton, Tenn.							h1147				3 35					
▲Pulaski							f				f					
Waco							12 30				4 20				11 05	
▲Columbia							f				f				11 50	
Spring Hill							1 00				4 55					
▲Franklin							2 15				5‖30	5‖30	9#50		12 40	12#45
▲Nashville Ar	3#00															
Nashville, Tenn. (410) Lv							2 15				7 00					1 10
Evansville, Ind. Ar							5 55				10 40					4 50
St. Louis, Mo. (CT) Ar							11 55									10 30
Atlanta, Ga. (ET)(350) Lv		10 55				3 10		8 40			1 30				6 45	
Chattanooga, Tenn. (ET)(410)		1 25				6 45		11 30			4 00				10 15	
Nashville, Tenn. (CT) Ar		3#00				9 40		1‖05			5 55				12 15	
Memphis (215) Lv				1 20		7 00			9 30		1 15			5 15		8 15
Jackson				3 15					11 50		3 15			7 30		10 10
Nashville Ar				5‖40		11 00			3 15		5 45			9#55		12 35
▲Nashville Lv	3 30	3 35	6 00	6 15		11 15		1 45		4 30	6 25	6 10	10 15	10 15		1 10
Goodlettsville										4 50	f					
Millersville										5 00	6 50					
▲White House										5 16						
Mitchell, Tenn.										5 25						
▲Franklin, Ky.			7 20	7 10		12 10		2 40		w600	7 50			11 30		
▲Bowling Green			7 55	7 45		12 45		3 15		6 33						
▲Park City			8 05			1 20		3 50		6 43						
▲Cave City			8 10			1 30				6 48						
▲Horse Cave			8 25			1 35				7 02						
▲Munfordsville			f			1 50				f						
Bonnieville (CT)						f				f						
Upton (ET)						3 25		5 45		8 45	10 15					
▲Elizabethtown		6 55	10 10			3 50				f	9 10					
Radcliffe						HS			HS	f						
▲Fort Knox						HS			HS	HS						
West Point						HS			HS	HS						
Valley Station						4 35			6 35	9 55						
▲Standiford Field						4‖50			6‖50	6‖50	10 10	11#10	10#35	2#40	2#45	5‖35
▲Louisville, Ky. Ar	7‖55	8‖00	11‖15	11‖05				5 45								
Louisville, Ky. (ET)(355) Lv		8 45	11 45			5 15		7 45			11 15		3 00		6 00	
Indianapolis, Ind. (EST) Ar		10#00	1#25			7 45		9#00			12#30		4 15		8 25	
Indianapolis, Ind. (EST) Lv		10 45	1 45					9 20			4 00		4 30		8 40	
Chicago, Ill. (CT) Ar		3 05	5 20					1 50			4 45		9 15		1 45	
▲Louisville, Ky. (ET) Lv	8 40			11 45	1 45	5 20			7 30		11 30		3 05	3 15		6 10
Jeffersonville, Ind.									7 40							
New Washington (ET)									f							
▲Madison, Ind. (EST)									7 41							
Prospect, Ky. (ET)		f							f							
Bedford		f														
▲Carrollton	10 00				2 50				9 02							
Ghent	10 10								9 12							
▲Warsaw	10 21								9 23							
Florence	D								f							
▲Covington, Ky.	11 20			1 35	3 50	7 15			10 20				5 05		8 05	
▲CINCINNATI, OHIO Ar	11‖30			1#45	4#00	7#25			10 30		1#30		5#15		8#15	
Cincinnati, Ohio (345) Lv	12 15			2 15	4 30	7 50				12 25	2 15			6 00		8 50
Columbus Ar	2 20			4 30	6 50	10 00				1 30	3 05			8 00		11 30
Akron				8 00	10 30					4 50	#7 45			12 25		5 00
Youngstown				9 20	11 35					6 25	#9 10			2 55		#6 20
Cleveland, Ohio Ar	5 40			7 55	10 50	1 15				6 10	7 40			12 15		2 55
Cincinnati (350) Lv	12 05			2 25	4 35	9 30				12 25	2 00		6 05		8 40	
Dayton Ar	1 25			3 40	5 40	10 40				1 30	3 05			9 55		9 55
Toledo, Ohio	5 10			8 20	10 40	2 40				4 50	6 25		9 55		2 40	
Detroit, Mich. Ar	6 30			9 50	12 10	4 05				6 10	8 10		11 25		4 00	

Destinations shown in italics are taken from connecting schedules.
Table numbers of those schedules are in italics enclosed by parentheses.

SCHEDULE Nos. → 290

Folder No. 72 — 9-6-78

EASTBOUND READ DOWN

	1358	4470	4452	1350	3884	2098	4372	1352	1354	1334	1356
△INDIANAPOLIS, IND. Lv	6 50		11 45	3 00		3 50		7 25	10 20	1 00	3 30
Greenfield	f					f		f			
Knightstown	f							f			
Lewisville	f										
Dublin	f										
△Cambridge City	8 15					5 10					
Centerville											
△Richmond, Ind. (EST)	8 45		1 10			5 45		8 50		2 25	
△Eaton, Ohio (ET)						⊠730					
△DAYTON Ar	10 45		3 10			⊠815		10 50	1 45		6 55

(Thru Bus via New York / Via Fort Wayne to New York / City to New York notations shown in vertical columns)

SCHEDULE Nos. → 290

Folder No. 72 — 9-6-78

WESTBOUND READ DOWN

	1351	2099	1341	1353	1361	1355	4373	1357	4453	1359
△DAYTON Lv	7 15	▽800	10 15		3 55	6 00		11 45		2 10
△Eaton, Ohio (ET)		8 45								
△Richmond, Ind. (EST)	7 15	8 25	10 15			6 00		11 45		2 10
Centerville										
△Cambridge City		8 45				6 20		12 10		
Dublin						f		f		
Lewisville						f		f		
Knightstown						f		f		
Greenfield						f		f		
△INDIANAPOLIS, IND. Ar	8#40	10 10	11#40	12#40	5‖20	7‖55		1‖40		3‖35

(Thru Bus / Via Fort Wayne notations in vertical columns)

NEW ORLEANS—MEMPHIS—CHICAGO

READ DOWN

SCHEDULE Nos. → 400

Folder No. 80 — 9-6-78

	1204	1206	2030	5234	1208	5288	1210	5290	1200	5286	5240	1202
△NEW ORLEANS Lv			4 15		7 30		11 00				4 30	10 00
Charity Hospital							f					
Tulane and Broad							f					
△Metairie (N. Causeway B.)					7 50		▼				▼	
Norco					f		f				f	
△La Place					11 52						5 25	
Manchac					f		f				f	
△Ponchatoula			5 20		8 40		12 40				6 12	11 10
Covington							f				f	
△Hammond Ar			5 30		9#15		12#50				6 22	11 20
△Hammond Lv			5 40		9 25		1 00				6 35	11 20
△Independence			5 55								6 50	
△Amite			6 05		9 55		1 30				7 00	Ⓛ1135 11 45
Roseland			f		f		f				f	
Fluker			f		f		f				f	
Tangipahoa			f		f		f				f	
△Kentwood, La.			6 25		10 15		1 55				7 25	12 05
Osyka, Miss.			f		f		f				f	
Magnolia			f		f		f				f	
△McComb			7 00		10 50		2 30				7 55	12 35
Summit			f		f		f				f	
Bogue Chitto			f		f		f				f	
△Brookhaven			7 45		11 25		3 10				8 30	1 05
△Wesson			7 58				3 23				8 43	
△Hazlehurst			8 15				3 45				9 05	
△Crystal Springs			8 29				3 59				9 14	
Terry			f				f				f	
△JACKSON Ar			9‖15		12‖35		4‖50				9 50	2#15
△JACKSON Lv		6 45	9 30		1 05	1 35	5 15	5 10	7 20			2 30
△Flora		7 20	10 05					5 45	7 55			
△Bentonia		7 30	10 15					5 55	8 05			
△Yazoo City		7 50	10 35			2 35		6 15	8 25			
Louise			11 00					6 40				
Midnight			f									
△Belzoni			11 25					7 05				
△Isola			11 40									
Inverness			11 50					7 25				
△Indianola			12 20					7 35				
Moorhead												
Sunflower												
△Ruleville			12 47									
Drew			12 55									
Parchman			f									
△Tchula			f									
△Greenwood Ar		8 31			3 15				9 00			
△Greenwood Lv		9 10			3 50				9 15			
△Webb		9 15			3 55				9 35			
Tutwiler		10 00			4 40				10 20			
△VICKSBURG, MISS. Lv	6 15				10 15				6 45			
△Cary	6 58				10 58				7 28			
△Rolling Fork	7 15				11 05				7 35			
△Anguilla	7 28				11 18				7 48			
△Hollandale	7 48				11 38				8 08			
Arcola Jct. (½ Mi.)	f				f				f			
△Leland	8 10				11 59				8 29			
△Greenville Ar	8#30				12#20			8 00	8#50			
△Greenville Lv	8 45				12 35			8 20	9 10			
△Leland	9 05				12 55				9 30			
△Shaw	9 25				1 15				9 45			
Boyle	f											
△Cleveland	9 40				1 30				10 00			
Merigold	f											
△Mound Bayou	9 55				1 45				10 15			
Shelby	10 05				1 55				10 25			
Duncan	f											
△Clarksdale Ar	10 35	10#40	1#40		2 30	5#15		11 00	10#55			
△Clarksdale Lv	10 45	10 55	2 00		2 35	5 30		11 10	Ⓛ1110			
Jonestown Jct. (3¼ Mile)	11 04	11 14	2 19		2 54			11 28	11 28			
△Rich Jct. (1½ Mile)	11 10	11 20	2 25		3 00			11 34	11 34			
△Tunica	11 35	11 45	2 50		3 25	6 20		11 59	11 59			
Robinsonville Jct. (1 Mile)	f		f					f	f			
Walls, Miss.	f		f					f	f			
△MEMPHIS, TENN. Ar	12‖35	12‖45	3 50		4‖25	5‖00	7 20	9#10	1#00	1 00		6‖25

(Vertical column notations: "For Complete Service See Table 434"; "Except Sundays and Holidays"; "Thru Bus Vicksburg to Milwaukee"; "Thru Bus Vicksburg to St. Louis"; "×")

DETROIT—INDIANAPOLIS—EVANSVILLE—MEMPHIS

SOUTHBOUND READ DOWN | NORTHBOUND READ UP

SCHEDULE Nos.
Folder No. 80
401
9-6-78

1403	1221	1743	5321	5329	1171	1741	1225	5319	1223		5318	5320	5330	1406	1222	5326	1742	5328	1224	1220
																	Fri			
4 45	2 15			8 40	6 30		5 00		12 30	Lv **DETROIT, MICH.** (388) **GL** Ar			9 50	10 55			4 05	8 30	1125	2 45
5 05	2 35			9 00	6 50					Lincoln Park			9 25	D1030						
5 25				9 40	7 35					Flat Rock										
5 50				9 30						Monroe, Mich.									1035	
6 30	3 40			10 20	8 05		6 15		1 45	Ar **Toledo, Ohio** (388) Lv			8 25	9 30			2 45	7 15	1000	1 30
	12 55			6 30			3 55		9 30	Lv Cleveland, Ohio (285) Ar				1 15			7 20	10 50		4 35
	3 40			9 15			6 20		11 55	Ar Toledo, Ohio Lv				10 50			4 30	8 10		1 45
6 35	3 45			10 25	8 10		6 35		1 50	Lv **Toledo, Ohio** R Ar			6 45	8 20	9 25		1 55	6 40	9 55	1 25
							6 50			Maumee R			D6 30				D625			
							f			Waterville			f				f			
							f			Grand Rapids Jct. 1 Mile			f				f			
	4 34			11 14			7 35			Napoleon			5 50	1 00			5 40			12 27
	5 00			11 40			8 00			**Defiance**			5 25	12 35			5 15			11 59
	f			f			f			Antwerp, Ohio (ET)			f				f			f
	f			f			f			New Haven, Ind. (EST)			f				f			f
	5#10			11 50			8#15		3#00	Ar **Fort Wayne** Lv			3 15	6 15			10 30	3 10		9 55
	5 30			12 20			8 30		3 20	Lv **Fort Wayne** Ar			2#55	5#50			10#10	3 05		9#40
				HS			HS			Roanoke			HS							HS
	6 10			12 59			9 05			Huntington			2 15	5 10			9 30			9 05
	6 46			1 30			9 40			**Marion**			1 40	4 35			8 55			8 30
				2 07			10 10			Alexandria			1 00				8 00			8 00
	7 35			2 30			10 30			**Anderson**			12 40	3 45			8 05			7 40
										Pendleton (Jct. 67 & 38)½ Mile			HS							
										Indiana State Ref.			f							
										Fortville			f							
	8#45			3#40			11 40		5 40	Ar **Indianapolis, Ind.** Lv			11 30	2 40			7 00	12 45		6 30
	9 20			4 30			2 20	6 00		Lv Indianapolis, Ind. (EST) (290) Ar			10 55	2 25			6 45	9 55		6 10
	2 15			10 10			7 15	10 55		Ar St. Louis Mo. (CT) Lv			5 00	9 20			1 30	4 20		1 25
	12 10			4 00			12 10	7 00		Lv Indianapolis, Ind. (EST) (355) Ar			10 00	1 25			12 30	11 15		4 15
	12 45			7 15			3 40	11 25		Ar Louisville Ky. (ET) **GL** Lv			8 45	11 45			11 15			3 00
	5 25			11 15			7 40			Lv South Bend, Ind. (EST) (1315) **IMB** Ar	12 30	4 10			9 05					12 30
	9 10			3 10			11 35			Ar Indianapolis, Ind. (EST) **IMB** Lv	8 35	1230			5 15					8 35
	5 15	3 00		10 45			7 25		11 30	Lv Chicago, Ill. (CT) (355) **GL** Ar	1 45	5 20		6 50	10 25	9 55		4 45		11 50
	8 50	7 30		3 10			11 20		3 15	Ar Indianapolis, Ind. (EST) Lv	8 40	1 45		2 30	6 20	5 30		1 00		8 15
	1 45		7 00	7 10			2 00		11 00	Lv New York, N.Y. (ET) (290) Ar		7 40		8 00	11 35	5 10		4 05		4 05
	12 20		4 50	10 15			12 30		9 05	Pittsburgh, Pa.		1025		11 35	7 15	12 35		10 50		5 55
	8 40		10 00	12 15			4 40		2 10	Columbus, Ohio (ET)		4 35		7 15	12 35	1 00		5 25		4 45
	8 40		1 40	3 35			7 55		5 20	Ar Indianapolis, Ind. (EST) Lv		1145		3 00	7 25			1 00		6 50
	9 10	7 45	5 45	4 15		2 30	12 30	8 45	6 30	Lv **INDIANAPOLIS, IND.** Ar	8 30	1120		11 50	5 10	5#00		11#55		5 20
	D9 50	9 00	7 05	5 00			1 15	9 30	7 15	Martinsville	7 40	1035		1 05	4 25			11 05		
	10 20			5 30		3 45	1 45	10 00	7 50	**Bloomington**	7 10	1005		12 35	3 55	4 00		10 35		4 10
	HS									Oolitic										
				6 05			2 25		8 30	**Bedford**			11 59	3 20			10 00			3 40
		Sunday only See Note		30					20	Rest Stop (The Gables)			25			Friday only See Note	25			
	11 45			7 15				9 25		Shoals			10 55				8 45			
				7 26				9 35		Loogootee			10 45				8 05			
				7 46				9 55		**Washington**			10 25				8 25			
							HS			Mitchell				fhs						
							3#00			Ar **Orleans** Lv			2 50							
							3 15			Lv **Orleans** Ar			2#35							
							3 30			Paoli			2 20							
							3 47			West Baden										
							4 25			**French Lick**			2 05							
							4 40			Jasper			1 15							
							4 52			**Huntingburg** (EST)			1 03							
										Dale (CT)										
										Gentryville										
							5 31			**Boonville** (CT)			12 24							
								10 15		Petersburg (EST)			9 51					7 50		
				8 19				10 30		**Oakland City** (CT)			8 55	11 55				7 00		1 30
	1#00			9 15			6 00	11 25		Ar **EVANSVILLE** Lv										
	1 20						6 45	12 15		Lv **EVANSVILLE, IND.** Ar	8 25			6 15				12 50		
	1 40						7 10	12 40		Henderson, Ky.	8 00			5 50				12 30		
	f									Corydon	f			f				f		
	D						7 40	1 10		Waverly	f			5 20				D		
	2 15						7 45	1 15		Camp Breckenridge	7 30			5 15				11 55		
	2 30						8 00	1 30		Morganfield	7 25			5 00				11 40		
										Sturgis	7 08									
	2 55						8 30	2 00		Sullivan										
	3 10						8 45	2 15		**Marion**	6 42			4 30				11 15		
	3 20						855	2 25		**Salem**	6 30			4 15				11 00		
							f			Burna	6 20			4 05				10 50		
	3#45						9 40	3#10		Smithland										
										Ar **Paducah** Lv				5 45				3 30		10 15
	4 00						11 00	3 45		Lv **Paducah** Ar				5 30				11 55		9 55
	4 45						11 45	4 30		Mayfield				4 45				11 10		9 10
	5 15						12 10	5 00		Fulton, Ky.				4 15				10 35		8 40
	5 35						12 30	5 20		Union City, Tenn.				3 50				10 10		8 20
	6 15						115	6 10		Dyersburg				3 05				9 20		7 30
	7 00						1 45	6 45		Ripley				2 35				8 45		6 55
	7 25						2 10	7 10		Covington				2 15				8 20		6 30
	7 55						2 40	7 40		Millington				1 45				8 00		6 00
	8 15						3 00	8 00		tFrayser				1 25				7 40		5 45
8 00	8 25			1240			3 10	8 10		Ar **MEMPHIS, TENN.** Lv	1 20			1 00				7 30	5 15	5 30
8 40				1255				8 45		Lv Memphis, Tenn. Ar				1 00	1 00			6 25	5 00	
4 40				1225				7 20		Ar New Orleans, La. (CT) (400) **GL** Lv				11 00	11 00			10 00	7 30	

Thru Bus Detroit to Dallas via Louisville — See Tables 350 and 365 for detail

Thru Bus Detroit to Memphis via Cincinnati and Louisville — See Tables 350 and 365 for detail

Thru Bus Dallas to Detroit via Louisville and Cincinnati — See Tables 350 and 365 for detail

Memphis to Detroit—Connection in Nashville — See Tables 350 and 365 for detail

For Complete Service See Table 400

SOLUTIONS

Problem #1

This problem has *two* good solutions. If you keep yourself occupied in New Orleans until 6:30 or 7:00 a.m., Solution A is best because it requires fewer bus changes and less immobile time in Birmingham and Indianapolis.

On the other hand, if you want to leave New Orleans earlier and get right to sleep on the bus, you may prefer Solution B.

SOLUTION A

Lv.	New Orleans	--	7:30 a.m.⎫
Ar.	Memphis	--	5:00 p.m.⎬ 400
Lv.	Memphis	--	5:30 p.m.⎫
Ar.	Ft. Wayne	--	9:40 a.m.⎬ 401
Lv.	Ft. Wayne	--	10:00 a.m.⎫
Ar.	Decatur	--	10:40 a.m.⎬ 1390

Arrival is on Friday.

SOLUTION B

Lv.	New Orleans	--	5:15 a.m.⎫
Ar.	Birmingham	--	2:50 p.m.⎬ 216
Lv.	Birmingham	--	6:00 p.m.⎫ 365 &
Ar.	Indianapolis	--	4:15 a.m.⎬ 355
Lv.	Indianapolis	--	6:30 a.m.⎫
Ar.	Ft. Wayne	--	9:40 a.m.⎬ 401
Lv.	Ft. Wayne	--	10:00 a.m.⎫
Ar.	Decatur	--	10:40 a.m.⎬ 1390

Arrival is on Friday.

DID YOU NOTICE... that you can ride free from Metairie to the New Orleans Greyhound Depot? Your delivery would have been in time for you to catch the only Greyhound serving Metairie eastbound, all day. With your bus pass, you could ride it:

Lv.	Metairie	--	6:25 p.m.⎫
Ar.	New Orleans	--	6:45 p.m.⎬ 216

Problem #2

Interception of the morning A.B.C. bus to Decatur is impossible with the schedules provided here. But the afternoon bus can be taken north from Richmond using either of these itineraries:

SOLUTION A

Lv.	New Orleans	--	10:15 a.m.⎫
Ar.	Birmingham	--	7:15 p.m.⎬ 216
Lv.	Birmingham	--	8:10 p.m.⎫
Ar.	Nashville	--	12:40 a.m.⎬ 365,
Lv.	Nashville	--	12:45 a.m.⎬ 355
Ar.	Indianapolis	--	8:25 a.m.⎭
Lv.	Indianapolis	--	11:45 a.m.⎫
Ar.	Richmond	--	1:10 p.m.⎬ 290
Lv.	Richmond	--	2:30 p.m.⎫
Ar.	Decatur	--	4:28 p.m.⎬ 1390

SOLUTION B

Lv.	New Orleans	--	10:15 a.m.⎫
Ar.	Birmingham	--	7:15 p.m.⎬ 216
Lv.	Birmingham	--	8:10 p.m.⎫
Ar.	Nashville	--	12:40 a.m.⎬ 365,
Lv.	Nashville	--	12:45 a.m.⎬ 355
Ar.	Cincinnati	--	8:15 a.m.⎭
Lv.	Cincinnati	--	8:40 a.m.⎫
Ar.	Dayton	--	9:55 a.m.⎬ 350
Lv.	Dayton	--	11:45 a.m.⎫
Ar.	Richmond	--	11:45 a.m.⎬ 290
Lv.	Richmond	--	2:30 p.m.⎫
Ar.	Decatur	--	4:28 p.m.⎬ 1390

Arrival in both cases is on Tuesday.

Notice the time situation from Dayton to Richmond in Solution B. Ohio is in the Eastern Daylight Savings Time Zone. Indiana's staying on Eastern Standard Time during the summer has the effect of moving that state into the Central Daylight Time Zone. (Eastern Standard and Central Daylight are identical.)

Problem #3

You can reach Indianapolis by 4:15 a.m. on Friday, and easily connect from there. But you might find it more desirable in terms of sleep to use the itinerary below, which utilizes the last half of the "Cincinnati Trampoline" technique:

Lv.	Decatur, Alabama	--	2:00 p.m.	365
Ar.	Cincinnati	--	1:30 a.m.	
Lv.	Cincinnati	--	2:15 a.m.	350
Ar.	Toledo	--	6:25 a.m.	
Lv.	Toledo	--	6:35 a.m.	401
Ar.	Fort Wayne	--	8:15 a.m.	
Lv.	Fort Wayne	--	10:00 a.m.	1390
Ar.	Decatur, Indiana	--	10:40 a.m.	

Notice the slight fluctuation in times in Table 350 between the older schedule used to describe the "Cincinnati Trampoline" on page 74, and the more recent schedule used for these problems. It is for this reason that you should always verify schedules, unless you use a current Russell's Guide. (A shift of just 15 more minutes, and the "Cincinnati Trampoline" technique, as well as the above itinerary, would have become as extinct as the dinosaurs. It would be disastrous to actually be en route on a return trip, and suddenly learn that a formerly reliable connection no longer existed!)

None of these three problems required you to use footnotes and reference marks in their solution. Remember, though, that just about the time you begin ignoring them is when they'll become important. Just how important they can be is illustrated by the fact that the only direct bus link to Decatur, Indiana does not run on weekends or holidays. Don't learn to check reference marks the hard way. Always keep it in mind.

APPENDIX C

EASY ALTERNATIVES TO TURNPIKES AND TOLLWAYS

Toll highways are an anachronism -- a remnant of the distant past, with no place in the late 20th century. When the first turnpikes were built in the Colonial Days of early America, the people were so angered at the notion of paying a toll to travel, they built roads in many places to provide free bypasses *around* the turnpikes. These became known as "shunpikes", because they allowed travellers to *shun* the turnpikes.

Today, there exist far more excellent shunpikes than many state authorities would like for us to know about. There are too many to list here, so some of the *best* ones are presented, to enable you to plan your routes accordingly.

Even if you work for a company that pays your tolls (and most do), think how much better it would be if *no one* had to pay this outmoded form of taxation. Using the shunpikes listed below, you can save money for all concerned -- your company, the dealer, the customer, or even you, yourself.

THE NEW JERSEY SHUNPIKE

Approximately half the length of the New Jersey Turnpike can be bypassed very easily on a freeway that runs parallel to it, usually only a mile or so away.

Going south, get off the New Jersey Turnpike at Exit 7, and cross over to I-295. The Turnpike and I-295 merge without difficulty immediately before reaching the Delaware Memorial Bridge.

Going north, simply *stay* on I-295 after crossing the bridge from Delaware, and then transfer onto the the New Jersey Turnpike at the Turnpike's Exit 7.

THE KANSAS SHUNPIKE

To save $1.50 or more, get off of I-70 west of Kansas City where it intersects Kansas Route 32 (the Bonner Springs exit). Continue west on Route 32 until it ends at U.S. Route 40, just east of Lawrence. Then continue west on U.S. 40 to Topeka. Before you hit city traffic, you will see signs directing you to I-70. Re-join I-70 at that time, and take it across the city and on westward. This routing permits you to avoid all contact with the Kansas Turnpike, and generally consumes no more than 10 or 15 extra minutes.

SHUNPIKES AROUND THE NEW YORK STATE THRUWAY

There are many excellent ways to get around this overpriced highway, but
New York State doesn't advertise them. Here are a few of the best ones.

1. The Capital District Shunpike

The Interstate 90 Freeway is one of America's best shunpikes. Using it
saves well over $1.00 in tolls, several extra miles of travel, and several
minutes of time. (See the map on the facing page.)

It is unfortunate that the Thruway Authority has been so blatantly
deceptive about the usefulness of this freeway. Travellers not familiar with
the Capital District would never guess from the signs posted in four critical
locations that such a handy freeway even exists.

A few years ago, the author attended a public meeting in Albany, scheduled
by the Thruway Authority, and spoke in favor of making the signs honest. The
officials present publicly admitted that a good point had been made -- but to
date nothing has been done to remedy the situation.

How ironic, in these times of government encouragement to save energy,
that a New York State agency would perpetuate a practice which causes people
to use *more* gasoline! (The Thruway dogleg is *longer* than the I-90 Freeway
shortcut.)

2. The Buffalo Shunpike

Another example of such deception exists on the Niagara Frontier, in
western New York.

If one gets off the mainline Thruway at Buffalo with the intention of
going downtown, he finds that an extension of the Thruway for that purpose,
toll and all, is ready and waiting. Almost immediately upon leaving the main
Thruway, however, the driver is informed of an exit to N.Y. Route 33 to downtown Buffalo.

Those unfamiliar with Buffalo, given only that much information, often
envision a two-lane road full of stoplights and congested traffic leading
tediously toward the Buffalo skyline, off on the horizon.

In actuality, N.Y. Route 33 westbound from this location is a limited-
access *freeway* -- and the signs *should* make that fact known.

3. The Trans-New York State Shunpikes

East-west travellers crossing the full length of upstate New York save
a lot of money by using the Southern Tier Expressway (N.Y. Route 17). This is

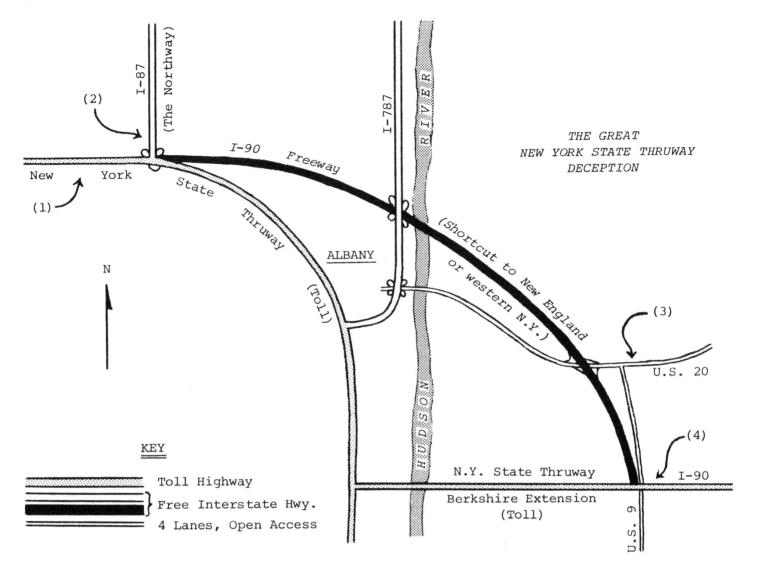

THE GREAT
NEW YORK STATE THRUWAY
DECEPTION

KEY

▨▨▨▨▨ Toll Highway

▬▬▬▬▬ } Free Interstate Hwy.

═════ 4 Lanes, Open Access

(1) -- Eastbound traffic sees a sign telling of an exit to
Albany and The Northway. Small signs on top of the
larger one indicate I-90 and I-87. There is no
indication that this exit could even be used to go
to Boston or New England. A sign *should* be erected
to inform travellers that <u>this</u> exit is the fastest
and shortest way to go to Massachusetts & Boston.

(2) -- Southbound traffic is told that I-90 eastbound at
this exit goes to *ALBANY*. There is no mention of
Boston, whatsoever.

(3) -- Westbound traffic is told to turn south on U.S. 9
to go to the Thruway. There is no indication that
the best Thruway entrance for westbound traffic
still lies *ahead*, on I-90. At this location, I-90
is still just out of sight, half a mile ahead.

(4) Westbound traffic on the Berkshire Extension is
told that this is the exit for Hudson & Rensselaer.
At the top of the sign is a small I-90 symbol. There
is no indication that this is the best exit to use
to reach downtown Albany, let alone points farther
west in New York State.

a freeway of Interstate Highway quality that allows one to bypass the N.Y. State Thruway almost in its entirety.

Except for a few miles of two-lane highway, mostly at the western end of the state, the freeway links New York City to the Pennsylvania line, near Erie.

Travellers going to and from Albany can use N.Y. Route 7 and the recently-constructed I-88 to connect with the Southern Tier Expressway.

If one is crossing the state between Albany and Buffalo, U.S. Route 20 makes a good shunpike. Much of it is 4-lane highway, and traffic usually is light. Only in the cities of Geneva and Auburn does one encounter some slow driving and congestion. One can can cross the state within about one hour of the time it normally takes to make the trip via the Thruway.

SHUNPIKES FOR THE ILLINOIS TOLLWAYS

1. Chicagoland Shunpikes

The best way to travel to points north and west of Chicago from Indiana is to "Shoot the Loop". This technique requires you to take I-94 north from I-80, almost immediately after crossing into Illinois (see the map on the facing page). I-94 soon becomes the Dan Ryan Expressway, which takes one directly to the Chicago Loop, toll-free. If travelling northwest toward Rockford, Illinois or northeastern Iowa, he should take the Eisenhower Expressway westbound upon reaching the Loop. (The Eisenhower Expressway is joined almost at the base of the world's 2nd-largest building, the Sears Tower. You can't miss it!)

The Eisenhower Expressway is I-90, and this route provides one with the longest possible stretch of freeway before connecting with the Northwest Tollway. (The Northwest Tollway becomes I-90 as well, from that point westward.)

Traffic continuing north, instead, to such points as Milwaukee, Madison, Minneapolis, and beyond, should continue on I-94 past the Loop (Kennedy and Edens Expressways). Eventually, one gets a choice of continuing on I-94, or taking U.S. Route 41. To stay on U.S. 41, just continue straight ahead. It is very close to freeway quality, having only a very few stoplights.

I-94 becomes part of the Tri-State Tollway (the I-294 route number ends where I-94 meets it). Bypassing it saves sixty cents. At the Wisconsin state line, U.S. 41 merges with I-94, and I-94 again becomes *freeway*.

CAUTION -- "Shooting the Loop" is recommended only for certain times of day: between 10:00 p.m. and 6:00 a.m., and on ordinary weekends. Any other time the technique carries the risk of involving you in a traffic jam that could easily cost an hour or more.

During daytime and early evening hours on weekdays, use of I-294 (the Tri-State Tollway) around the city is usually more cost-effective, and is strongly recommended.

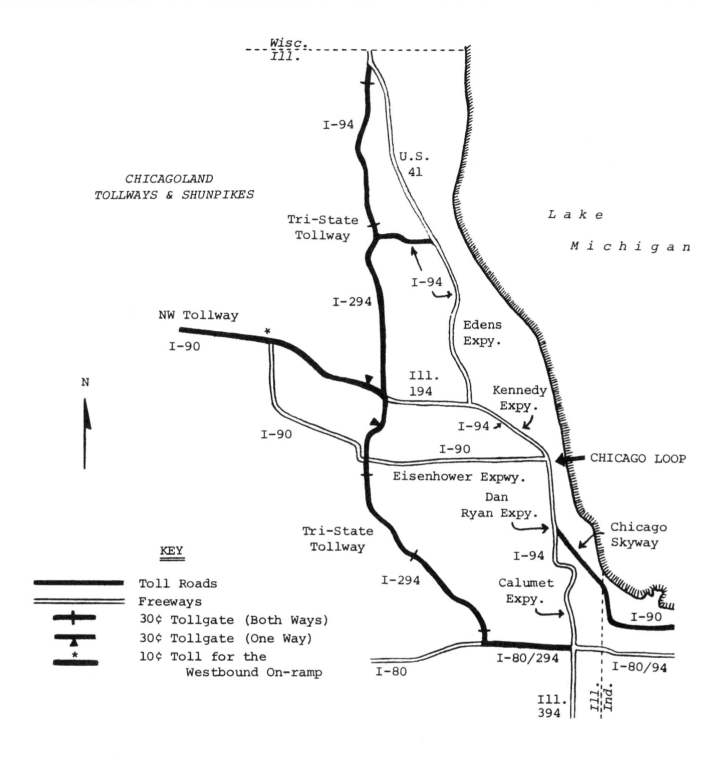

CHICAGOLAND
TOLLWAYS & SHUNPIKES

N

KEY

▬▬▬▬▬	Toll Roads
═════	Freeways
╂	30¢ Tollgate (Both Ways)
▬▲▬	30¢ Tollgate (One Way)
＊	10¢ Toll for the Westbound On-ramp

Finally, *do not* use the *Express Lanes* of the Kennedy Expressway if you intend to go toward Rockford. Traffic is not allowed to cross the expressway from the Express Lanes to the Rockford exit, and police frequently lie in wait for those who would try it.

You can save 20¢, going toward Rockford via the Tri-State Tollway (I-294) if you take I-90 when you *first* contact it (rather than exit onto Ill. Route 194, westbound). This bypasses a major tollgate (30¢) and substitutes a lesser one (10¢) where you join the Northwest Tollway.

2. *Genoa Road Shunpike*

Going toward Dubuque, Iowa from Chicago, take the Genoa Road exit from the Northwest Tollway, onto Bypass U.S. Route 20. (Turn right at the end of the exit ramp to reach it.) Then go west on Bypass U.S. 20. You save 30¢.

Know of a really good shunpike that isn't included here? We'd really like to know about it, for future editions. Let us know any extra information you can provide, too, if possible, such as deceptive directions on highway signs that ignore or hide the presence of the shunpike.

Please use this address:

"Shunpikes"
c/o Craig Chilton
Box 424
East Greenbush, NY
12061-0424

Thank you!

APPENDIX D

MAKING MONEY BY SAVING MONEY

Don't be disheartened by the mathematics shown in this Appendix. Having a *hand calculator* makes the operations quite simple to perform -- and there are only a few basic operations.

After one or two runs, these procedures become second-nature.

The Log Book

For illustrative purposes, more mathematical functions and descriptions are shown in the log sample than you will ever be likely to write down, in actual practice. *As you gain experience, you will develop a "shorthand" of your own with which to make log notations.* The entire run shown, when shortened to normal length, would fill no more than a *page or so* of a wire-bound notebook. (Medium-sized wire-bound notebooks, incidentally, make ideal log books.)

There are four main reasons for keeping a log:

(1)   The data aids the driver in making decisions *during* a run.

(2)   *After* the run, the driver can objectively examine his patterns of driving, and seek ways to improve his performance and overall speed.

(3)   Information on times and expenses can easily be transferred to the *budget book* after a run, so that the driver doesn't have to maintain both books while he's driving.

(4)   It provides comparative data to which the driver may refer when making future runs along the *same* routes.

NOTE: Nearly all of the information contained in *The XANADU System* was *first* written down, at one time or another, in *log books* maintained by the author!

Some companies require drivers to use the official Department of Transportation log books as used by the trucking industry, but most do not. This Appendix deals only with the log book that drivers often maintain for their *own* personal use.

Log books can be set up in various ways, but the author's experience has been that it is best to log everything in chronological order. Then it is easy to locate information simply by recalling the portion of the run in which it was obtained and recorded.

- 165 -

The Odometer Check

If you wish, you may lightheartedly skim over this section, for you *can* manage without it. However, you should remember that what you *get out* of anything often depends upon what you *put into* it.

Always assume that your unit's odometer is inaccurate. Over 99% of them *are*. It will be necessary to run an odometer check at some point during the run, in order to be able to refer back to your log later to calculate actual distances between points ... *and*, for you to be able to calculate your gas mileage accurately, en route.

Ideally, this is done early in the run, especially if you have decided to drive at marginal speeds.

> *Example:* Your odometer check may tell you that you are *actually travelling* only 58 mph when the speedometer *reads* 62. If your intention is to drive at the *actual* speed of 62 mph, you would have to drive at a higher *indicated* speed.

When starting the odometer check, keep in mind that <u>none</u> of the following three things must occur while the check is in progress:

1. You must not cross a state line (or, in California, a county line), as this will end the system of mile markers with which you are working.

2. You must not change course even slightly (such as: reverse direction, stop at a rest area, or exit from a freeway) -- for obvious reasons.

3. You must not make a route change (the new route will either have a different set of mile markers, or none at all).

Plan your odometer check in advance, to avoid these disrupting factors. Be sure that no rest stops nor gasoline will be required during the check. Then, proceed as follows, for best results:

1. Select a segment of highway having regular mile markers. The segment can be any length, but try not to settle for less than 10 miles. Fifty or 100 miles is better still, in terms of accuracy, but any length will suffice if you have a pocket calculator along to simplify the process and save time.

2. When approaching the mile marker you wish to use to start your check, look at the odometer *at the exact instant* you pass it, and note its reading. Do this to the nearest tenth, if you must, but for greater accuracy, it is suggested that you estimate to the nearest hundredth.

In our example, we shall suppose that your starting mile marker reads: Mile 162. You mark your log as follows:

Odo. ✔ -- 36.37 Mile 162

3.   In most of the USA, when travelling on Interstate highways, mile markers decline when going south or west, and increase when going north or east. For this example, let us assume that you are going west. If you wished to make a 50-mile check, you therefore would watch for Mile 112.

The *instant* you reach the mile marker selected for the end of the check, note your odometer reading, and then record all figures on the log. It now should look like this:

```
Odo. ✓ --    36.37    Mile 162
             88.71    Mile 112
```

4.   Next, find the differences by subtracting the smaller number from the larger, in each case:

```
Odo. ✓ --    36.37    Mile 162
             88.71    Mile 112
             52.34           50 miles
```

In this case, the odometer reading is too high; it is *adding* more miles than the distance actually being travelled. The rate is 2.34 extra miles for every 50 miles travelled, which would be the same as 4.68 extra miles indicated for every 100 travelled. (The error here is almost 5%.)

5.   Next, you must arrive at a *Correction Coefficient* (cc). This is done by dividing the Indicated Miles Travelled (52.34) *into* the Actual Miles Travelled (50):

$$cc = \frac{AMT}{IMT}$$

$$cc = \frac{50.00}{52.34} = 0.9553$$

6.   Now that you have the cc, you can determine the *actual* number of miles travelled between gas fills, and thus accurately determine your gas mileage for any given segment of the trip.

Simply multiply the cc times the *indicated* number of miles in the segment, and you'll have the *actual* distance travelled:

$$cc \times IMT = AMT$$

For our example, let's assume that the indicated number of miles travelled between gas fills was 235.7. We convert this to actual miles, thus:

$$0.9553 \times 235.7 = 225.2 \text{ actual miles}$$

7.	Using the cc, you *also* can discover the *indicated* speed you will need to travel (as displayed on your speedometer) in order to proceed at a *desired* (actual) rate of speed.

Simply divide the cc *into* your Desired Rate of Speed (DRS) to obtain the Indicated Rate of Speed (IRS) at which you must drive. Let's assume that you want to drive at the *actual* speed of 60 mph:

$$IRS = \frac{DRS}{cc}$$

$$IRS = \frac{60}{0.9553} = 62.8 \text{ mph}$$

In this example, you will have to drive at a speed of about 63 mph (on the speedometer) in order to travel at an *actual* speed of 60 mph.

You can see why it is helpful to obtain this information *early* in the run!

(Remember, the speedometer and the odometer both are driven by the *same* cable -- so the cc is accurate for *both* instruments.

8.	A typical complete log notation for an odometer check might look like this:

Odo. ✔ --	36.37 Mile 162
            88.71 Mile 112
            52.34   50 miles
            cc = 0.9553
            60 mph = Indicated 62.8 mph

The Gas Mileage Check

This section is developed in great detail. It might seem like a "long trail a-winding," but don't let it raise your blood pressure!

In this age of energy hoaxes, a dashboard gauge which informs the driver of his gas mileage at a glance, *should* be standard equipment on all motor vehicles having four or more wheels. Since it is not, the gas mileage check is the best substitute.

IMPORTANT *NOTE:*	One should always run the gas mileage check at a very consistent speed. Ideally, he should wait until he reaches a stretch of freeway or Interstate where he can be assured that nothing is likely to cause him to have to change speed or stop for at least 30 miles. (Varying speed during the check invalidates the results.)

For units having cruise control, the speed should be punched in and allowed to stabilize at the desired level, *before* starting the check. For units without cruise

control, speed should be maintained as steadily as
possible throughout the check.

Your assigned RV will have either one or two gas tanks. (If not, you're
in big trouble!) Most Class "A" motor homes have an auxiliary tank.
Checking gasoline mileage with a two-tank unit is the simpler process, so
we'll discuss it first.

Two-Tank Mileage Check

1.   At the beginning of the trip, put any desirable amount of
        gasoline into the *main* tank. Then put *exactly* three gallons into
        the reserve (auxiliary) tank.

2.   Wait until the odometer which reads out to the nearest tenth
        of a mile (in some units, this will be the *trip* odometer) reaches
        an *even mile* exactly, and at *that instant*, flip the switch, convert-
        ing you to the reserve tank. Note this mileage in your log.

3.   In a few miles, the tank will be drained; when the unit falters,
        switch back to the main tank. At *that* instant, take note of the
        odometer reading in miles and tenths, and enter it in the log. (If
        possible, estimate that reading to the nearest hundredth of a mile.)

4.   Subtract the smaller figure from the larger one. Then divide
        the result by three (the number of gallons of gasoline consumed),
        to obtain your gas mileage. Be sure that the log shows the *speed*
        at which you conducted the test. Your log notations should look
        like this:

                        SAMPLE

        Gas Mileage ✓ @ 58 mph
                Start: 14.00 ⎫
                  End: 35.44 ⎬ 21.44 miles

                        21.44 ÷ 3 = 7.147

If your gas mileage check proves satisfactory to you (as it should, if
it yields a result of 6 m.p.g. or better), chances are you won't want to
bother with more of them.

But -- should you want to double-check your findings (i.e., you got
results of 4.3 m.p.g. or some other abominable figure), or you wish to
determine your gas mileage at a *different speed,* it will be necessary to
run one or more additional checks.

If you ran the first check properly, chances are good that it was
accurate. On most units, all but a few ounces of gasoline are drawn from the

tanks when they are drained, so a second check with all conditions held the same will probably yield either the same result, or perhaps only a tenth or two of a mile per gallon better. Therefore, *an abysmal rating may deem it logical for you to try another check at a lower speed.* The results of this second check will tell you if sufficient additional fuel economy is gained by maintaining the lower speed, to make continuation of the run at that speed worthwhile. (Remember, though, to keep your scheduling conditions at your destination in mind -- tradeoffs frequently need to be weighed against each other, as discussed in Part III, Chapter 4.)

A final word... I have purposely recommended the use of exactly three gallons of fuel for the check for two reasons:

1.   Using a small amount of fuel will permit you to make checks more frequently at the beginning of the trip, if necessary.

2.   Three gallons of fuel will propel one for less than 30 miles in most coaches. A reasonable distance, especially since speed must be held constant throughout the check.

3.   The electric switching mechanism has been known to malfunction on a two-tank coach. This is extremely rare, but if it were to occur with only three gallons in the reserve tank, you probably would stand to lose only $2.00 or less in fuel that had become unavailable. (With *more* fuel in the reserve tank, your loss would be greater.)

In short, the gas mileage check on a two-tank coach is two tests in one: the gas mileage, and the switch-over mechanism.

Single-Tank Mileage Check

It is impossible, unfortunately, to conduct a gas mileage check on this type of vehicle with the precision and accuracy possible with the method described above. The only way to do it is to start out with the tank filled to the very top of the fill spout. (Watch carefully for leaks!) Record your mileage, and then drive down the road a few miles and fill it again, to see how much was consumed in the distance travelled. Then divide the number of miles travelled by the quantity of gasoline added, thus:

$$\text{m.p.g.} = \frac{\text{Total Miles since First Fill}}{\text{Total Gallons Added on Second Fill}}$$

Several factors and tradeoffs come into play here, and it would be helpful for you to be aware of them:

1.   The lowest gasoline price in your city of origin may be considerably higher than the price of gasoline in another location along your route,

less than one full tank of travel away. (Decatur, Indiana is notorious for this; one can nearly always find lower gasoline prices within a half-hour to 2 1/2-hour drive from Decatur, in any direction -- so it seldom pays to fill up there.

2.   Terrain can make a great difference. This factor is negligible on the flat lands of Indiana, but if you are based in California, you generally will cross mountain ranges soon after departure. And *a gas mileage check taken while crossing mountains is worse than useless*. (Also, the terrain factor may cause you to have to drive out a considerable distance before you can make an accurate check.)

Sooner or later, though, you should achieve a feel for the mileage you are getting -- and this knowledge *will serve you well* as you get within a tankful of gasoline of your destination.

Clearly, it is in your best interests to arrive at the dealership "on fumes", if possible. No one will praise you for leaving gas in the tank. You simply lose the money you invested in it!

Calculating your mileage this closely at the end is more of an *art* than a science, and your ability to accomplish the feat comes with experience. Be aware of factors that affect gas mileage during your homestretch.

Ask yourself --

1.   Is the *terrain* different at the end of the run than near the beginning? Hilly or mountainous terrain causes a reduction in fuel economy, and could cause you to fall short.

2.   Is the *altitude* (elevation above sea level) greater near the end? In my experience, a large motor home will average almost one mile per gallon less in the High Plains of western Nebraska or Kansas, or eastern Colorado, than it does in the lower elevations farther east.

3.   Has the break-in process caused the unit to experience an improvement in gas mileage? This can be an important factor in runs of 1,000 miles and more. Awareness of this possiblity can save you money.

4.   Has the wind changed direction? If so, you may be in for a big surprise -- one of two types. Neither one is pleasant.
         Wind is the greatest single external factor governing your gas mileage. It can either be a benevolent friend, or a malevolent foe.
         A tailwind -- especially a strong one -- can boost your gas mileage to unbelievable heights. A crosswind will cut your mileage back somewhat. But a strong *headwind* is pure and unadulterated

disaster!

If you've been bucking a headwind, or have been experiencing crosswinds throughout a run, and the wind suddenly switches around to become a *tailwind* during the last leg of your trip, you may find yourself making a gift to the dealer of $5 to $10 worth of gasoline. (The money could still be in your wallet, if only you could have known it would happen.)

That's Unpleasant Surprise #1. But it is preferable to its counterpart.

Unpleasant Surprise #2 occurs if the reverse happens -- a tailwind becomes a headwind -- and you don't realize it in time. You run out of gas!

Believe me, no matter how long you've been driving, it can happen to you!

It happened to me, after nearly a year of driving motor homes. 'Way out in the boondocks, on the prairies of Saskatchewan.

Boy, was that ever a near-disaster.

Throughout the trip, I had been blessed with a tailwind that enabled a Class "A" motor home to consistently get over 6 m.p.g. (I say blessed, because in a dead calm, that turkey probably would have been getting only between 4 and 5 m.p.g.)

The weather had been beautiful. Fleecy fair-weather cumulus clouds were sprinkled across azure skies.

(Radical wind shifts usually are accompanied by some visible change in the weather. This one wasn't.)

At Weyburn, I added a pre-calculated amount of gasoline to the empty reserve tank -- which should have been enough to reach Regina (my destination), with 10 miles to spare.

The main tank ran dry at the predicted location, and my confidence was bolstered. Soon, the skyline of Regina shimmered like a mirage on the distant northwest horizon. And *that* is where the reserve tank ran dry, and I coasted to a disheartening stop. Between the expiration of the main tank and this location, the wind had shifted 180 degrees, and I hadn't been aware of it.

Mentally reviewing the drive from Weyburn, I recalled something that should have warned me...

If the unit has been running comfortably, on cruise control, at the desired speed, and then suddenly begins cruising *a few miles per hour slower* -- _and,_ if the terrain hasn't changed -- one *probably* has acquired a *headwind*.

If that happens to you when you are running on a quantity of fuel pre-calculated to reach your destination, *don't ignore it! Assume that*

*your gas mileage has been cut squarely in half, and stop at the
first available gas station -- even if it's not a cut-rate. The
extra expense is far outweighed by the frustration of running
out of gas.*

(In the Saskatchewan example above, the gas mileage dropped
within moments from 6.3 m.p.g., to only 3.75!)

(Incidentally, that trip was a near-disaster because the
lost time caused me to reach the dealership with only five
minutes to spare!)

A Practical Example

Sample log book entries for a typical run are shown below. (Italicized
entries are for purpose of explanation, and would not be shown in an actual
log book.)

COACH: Class "A" Sun Rover #6837   B/L #007-4683 *(Bill of Lading No.)*
FROM: Sun Rover Corporation, San Bernardino, California
TO: Exotic Vehicles, Inc., 98267 W. Florin Road, Sacramento, Calif.
DISTANCE: 437 miles   PAYMENT: $131.10   *(@ 30¢/mi.)*

September 11, 1979 (Tuesday) --

Gas -- San Bernardino -- "Spilco"   00039.6
    Main tank: 38.67 gal. @ 58.9 = $22.78
    Aux. tank: 3.00 gal. @ 58.9 = $ 1.77
       Total: 42.67 gal. @ 58.9 = $24.55
Departure: 5:50 am
Calif. Rte. 138 Odo. ✓ --   72.54 Mile 78
                            98.32 Mile 53
                            25.78   25 miles

                          25.00 ÷ 25.78 = 0.9697

        <u>Actual</u> 62 mph (÷ 0.9697) = 63.9 Indicated mph *(on Speedometer)*
Gas Mileage ✓ @ 64 mph (indicated speed)
            Start: 99.00 ⎫
              End: 115.37 ⎬ = 16.37 indicated miles
            16.37 x 0.9697 = 15.87 actual miles
            15.87 ÷ 3.00 *(gallons)* = 5.29 m.p.g.

STOP -- Gas; Food -- Lancaster -- "7-11"   00116.4 7:21-7:43 am
    Main tank: 13.97 gal. @ 61.9 = $ 8.65
    Aux. tank: 3.00 gal. @ 61.9 = $ 1.86
       Total: 16.97 gal. @ 61.9 = $10.51   Food: $1.85

Gas Mileage ✓ @ 60 mph (Indicated speed)

  Start: 123.00 ⎱ = 18.22 indicated miles
    End: 141.22 ⎰

       18.22 x 0.9697 = 17.67 actual miles
       17.67 ÷ 3.00   = 5.89 m.p.g.

  (In this case, using a lower speed caused a significant savings.)

STOP -- Gas -- Mojave -- "Barfco"   00143.1   8:13-8:23 am

   Miles Out: 143.1 - 39.6 *(Odometer reading at the start of run)*
             = 103.5 indicated miles
        103.5 x 0.9697 = 100.36 actual miles

   Miles to Run: 437 - 100.36 = 336.64 actual miles
   Gasoline Required *(to complete the run)*: 336.64 ÷ 5.89 = 57.15 gallons

(This is the actual amount of gasoline that should be needed to complete the run, if speed is held steady at an actual 58.2 mph -- which shows on the speedometer as 60 mph. In making this gas purchase, the driver must next consider the fact that the main tank lost approximately 1.5 gallons of fuel while it was used to drive 8.5 miles of the distance from Lancaster to Mojave -- the miles that were not included in the gas mileage check. Since we learned, upon filling the main tank in San Bernardino, that its capacity probably is 40 gallons (since it took nearly 39 gallons to fill it), we can assume that it now contains 38.5 gallons. Of this, we shall consider that at least 38.00 gallons are available to the fuel line.

The auxiliary tank was emptied on the gas mileage check. If 57.15 gallons are needed to finish the run, then 19.15 gallons more than we now have will be required. (57.15 - 38.00 = 19.15). Of this we shall add only 16.15 gallons, here in Mojave, leaving 3.00 gallons more to add later.

The reason for this is precision. If we added all of it now, we would empty one tank en route, and nearly empty the other one as well. We would therefore have no real indication, near the end of the run, of how well the gas mileage was holding stable. This will become more clear, later.)

   Aux. tank only: 16.15 gal. @ 62.9 = $10.16   (Staying on main tank.)
       (ALWAYS note in the log which tank you currently are using!)

Main tank empty --   00380.1   12:27 pm

            380.1 - 143.1 = 237.0 indicated miles
            237.0 - 0.9697 = 229.8 actual miles
            229.8 ÷ 38 *(estimated amount of useful gas in main tank, at
                 Mojave)* = 6.05 m.p.g.

(Notice that gas mileage has improved. This might be due to improvement through break-in of the engine. But one must also consider terrain and wind. The gasoline savings may be a result of our having dropped 3,000 feet of elevation in eight miles, at the Grapevine (Tejon Pass). Except for the Grapevine, most of the miles have been driven on the relatively flat plateau of the Upper Desert, and in the flat Central Valley of California. To be safe, we'll still add those three gallons to the main tank when we get closer to the destination.)

STOP -- Gas, Lunch -- Lodi -- "Gypco"   00399.5   12:50-1:10 pm

> Main tank only: 3.00 gal. @ 63.9 = $1.92   Food: $2.58
>
> Staying on aux. tank.

Aux. tank empty --   00478.7   2:39 pm

> 478.7 - 380.1 = 98.6 indicated miles *(Total miles run on the 16.15 gallons that we put in at Mojave)*
>
> 98.6 x 0.9697 = 95.6 actual miles
>
> 95.6 ÷ 16.15 = 5.92 m.p.g. *(The improvement noticed earlier probably <u>did</u> result from the boost from the Grapevine.)*
>
> Miles Out: 478.7 - 39.6 = 439.1 indicated miles
>
>   439.1 x 0.9697 = 425.8 actual miles
>
> Miles to Run: 437 - 425.8 = 11.2 actual miles
>
> Predicted Amount of Gas Remaining upon Arrival: (3 x 5.92) - 11.2
>
>   = Enough gas to go an additional 6.56 miles
>
>   Or... 6.56 ÷ 5.92 *(Our latest gas mileage figure)* = 1.11 gal.

(You have enough gasoline to complete the run, no matter <u>what</u> the gas gauge reads. The reason for ending the trip with a tank holding only 3 gallons was to permit this degree of exactness. It has enabled us to complete the run with only 1.11 extra gallons remaining -- a good safety margin, costing us about 73¢. That tiny expenditure is well worth the assurance of not running out of gas.)

STOP -- DESTINATION -- Exotic Vehicles, Sacramento -- 00490.3 2:55 pm

> Actual Miles Run: (490.3 - 39.6) x 0.9697 = <u>437.2</u>

* * * * * * * * * * *

The important things to remember are:

1.   Precision, such as we obtained in the above example, is somewhat better than one could expect to get with a single-tank unit.

2.   The cc (Correction Coefficient; in the above example, 0.9697) is always <u>*multiplied*</u> times the *indicated* distance or speed, in order to obtain the *actual* distance or speed.

3.   To obtain *indicated* speeds or miles, always <u>*divide*</u> the actual figure *by* the cc.

4.   Two *figures* are vitally important throughout the run: (1) the *total mileage* of the run, and (2) the mileage on the odometer at the *start*. (Notice the number of times the figures *437* and *36.9* were used in the example!)

If your company uses a bill of lading, the mileage of the run is usually shown on it. If you are unsure of the mileage, ask your dispatcher. After you have reached a destination once, you will always know the *exact* mileage (using identical routes), obtained from your log notations.

The Budget Book

Your best barometer of success is the budget book. It not only helps you keep your records straight, but also shows how well you are doing in all phases of your unique lifestyle.

Various account books serve well, but I have found two to be particularly handy and easy to use in terms of their size and columnar arrangement. One is the 12-column *Columnar Book No. 2580* by Herald Square, distributed and sold by the F.W. Woolworth Company. It is commonly found in Woolworth's and Woolco stores.

The other is the *Simplex Column Book #91-522* (12 column) produced by the National Blank Book Co., Inc., Water St., Holyoke, Mass. 01040. Look for this one at Kresge and K-Mart stores.

The budget book is used in the normal fashion, but with every trip kept separate. Following each run, you can record a *Trip Summary*, compiled from information gleaned *both* from the budget book *and* the log book.

Having a 12-column book will enable you to break down most of your expenses by categories. Not only will this enable you to keep tabs on your income and expenses, but at tax time, you'll find that your expenditures are orderly enough to greatly simplify your tax preparation.

The next page illustrates a sample budget book page from a typical medium-length run -- the *same* run used to illustrate the use of the log book, earlier in this Appendix. The Trip Summary was compiled from information recorded in both books.

Only four of the 12 columns are shown. (These columns comprise the first two and the last two used by the author in his own budget books. Some of the other headings include: *Tolls & Public Transportation*, *Phone Calls*, *Work-Connected Expenses*, *Payments, etc.*, *Entertainment*, and *Miscellaneous*. Should you choose to use these, you still will have two columns remaining for headings of your own choosing.

The Trip Summary

You may want to include more or less information than shown here, or change some of the entries. Here is how the ones displayed are derived:

1. *Total Mileage* -- Taken directly from the log book. (*Actual* miles)
2. *Total Gas Purchased* -- Sum of all gallons purchased. Use either book, but it is easier to compile from the budget book.
3. *Average Price per Gallon* -- Divide total amount spent on gasoline by the total gallons purchased.
4. *Estimated Total Gasoline Consumed* -- <u>Add</u> the total number of gallons purchased to the estimated amount of gasoline in the tank before your first gas fill. *Then*, <u>subtract</u> the approximate amount of gasoline remaining at the end of the run.

SAN BERNARDINO to SACRAMENTO, CALIFORNIA (SUN ROVER "A", #6837)

DATE	PLACE AND DESCRIPTION	GASOLINE	FOOD	INCOME	BALANCE
9-11-79	B/L #007-4683 to EXOTIC VEHICLES			131 10	131 10
9-11-79	"SPILCO" - 42.67 gal. @ 58⁹ - SAN BDNO.	24 55			106 55
9-11-79	"7-11" - 16.97 gal @ 61⁹ - LANCASTER	10 51			96 04
9-11-79	"7-11" - BREAKFAST - LANCASTER		1 85		94 19
9-11-79	"BARFCO" - 16.15 gal. @ 62⁹ - MOJAVE	10 16			84 03
9-11-79	"GYPCO" - 3.00 gal. @ 63⁹ - LODI	1 92			82 11
9-11-79	"GYPCO MINI-MART" - FOOD - LODI		2 58		79 53
	TOTALS	47 14	4 43	TOTAL EXPENSES:	51 57

TRIP SUMMARY

TOTAL MILEAGE:	437.2
TOTAL GAS PURCHASED:	78.79 gal.
AVERAGE PRICE PER GALLON:	59.8¢
EST. TOTAL GAS CONSUMED:	APPROX. 77.5 gal.
TRIP GAS MILEAGE:	5.64 MI/GAL.
GAS COST PER MILE DRIVEN:	9.41¢
FOOD COST/MILE TRAVELLED:	1.01¢
% OF INCOME SPENT ON GAS:	35.96 %
% OF INCOME SPENT ON FOOD:	3.38 %
TOTAL % OF INCOME SPENT:	39.34 %
% OF INCOME REMAINING:	60.66 %
ACTUAL DRIVING TIME:	8 HRS. 13 MIN.
TOTAL OUTBOUND TIME:	9 HRS. 5 MIN.
SLEEP TIME OUTBOUND:	NONE
AVERAGE DRIVING SPEED:	53.2 MPH
AVERAGE SPEED (OVERALL):	48.1 MPH
% OF TIME IN MOTION:	90.46 %

5. *Trip Gas Mileage* -- <u>Divide</u> the *Total Mileage* figure by the *Estimated Total Gasoline Consumed* figure.

6. *Gas Cost per Mile Driven* -- <u>Subtract</u> the estimated value of the gasoline you estimate remained in the tank at the end of the run, from the total amount spent on gasoline. *Then*, <u>subtract</u> the estimated value of the quantity of gasoline in the tank <u>before</u> the first gas fill. Finally, <u>divide</u> this result <u>into</u> the *Total Mileage* figure.

7. *Food Cost per Mile Driven* -- <u>Divide</u> total food cost by *Total Mileage*. (If you are on a diet, or just frugal, you'll find it a challenge to keep this figure under one cent!)

8. *% of Income Spent on Gas* -- <u>Divide</u> total amount spent on gasoline by total income for the run. (This figure should be under 42% if you work for a manufacturer, or should not exceed 60% if you work for a transporter company. If these upper limit figures *are* exceeded, discuss with your employer the possibility of a raise due to gasoline price inflation. Everyone in the RV industry is acutely aware of this problem, and generally increases pay scales periodically to keep ahead of it.)

9. *% of Income Spent on Food* -- <u>Divide</u> total amount spent on food by total income for the run. (A good barometer of your eating habits. If the figure exceeds 6%, watch your weight. If over 10%, step on scales very gingerly!)

10. *Total % of Income Spent* -- <u>Divide</u> the total amount of money spent (on everything) on the run, by total income for the run.

11. *% of Income Remaining* -- <u>Divide</u> final "Balance" figure, at the end of the run, by total income for the run.

12. *Actual Driving Time* -- Taken from log book. <u>Subtract</u> all time that vehicle was *not moving* from the total duration of the run, from departure to delivery.

13. *Total Outbound Time* -- Total time spent from departure to delivery.

14. *Sleep Time Outbound* -- Total time spent sleeping en route.

15. *Average Driving Speed* -- Convert the minutes of *Actual Driving Time* to decimal equivalent by <u>dividing</u> the number of minutes (unless zero) by 60. <u>Add</u> this to the number of hours. (In this example, 8 hrs. 13 min. = 8.21667 hours.) *Then*, <u>divide</u> this figure <u>into</u> the *Total Mileage* figure.

16. *Average Speed (Overall)* -- Convert hours and minutes as in #15, above, for *Total Outbound Time*. *Then*, <u>divide</u> this figure <u>into</u> the *Total Mileage* figure. (The average speeds in #15 and #16 help you to gauge your performance. They should improve over time, and then stabilize at a reasonable level.)

17. *% of Time in Motion* -- <u>Divide</u> the decimal equivalent of time found in #15 <u>by</u> the decimal equivalent found in deriving #16. (If you waste too much time on some of your runs, this is the easiest way to compare and evaluate your time losses.)

The budget book sample page is typical for a driver having *Interlock* established with another company in Sacramento. A driver who returns by bus to San Bernardino should continue making expense entries during the return trip, and then evaluate all time spent while away from San Bernardino.

In that case, non-*Interlock* drivers probably will want to add another line or two to the Trip Summary to cover bus-related time and expanses.

<u>A FINAL NOTE</u>: *Many of the mathematical operations in this Appendix are <u>meant</u> to be performed with a hand calculator. <u>With</u> this device, the operations are performed simply and quickly. <u>Without</u> it, the math would be more trouble than it is worth -- you would waste too much time on it!*

If you do not currently own a hand calculator, I would strongly recommend that you make it your very first investment, as a Road Rat. Excellent ones now sell for $5 and less in stores such as K-Mart.